2 Minute *Devotionals*

How to
Launch Your Day

365 Daily Devotionals

Albert H. Epp

Stairway Discipleship, Inc.
P.O. Box D, Henderson, NE 68371

How to Launch Your Day

Scripture taken from the New King James Version®.
Copyright © 1982 by Thomas Nelson, Inc. Used by permission.

Scripture taken from the Holy Bible, New International Version®, NIV®
Copyright © 1973, 1978, 1984, 2011 by Biblica, Inc.™
Used by permission of Zondervan. All rights reserved worldwide.
www.ZONDERVAN.com

Cover design, book design and layout by Jim L. Friesen

Library of Congress Control Number: 2013947415

International Standard Book Number: 978-0-9638185-0-8

Printed in the United States of America by Mennonite Press, Inc.,
Newton, KS, www.mennonitepress.com

PREFACE: REASONS FOR WRITING

This book is designed to be informational, inspirational and motivational. Having been reared on a Kansas farm, in a Christian family, under the influence of a traditional wholesome country church, my upbringing was marked by solid educational principles. After studying at Christian high schools and colleges, I landed at Fuller Theological Seminary, in the mid-1950's, under the teachings of outstanding Evangelical scholars. After a 13-year pastorate in Downey, California, I returned to Fuller for doctoral studies.

The focus of my graduate work was "Convert-Care" in churches. Why do many people enter a church, profess faith, and gradually lose interest, escaping out of the back door? In our homes we learn quickly that child-care is tedious but so rewarding! Why can't churches learn the value of convert-care? It may be very time-consuming, but highly profitable! To me, it becomes apparent, that winning new people is more exciting, than devoting time to loving and nurturing the converts! However, our Risen Christ gave us a mandate to "make disciples," which includes a baptismal commitment, an identity with our Lord and Savior, and it requires vigorous Biblical teaching and training (Matt. 28:19-20)!

In our second church, in Newton, Kansas, we developed Fellowship Groups, where a Shepherding Couple was assigned to about 30 members. The shepherds periodically assembled their flocks for fellowship, and organized so each ones needs were met. In our third church, at Henderson, Nebraska, we were more intensive. We formed Covenant Discipleship Groups, with eight to twelve persons. I myself discipled 128 men in ten years. I trained two extra disciplers, and recuited four ladies to disciple 100 women. Men met morning or evening, women met midday.

The group-dynamics were powerful—full-circle prayer, Bible lessons, sharing their personal faith-stories, and reading growth books. I could spend hours telling you exciting happenings that grew out of this discipling. Neighboring churches once kept stealing our sheep through their home studies. Our discipleship work stopped that completely! Every sacrificial effort was worth it. That's why I say, our goal in writing this book is to inform, inspire and motivate!

FOREWORD

FIRST OF ALL, we have chosen Bible passages for each of our 365 devotionals. Audible reading requires only two minutes to read each. We do encourage you to use a one-year-through-the-Bible reading schedule as well. Our scriptures require meditation, or even memorization! We must store God's word in our hearts (Psalm 119:11). Spiritual growth depends upon it! It gives daily joy and victory.

SECONDLY, this book highlights 20 distinct conversions to Christianity. My favorite case is Jim and Alice Vaus—accepting Christ—at Billy Graham's crusade. God led Jim to New York's worst crime area (Harlem) to organize clubs for youth. After six years, juvenile crimes dropped 40%; Jim kept youth out of prison, and off welfare!

THIRDLY, we include stories where prayers and miracles intercept. Frank Foglio of Full Gospel Business Men urged thousands to pray for his daughter, a car accident victim. She was comatose seven years. When Frank dropped his anger, praising God—instantly she woke up. The guards and nurses wept. Today she is at home!

FOURTHLY, we explain doctrines like Forgiveness, Justification and Sanctification. As we become more Christlike, we stress Discipleship (Matt. 28:19-20). We encourage church participation, as we pursue spiritual advance with great vigor.

FIFTHLY, we quote famous leaders: Henrietta Mears, Mother Teresa, C.S. Lewis, Archibald Hart, K.S. Lautourette and others. Today I mention Paul Harvey, once our favorite newscaster. He told of a woman who inherited three million dollars. She required a nephew and niece, living with her, to read the Bible daily. Then, unexpectedly she died. The lawyer read the will. Many benefactors got money, but the nephew and niece each got a Bible. In disgust both left town. Thirty years later in Cleveland, Ohio, two Bibles were found, containing money—$800,000!

FINALLY, we highlight our own family. Susan Joann and I are married over 50 years. We enjoy our grandchildren. We took Jordan fishing at Lake Alpine. He won a local contest (24 inch trout). We watched Anthony and Hans win the Nebraska State Championship in Cross-Country. We witnessed Zach perform the winning kick in an overtime soccer tournament in Los Angeles! Cydney brought her family from Indiana to visit us when she won the $25,000 Danimal's video-contest on the internet, winning a four-day trip to Hollywood's Universal Studio. And Grandma flew to Kansas for Sally's Senior Piano Recital at Tabor College.

"I have fought the good fight, I have finished the race, I have kept the faith. Now there is in store for me the crown of righteousness, which the Lord, the righteous Judge will award to me..." (2 Timothy 4:7-8 NKJV)

As the athlete trains mile by mile to win the cherished trophy, the Christian lives day by day to claim the Judge's heavenly crown. No athlete will excel unless he commits himself to hours of disciplined training, striving to please his coach. Neither will the Christian please his Lord unless he or she lives a structured life of discipline and wholehearted devotion. No casual easy-go-lucky halfheartedness will do! Christ gave His all—and demands our all.

One day we received an urgent phone call from our grandsons, Anthony and Hans. "Grandpa and Grandma, our school, Nebraska Christian High is going to state in Cross Country and you must come to see us run!" So, one week in October we drove the 1400 miles to the city of Kearney. How exciting! At the starting gun, 120 boys sprinted forward. By design, our grandsons and their two teammates stayed at the back, and then in the second mile they sped up. They passed 100 runners. The four of them finished with only nine seconds separating the first and the last. The local newspaper photographer in one photo showed these four boys coming in together. What an honor—for the first time Nebraska Christian of Central City won the state Championship Trophy! They alone had four runners in the top 20.

Likewise, in our Christian endeavor, we race toward the Pearly Gates. In the name of Christ we are victorious in every battle, with God's power we persevere to the end! If a sinner's prayer rings the bells of heaven, then certainly heaven applauds when each runner enters in!

SHINE YOUR LIGHT   January 2

"You are the light of the world. A town built on a hill cannot be hidden...In the same way, let your light shine before others, that they may see your good deeds and glorify your Father in heaven." (Matthew 5:14-16 NIV)

Jesus said that his followers, by the way that they live, shine as lights in a dark world. In my third pastorate, in the 1980's, I learned a profound lesson. My doorbell rang and a parishioner brought a stranger to my door. The man was looking for the pastor since he needed gas to continue east on Interstate 80. I promised to phone the freeway gas station and they would give him $10.00 of gasoline. I closed the door and felt good about my generosity! Unknown to me, my church member had his five children in the car. They asked whether the strangers had food? So after a serious debate, my member drove three miles to the interstate, to the strangers getting gasoline, and asked if they would come to his house for dinner. They gave a grateful, "YES!" So, he led them back into town. When the station wagon stopped in front of their house—eleven people climbed out including three full grown men! Our parishioners were cordial hosts, kindly visiting and, of course, praying as usual before the meal. In this little story, guess who resembled a car driving with his lights on dim, and who resembled a car driving with a high beam, all for the glory of God?

Think of the impression left on those five children. One hundred admonitions of "Be kind to strangers" would have made less of an impact than this one dinner that day in Nebraska! Children are far more influenced by parental example than by a bunch of words!

SHOW YOUR LOVE   January 3

"A new commandment I give to you, that you love one another as I have loved you...By this all will know that you are My disciples, if you have love one for another." (John 13:34-35 NKJV)

Jesus Christ our Lord gave this strict mandate to His followers—TO LOVE, and declared that this was indeed a distinguishable mark of a Christian. This rules out hatred and sets a lofty standard for each of us. According to John 3:16 we are simply imitating the actions of our gracious and merciful Heavenly Father.

Our three sons were born while we lived in Southern California. My first pastorate was in the suburb of Downey. One day when our boys were about eight, five and three, I was in the parsonage and the boys were playing in the backyard. Suddenly I heard a loud scuffling brawl outside. Promptly I ordered my boys into the house and began a lengthy lecture: "Boys, we are Christians, but what will our neighbors think when they hear your backyard fight? It sounded awful. Jesus said, 'By this all will know that you are My disciples, if you have love one for another.' I have one requirement—not one of you will leave this room until you have memorized John 13:35!" Repentantly they obeyed. One by one the boys left the room—having learned one of the greatest utterances ever given to the church of Jesus Christ.

It was said of the Early Church "How they loved one another!" We know that no quality in a church is more magnetic, in drawing people in, than genuine love. In evangelism few things supersede the importance of Love. When we allow unforgiveness and grudges to take root in ourselves, love will be choked out by resentment and bitterness!

GROWING OLD GRACEFULLY   January 4

"O God, You have taught me from my youth; and to this day I declare Your wondrous works. Now also when I am old and grayheaded, O God do not forsake me, Until I declare Your strength to this generation, Your power to everyone who is to come." (Psalm 71:17-18 NKJV)

My paternal grandfather, John Epp Sr., migrated from South Russia to Whitewater, Kansas at the age of 21 in 1883. As a devout Christian he came to the USA for religious freedom. I often vacationed at his farm in summertimes. Every breakfast included scripture from a German Bible. He ate his oatmeal with cream, and poured his coffee into his saucer to cool it off. His farm was only one mile east of us. When I was about four, I remember vacationing at his farm. At the hen house a large rooster chased me—nearly scaring me to death!

Every Christmas he had a big gathering for all his children and grandchildren. He died when I was 12 years old. At his funeral, Pastor Kauffman read the Bible verse that Grandpa had chosen for the occasion: "As it is appointed unto men once to die, but after this the judgment..." (Heb. 9:27). The pastor commented that he did not know why Grandpa chose this austere text. However, I can guess why. He knew he was accountable. He wanted to please his Lord. And praise God, Grandpa faithfully persevered to the end!

Older Christians often feel helpless, aimless and useless. However, the Psalmist (Ps. 71:18) saw it differently. He was goal-oriented. He wanted to exit life with a bang! As a grayheaded saint, he wanted to reveal the mighty power of God to the next generation. As long as God grants health and clear minds, the aged can always love, give and pray!

LOVE YOUR ENEMIES   January 5

"You have heard that it was said, 'You shall love your neighbor and hate your enemy' but I say to you, love your enemies, bless those who curse you, do good to those who hate you, and pray for those who spitefully use you and persecute you." (Matt. 5:43-44 NKJV)

The followers of Jesus have an awesome task, to be loving under all circumstances. The activities of each day test us repeatedly. It is simply impossible to obey the teachings of Christ without God's enabling power. We can't do it ourselves.

The example of my Grandfather has long inspired me. He migrated from Europe and settled in Kansas. The early years were tough. His first three children died, and soon his wife died. One night when he came home, in the moonlight he saw horses and wagon rush away from his barn. His hired man who had sleeping quarters in the barn, excitedly told him what he had witnessed. A certain man had stolen oats. The next morning Grandpa harnessed his horses, sacked up some oats and headed across the field to his neighbor. "Neighbor," he said, "I understand that you came to my barn last night and took some oats. I didn't know you needed it so badly. So I am bringing you some. Next time, feel free to come get it in the daytime!"

That is how my Granddad showed his Christian love to a potential enemy. What a reminder to all of us—each irritating encounter needs a careful prayerful response, so that the love of Jesus shines through. Often we respond quickly, and later think of what we could and should have done. Kind loving acts always have the potential of averting future revengeful deeds. The power of love supersedes the power of hate.

GIVE YOUR TITHE   January 6

"Give, and it will be given to you: good measure, pressed down, shaken together, and running over will be put into your bosom. For with the same measure that you use, it will be measured back to you." (Luke 6:38 NKJV)

It appears that many Christians feel that they can't afford to tithe their income. And as they get wealthier that feeling increases, because the tithe becomes ever larger. Yet, the Bible promises that when we give to God, He rewards us richly. Don't get me wrong, we won't all become millionaires, but we will experience His unusual benefits.

Let me share my Grandpa's experience. He came to this country in 1883 and settled on the prairies of Kansas. The early years were marked by hardship. His first wife and children all died. His house and barn burned down. Then on March 6, 1890 he married Anna, the oldest daughter of a local minister. His father-in-law was not an encourager! He said thoughtfully, "John, you better give up farming. It appears like you are not going to make it." However, John was determined to succeed. He was not about to quit. One day he made a vow to God—I will tithe of everything I get. It appears that this was a sacred moment where he placed his whole farm operation under the control of God! Soon things began to change. Each year he was able to pay down $1,000 on his farm loan. It was paid off by 1904. Over the next forty years, Grandpa became a generous giver to many Christian causes.

When we put God to a test (Malachi 3:10), He pours out blessings! Whether we work toward the ten percent gradually, or instantly, after we are there, we usually don't want to give less.

EXERCISE TRUE RELIGION   January 7

"Religion that God our Father accepts as pure and faultless is this: to look after orphans and widows in their distress and to keep oneself from being polluted by the world." (James 1:27 NIV)

The book of James states categorically that faith without works is dead. While the Bible states clearly that we cannot earn our own salvation by our deeds, yet good deeds validate our profession of faith. A concern for the needs of others is a clear mark of saving faith, and that the Bible calls True Religion.

My paternal grandfather was a wonderful model of caring compassion. Having migrated from Russia in 1883, he kept in contact with many friends and relatives. He sent numerous Care-Packages of food, clothing and other items. In 1943 I attended Grandpa's funeral. He was then 81 and I was a mere lad of 12. What I learned years later was that Grandpa had requested that he be buried in his white shirt and that his Sunday suit be shipped to a destitute family in Canada—the family he had recently sponsored, paying their ship fare from Russia to Canada. When that family had asked grandpa, "What do we owe you for paying our ship fare to Canada?" He answered, "not a cent, that was my gift to you!"

Because of chaos from wars, earthquakes and hurricanes our world is flooded with homeless refugees. Christian organizations operate huge programs of relief--giving food, clothing and medicines. Yet the needs are astronomical! Many Christians support orphanages in Asia, Africa and Europe. Our local church supports orphanages in Romania, India, and recently Thailand. There many parents had died of AIDS. Our missionaries secured a permit to open a home for orphans sick with HIV. What a beautiful model of compassion.

PROMOTE YOUR VISION   January 8

"Jesus said, '...Saul, Saul why do you persecute me...I am sending you to (Jews and Gentiles) to open their eyes, and turn them from darkness to light and from the power of Satan to God...' So then King Agrippa, I was not disobedient to the vision from heaven." (Acts 26:14-19 NIV)

Some church experts have said that one of the prime deficiencies in churches today is the loss of vision. If that is true of church executives, it is equally true of Mr. Average Church Member. In my promotion of better Discipleship training methods, I have suggested that Christians need five, ten and fifteen year goals. Why drift aimlessly?

My paternal grandfather, John Epp Sr. once had a great idea. He got news from Russia that many Mennonite children, as well as workhorses were all starving in a severe famine. John drove to Hillsboro and spoke to leaders of a new relief agency called Mennonite Central Committee (MCC). "Let's send tractors and plows to Russia and I will finance the first unit." The idea caught on and in two months—in 1922—50 Fordson tractors and 50 Oliver plows were shipped out of Detroit. My grandpa paid for the first tractor-plow unit ($500). That was the first major international MCC project—all in the name of Christ.

Some years ago I attended a Pastor's workshop at the Chrystal Cathedral in Garden Grove. The church founder, Dr. Robert Schuller, told of his vision to start his church. He used a striking illustration. A man went fishing, but threw all of the large fish away. People asked why? His answer, "My frying pan is only nine inches across." The lesson is obvious: many of us have great ideas, but we reject them—the idea looks too large. Why don't you and I grab a big dream, and ask God to help us fulfill it.

SEEK YOUR ASSURANCE   January 9

"If we confess our sins, He is faithful and just to forgive us our sins and to cleanse us from all unrighteousness. If we say that we have not sinned, we make Him a liar, and His word is not in us." (1 John 1:9-10 NKJV)

I grew up in a wonderful Christian home. The farm life was very wholesome. My parents promoted Bible reading at home, and always took us to Sunday School and Daily Vacation Bible School. The goal was obvious—as I look back—they wanted to raise us to be enthusiastic Christians.

For years I struggled with the issue of assurance. Some days I felt I was saved, and other days I doubted. When negative things happened, like a horse dying, or me catching the flu, or the report card having a dumb "C," the assurance waned. I remember the day I was in the field plowing with the Model G John Deere tractor. A sudden thunderstorm rolled in and the lightning began to flash everywhere. I was afraid. Our neighbor had been killed by lightning and I didn't want to be next. So I again prayed to ask Jesus into my heart.

In my high school days I attended Berean Academy, and there my fears were put to rest. Our Bible teacher, Waldo Harder, explained—The Bible never says "feel good" and you shall be saved. Then he explained how he came to assurance. He had been pointed to I John 1:9, "If we confess our sins, He is faithful and just to forgive us our sins…" Next he was asked, "Do you think God is a liar?" "Of course not." "So if you do your part, God will do His part!" That helped me as well. Feelings vacillate, but the Bible is constant.

ASSIMILATE THE WORD   January 10

"Blessed is the man who walks not in the counsel of the ungodly...But his delight is in the law of the Lord, and in His law he meditates day and night. He shall be like a tree planted by the rivers of water, that brings forth its fruit in its season..." (Psalm 1:1-3 NKJV)

Bible memory-work held a high priority in the Christian education system I was raised on. The psalmist urges us to meditate continually (24/7) on the Word of God. I recall memorizing Bible verses for Sunday School on a weekly basis. When I was in the sixth grade I attended six weeks of Daily Vacation Bible School, half-day German school and half-day Bible School. That year I memorized 275 verses.

The psalmist urges us to go beyond storing scripture in our memory bank, to assimilating it into our daily living! Hebrew scholars often compare the word "meditate" to a cow eating a healthy meal, then laying down to digest it (by chewing the cud). Yes, we need to absorb the Word of God into the very fabric of our daily schedules. Here is one reason: "Your word I have hidden in my heart, that I might not sin against You" (Ps. 119:11).

Here is another reason—it reminds us of our great Christian heritage. The Israelites were told to post scripture on their door posts, to remember how God had delivered them from Egypt. We can hang Bible verses on office desks, on bathroom mirrors, or on kitchen refrigerators, to remind us of our marvelous salvation through Jesus Christ. We have been transferred from the Kingdom of Darkness into the Kingdom of God's dear Son! Many of the elderly in their older sicker days draw soothing comfort from the Bible verses they memorized in childhood.

PRACTICE GOOD DISCIPLESHIP   January 11

"Jesus said, 'All authority has been given to Me in heaven and on earth. Go therefore and make disciples of all nations, baptizing them in the name of the Father and of the Son and of the Holy Spirit, teaching them to observe all things that I have commanded you...'" *(Matthew 28:18-20 NKJV)*

This passage is known as the Great Commission. In the Greek text there is one imperative, namely, "Make disciples" and three participles, going, baptizing and teaching. This has motivated the church for 2000 years. The Anabaptists of the Reformation were ahead of their times when they made this mandatory for every believer.

As I got into pastoral work, I noticed that many professions of faith were short-lived. I admired the Southern Baptists for their zeal in evangelism, yet when I researched their own writings, I found some were lamenting that only half of their members showed up on any given Sunday. One pastor wrote, "We dip them and drop them." My concern for convert-care kept growing.

Then in my third church my wife startled me, "Al, you keep brainstorming about discipling men by twelves. I'm getting tired of this! I'll make breakfast for 12 men next Thursday and you'll have 12 men there to eat it." Well, I was caught! I quickly phoned 12 men in their 30's. So on a Thursday, Feb. 25, they showed up for breakfast. I said, "I want to disciple you." So they asked, "What will you do to us?" I shared my plan: Full-circle prayer, Bible study of 2 Peter 1:1-11, Writing our faith story, and for homework we'll read books on parenting, marriage, doctrine, great conversions, spiritual gifts etc. Eleven said Yes. One said, "Looks too Personal." That was the start of discipling 128 men at our house in the decade of the 80's!

DEVELOP YOUR PRAYER-LIFE   January 12

"But when you pray, go into your room, close the door and pray to your Father, who is unseen. Then your Father, who sees what is done in secret, will reward you. And when you pray, do not keep on babbling like pagans, for they think they will be heard because of their many words. Do not be like them, for your Father knows what you need before you ask him." (Matthew 6:6-8 NIV)

As we developed our Golden Stairway Discipleship Course in that large rural church in Nebraska, we made prayer a high priority. We had taken in wives from various denominations and many were telling me that their husbands did not freely talk about spiritual things, even though they had joined their husband's church! I told my wife that these men were spiritually dysfunctional. If they shy away from spiritual discourse, they will never pray with their families.

So in recruiting men, I forewarned them that we would have full-circle prayers each time—no volunteers. And if they were uncomfortable praying in public, I encouraged them to bring a pre-written prayer which they could read while we all bowed our heads—that is until they felt comfortable praying off our prayer-request list. As we gathered prayer requests one fellow was so fearful that he said, "Pray that I will get through this prayer time!"

At the final banquet one man said, "When I joined Pastor Epp's group I was nervous. I had never prayed in front of others. The prayer page had a place for PTL's when we got an answer. I thought it would be embarrassing if we got only a few. As the weeks went by I was surprised at the number of PTL's. Some were near miracles! Now I believe in the power of group prayer!"

ENCOURAGE EACH OTHER   January 13

"Therefore, as God's chosen people, holy and dearly loved, clothe your-
selves with compassion, kindness, humility, gentleness and patience.
Bear with each other and forgive one another if any of you has a
grievance against someone. Forgive as the Lord forgave you. And
over all these virtues put on love, which binds them all together in
perfect unity." (Colossians 3:12-14 NIV)

As I started discipleship groups I was amazed at the caring
quality residing in a group. They showed beautiful concern for
each other. Loving compassion was evident over and over again.

One day a parishioner entered my office to declare forth-
rightly that she disagreed with my perception of my pastoral
job description. I was stunned! "You know, those group meetings at your house," she continued, "they have never been in
any previous pastor's schedule!" After she had talked a while, I
said, "Sister, you surprise me. I consider our discipleship work
the most significant thing we have done here in the past five
years. By the way, we meet either at 6:30 a.m. or 9:00 p.m.,
hardly a time to conflict with anything else in the church."

Then I gave her two explanations. First, a church in town
has been stealing our sheep, via their home Bible Study groups.
Our discipleship work is so effective that the flow has been shut
off! Secondly, this discipleship training greatly multiplies the
pastor's efforts. As the group assembles, they form a support
group. They pray for each other and their families. They minister to each other. It would cost the pastor countless hours of
counseling and visitation to provide the equivalent of attention,
help and care received, not to mention the spiritual growth!
The older ones always help the younger. The newer Christians
always thrive on this kind of attention. It is great!

UPHOLD YOUR BROTHER   January 14

"Brethren, if a man is overtaken in any trespass, you who are spiritual restore such a one in a spirit of gentleness, considering yourself lest you also be tempted. Bear one another's burdens, and so fulfill the law of Christ...and let us not grow weary while doing good." (Galatians 6:1, 2, 9 NKJV)

To bear the burdens of others is easy in a small group. First of all, a group needs to agree to confidentiality. One of my disciples once confided with our group that he wanted to quit his job and apply for one in our own town. It was of utmost importance that no one said a word, but we prayed about it. Three weeks later, he exclaimed, "Praise God, I have a new job!"

This matter of sharing is interesting. Groups do not always share intimately. In fact, I often tell groups to share only as deeply as they wish. Everyone tries to play it safe. If the trust level is strong, the group tends to move to a deeper level. Psychologically, I have noticed when one person really bares his soul, others will feel free to do the same. We feel that men should train men; and we're convinced that men share more freely when only men are present.

We also trained women to lead women's groups. Women also share more freely when no men are present. Whereas our men's groups met for two hours, our women usually needed three! Our women's groups had a different dynamic. It became obvious that any group could not tolerate more than one or two persons—with heavy chronic emotional needs. A few persons could dominate the whole session, robbing others of time to share their concerns. All in all, our small groups were a fantastic vehicle for lifting the burdens of others.

SHARE YOUR BURDENS   January 15

"Hear my prayer, O Lord, and let my cry come to You. Do not hide Your face from me in the day of my trouble; Incline Your ear to me; In the day that I call, answer me speedily. For my days are consumed like smoke, and my bones are burned like a hearth. My heart is stricken and withered like grass, so that I forget to eat my bread." (Psalm 102:1-4 NKJV)

As I have already stated, small groups potentially offer a deep caring quality. In the darkest hour, in the deepest pain, in the toughest heartache, help is at your side. There is great comfort in the presence of a support group.

One day as I was eating dinner with a men's group, the phone rang. One man was urged to rush home—his 12 year old daughter had been shot. The family SUV was missing, as was the 14 year old son. The funeral, sad as always, was a shining portrait of Christian compassion. My Discipleship Group of 1987, with their spouses, was sitting next to the bereaved family at the memorial service, a picture of loving solidarity.

The missing son was found sleeping in a US post office in central Kansas. In court, once convicted of murder, he was sentenced for life. Psychologists felt that "his kind" would not respond to treatment for decades. In the meantime queer sounds started at the house (footsteps on the stairs, refrigerator doors automatically opening), BUT NO PERSON VISIBLE! Christian friends prayed—delivering the house from demonic powers in Christ's name. Back to the boy, he was adopted from a Nebraska orphanage. He seemed normal at home, school and church, but was very quiet. Why did he kill his sister? What situation or person served as a conduit to bring this demonic influence into our community? We don't know.

CONCENTRATE ON CHRIST   January 16

"But He gives more grace. Therefore He says: 'God resists the proud, but gives grace to the humble.' Therefore submit to God. Resist the devil and he will flee from you. Draw near to God and He will draw near to you." (James 4:6-8 NKJV)

I do not often speak about Satan and his power to promote evil in the world. My goal is to keep my eyes on Jesus Christ our Risen Lord. Many foreign missionaries, as well as American pastors at times encounter demonic activities. C.S. Lewis in his book *The Screwtape Letters* warns of two extremes: a total disbelief in the existence of demons, or an unhealthy interest in them.

In the 1960's I attended the meetings of The Revival Prayer Fellowship in Southern California. One speaker was German Psychotherapist Kurt Koch. His hair-raising accounts astounded us! Out of his 20,000 counseling cases, 4,000 were linked to demonism, spiritism, or the occult. In recent decades this has come to America with demon worship, weird occult acts and attacks on Christians. Koch also warned against going to fortunetellers.

When my son bought his house in the San Francisco area, about 20 years ago, he was told that the former owners had hosted spiritualism séances in the house. Therefore, before he and Kim moved in, he invited Christian friends to join him, marching around the property, praying for its cleansing and deliverance from all demonic influences. Finally, I must emphasize that the Bible never tells us to fear the devil. We have victorious power over him through "the blood of the Lamb and the word of our testimony" (Rev. 12:10-11). And never forget that Jesus in the "Lord's Prayer" tells us to say, "Deliver us from the evil one." James says—first submit to God, then resist the devil.

INSPIRE YOUR CHILDREN   January 17

"I hope in the Lord Jesus to send Timothy to you soon…I have no one else like him, who will show genuine concern for your welfare…But you know that Timothy has proved himself, because as a son with his father he has served with me in the work of the gospel." (Philippians 2:19-20, 22 NIV)

The Apostle Paul poured his life into young Timothy, and in turn Timothy poured his life into the many converts that Paul brought into the Kingdom. Paul was so overwhelmed with him that he exclaimed, "I have no one else like him!" My Christian parents, on a farm in Kansas, raised a brood of eight. They poured their lives into ours.

The first daughter married a minister and served God for 40 years, starting in Nebraska, ending in Iowa. The second child went as a nurse to Ethiopia and Sudan, ending up in Wichita, teaching English to foreign women. I was third. I recall helping Dad at the north farm, standing by the silo, "Dad, I feel God is calling me. I don't think I will stay here to farm!" Dad's response, "That's wonderful." I pastored for 40 years, first in Los Angeles, later in Kansas and Nebraska. Fourthly, my sister took nurses training, married a minister and spent most of her life in Pennsylvania. The fifth child, my brother, went to Hong Kong as a PAX relief worker and became a pastor.

The sixth and seventh of us, two ladies, devoted their entire lives to teaching school in Leavenworth, Kansas. Our youngest brother, schooled in genetics, worked with bananas, pineapples, and alfalfa and recently helped a doctor in Wichita raise better health foods. Yes, I must say, our parents watched with eager anticipation as each child developed into a useful servant in the Kingdom of God.

HIGHLIGHT YOUR EXAMPLE   January 18

"Don't let anyone look down on you because you are young, but set an example for the believers in speech, in conduct, in love, in faith and in purity. Until I come devote yourself to the public reading of Scripture, to preaching and to teaching. Do not neglect your gift, which was given you through prophecy when the body of elders laid their hands on you." (1 Timothy 4:12-14 NIV)

Ponder for a moment the power of example. Why did five of my parent's eight children go into what we call "full-time Christian service?" Why did the other three, practice church attendance even though they took employment in the secular world? I would suggest Parental Example. Father and Mother were humble devout farm folks, taking us to church every Sunday.

Each Saturday we washed the car, shined our shoes and took our baths. On Sunday we dressed up for Jesus. On a blizzard-like Sunday, Dad feared the car might get stuck in the snow, so he hitched horses to a buggy and three kids joined him for a three mile trek to church. There must have been 100 people there—on a day when city folks normally cancel worship! In addition they took us to all Mission Conferences, and Revival Crusades. No wonder we caught the vision!

Dad even insisted that, after High School, we each get several years of Bible Institute training before we launched into our careers. Before we got electricity, in 1948, we only had a car radio. Most Sunday afternoons Dad and Mom sat in the garage, listening to the Old Fashion Revival Hour from Long Beach, California. Dr. Charles E. Fuller preached, Honey read the letters, the Fuller quartet sang and Rudy Atwood played piano. We kids listened as we played nearby.

DON'T AVOID ACCOUNTABILITY   January 19

"But you, man of God, flee from all this, and pursue righteousness, godliness, faith, love, endurance, and gentleness. Fight the good fight of faith. Take hold of the eternal life to which you were called when you made your good confession in the presence of many witnesses." (1 Timothy 6:11-12 NIV)

Here Paul urges his young disciple, Timothy, to practice strict accountability. When we published the Golden Stairway Discipleship course, our aim was to disciple men adequately, so the church dropout rate would decline. Churches are not grounding their converts properly. Commitments are often short-lived.

Once I conversed with a college president and outlined our small group requirements. One was to read a book per week. I said it may sound childish, but I go around the circle and ask each man how many pages he read. "That's not childish, that is accountability," he quickly said, "that is exactly what our churches lack today!" I agree. One of my recent groups (men aged 30-42) read an average of 149 pages per man per week. Our book list covered vital areas like Marriage, Great conversions, Holy living, Spiritual Gifts, Tithing, False Cults, and Revival History.

Reading a good book will enrich your life immeasurably. It will increase your resolve to be your best for Christ. Such reading has an amazing potential for impacting lives. In a day of rampant TV, and extreme busyness, members of a small group will still read if the Leader requires accountability. Men respond fondly, "We haven't read like this in years!"

Here is an alternate idea— where time is scarce, or language is a problem, or reading skills are lacking, leaders can circulate CD's or DVD's.

WRITE YOUR STORY   January 20

"From Attalia they sailed back to Antioch, where they had been committed to the grace of God for the work they had now completed. On arriving there, they gathered the church together and reported all that God had done through them and how he had opened a door of faith to the Gentiles." (Acts 14:26-27 NIV)

Paul and Barnabas returned from their missionary journey and gave a report to their home church at Antioch regarding what God had done through them. In the same way, in our discipleship groups we wrote out our pilgrimages of faith, recording what God had done in and through us. We told of our salvation commitment and our subsequent blessings and trials.

When we shared these life stories once a week, it became a nonthreatening way, in a group setting, to teach the dynamics of salvation assurance. Here is an example. One of my men shared his story, but he made no reference to a spiritual decision. So I thanked him, and in front of the group asked several questions—When did your parent's faith become yours? Did you ever pray for God to forgive your sins? Then I prayed asking God to bless this man's family.

The next week, at 10 o'clock at night my doorbell rang. "Pastor," this man said, "tomorrow I tell my life story. I want to tell them that I KNOW FOR SURE I'm a Christian. I made a profession of faith as a teenager and was baptized. But over the years I often heard a voice 'you're not a Christian.'" We carefully went through the Bible salvation promises. I emphasized, we are saved by faith, not by feelings. We both prayed. The next evening he said, "Last night I went for counsel, now I know with certainty that I'm a Christian!"

ENJOY YOUR CELEBRATION January 21

"Or suppose a woman has ten silver coins and loses one. Doesn't she light a lamp, sweep the house and search carefully until she finds it? And when she finds it she calls her friends and neighbors together and says, 'Rejoice with me; I have found my lost coin.' In the same way, I tell you, there is rejoicing in the presence of the angels of God over one sinner who repents." (Luke 15:8-10 NIV)

This parable of Jesus is the middle one of a trilogy (lost sheep, lost coin, lost son). In each case there is rejoicing when the lost is found. This is symbolic of the celebration in heaven when one sinner repents. In our program of discipling men by twelves, we also ended with a Celebration-Banquet in some restaurant. It was a climax. We would find a farmer who was delighted to finance the banquet. We invited the wives to be our guests. Each disciple was given three minutes to share what the three-month training had meant to him.

There were times when a person made a first time conversion commitment, but usually our men were Christians already. Nonetheless, they made the bells of heaven ring because they "REPENTED" of their relaxed, easygoing lives. They determined to follow Christ, using their Spiritual Gifts in the life of our church. Some started tithing, some ushering, some teaching, some joining the choir. Those with the gift of service took a new interest in disaster projects and relief service.

Yes, heaven rejoiced, but so did our wives on earth. More than one thanked us for helping train their husbands. Some men for the first time, were willing to take a leadership role in the spiritual development of their families. When men are role models in prayer, Bible reading and teaching children, it is thrilling!

CONTROL YOUR ANGER   January 22

"A gentle answer turns away wrath, but a harsh word stirs up anger. The tongue of the wise adorns knowledge, but the mouth of the fool gushes folly. The eyes of the Lord are everywhere, keeping watch on the wicked and the good. The soothing tongue is a tree of life, but a perverse tongue crushes the spirit." (Proverbs 15:1-4 NIV)

I have learned from experience that I must control my speech. I must think before I act! I relearned that recently. I was home alone. My wife had flown to Indianapolis to care for grandkids. On March 7, 2011, I got a letter from a Collecting Agency that we owed $312.86 for a delinquent bill. I was stunned! I phoned them, "This can't be, we always pay our bills." They told me which air conditioning company had sent this debt to them for collection.

So I phoned them, "This can't be. We always pay our bills. Why didn't you phone us?" "We sent you a letter," she claimed. "No, we never got one. Are you a reputable company? Why didn't you phone us?" I said again. The lady responded, "Do you want to continue being rude, or do you want my help?" I calmed down and replied, "I need help!"

She said, "I will check our records, but please check yours." In my wife's ledger I found that we had paid $180 (12-11-09) for furnace repair. My schedule book showed that the service man had come three times, but only charged us once. I phoned the store, "Yes, we paid $180, and I admit I was upset." She replied, "According to our records, we double charged. You owe us nothing. I'll notify the collectors!" We were falsely accused but a little patience resolved it all.

RETAIN YOUR MOMENTUM   January 23

"But thanks be to God, who gives us the victory through our Lord Jesus Christ. Therefore my beloved brethren, be steadfast, immovable, always abounding in the work of the Lord, knowing that your labor is not in vain in the Lord." (1 Corinthians 15:57-58 NKJV)

Our three month intensive Golden Stairway Discipleship Course climaxed in a banquet. This finished the weekly commitment. However, we highly recommend a continuity of fellowship. Thirteen weeks together would weld the bunch one to another by a special bond. While the women had many fellowship opportunities, the men did not. Of course, most men had a busy schedule, yet it seemed that a monthly get-together was workable for most.

For our men we planned monthly year-round support meetings hosted at the home of a deacon. Normally, they met at nine o'clock at night. The host provided dessert and a five minute devotional. Then the men handled their own prayer time. First they caught up on the latest. Then they updated the prayer page. This was followed by a full circle prayer. This took a full hour. This meeting for these men was extremely important. This was the only place the men had for a man-to-man prayer encounter. My first 1982 group continued to meet for ten years. Then they called me to a café for a dignified closure meeting. Some men were moving away, some were assuming different obligations.

These monthly prayer fellowships became the "launching pad" for adventures in service and witness. The twelve would grow, mature and dream together. As individuals tackled specific ministries for God, the whole group became involved with affirmation, encouragement and prayer. The support group became an immediate protection against discouragement and burnout. One man who nearly dropped out of the weekly meetings, became the strongest advocate for the monthly meetings.

EXPECT YOUR QUESTIONS   January 24

"But sanctify the Lord God in your hearts, and always be ready to give a defense to everyone who asks you a reason for the hope that is in you, with meekness and fear; having a good conscience, that when they defame you as evildoers, those who revile your good conduct in Christ may be ashamed. For it is better, if it is the will of God, to suffer for doing good than for doing evil." (1 Peter 3:15-17 NKJV)

Christians are asked to be a witness for Jesus Christ. We are fortunate when people ask us questions. Yet, too often we are caught by surprise—and appear to be unprepared.

Some years ago when I was working for Choice Books, we were delivering a book order to a Wal-Mart near Pasadena off the 210 Freeway. The store receiver noticed that these were Christian books, and immediately asked, "Do you read the Bible?" "Yes, I surely do," was my response. Then he continued, "I used to be with the Lord, but I have drifted. I have been living a very wicked life. Can God forgive me?"

I quoted a Bible verse: "Seek the Lord while He may be found. Call on Him while He is near. Let the wicked forsake his way, and the unrighteous man his thoughts; let him return to the Lord, and He will have mercy on him; and to our God, for He will abundantly pardon." "Where is that found?" he spontaneously asked. "In Isaiah, chapter 55, verses six and seven" I responded. "Please write it down on this piece of paper, so I can look it up in my own Bible," he said. While I never saw him again, I was happy that I had memorized a verse that answered his inquiry.

SURVIVE YOUR HARDSHIPS   January 25

"If I must boast, I will boast of the things that show my weakness. The God and Father of the Lord Jesus, who is to be praised forever, knows that I am not lying. In Damascus the governor under King Aretas had the city of the Damascenes guarded in order to arrest me. But I was lowered in a basket from a window in the wall and slipped through his hands." (2 Corinthians 11:30-33 NIV)

The Apostle Paul encountered vicious enemies who dogged his steps everywhere. They attacked his character and accused him of being a religious fraud, while they masqueraded as apostles of Christ! In reality they were deceitful apostles of Satan (2 Cor. 11:1-33). Paul did what he normally did not do. He defended himself, claiming that his credentials superseded theirs. He was an authentic Jew, and his sufferings surpassed theirs. He was jailed, stoned, shipwrecked, beaten with rods three times, and given 39 whip lashes five times.

When my wife and I delivered books in California, we also faced police opposition. One day I serviced Redlands. When I got to my motel, my briefcase was gone. I phoned my wife in a Wal-Mart in San Bernardino, "When you pass Redlands, stop to see if I left my briefcase there." At Redlands the police and store manager were blocking the door. "This is a lockdown," they said! My wife persisted, "I have to see—did my husband forget his briefcase?" "O, COME IN!" The police asked, "Is that briefcase in the aisle his?" "Yes." "What's inside?" "Store invoices." Gingerly, he carried it out, and opened it. "YES, INVOICES." Then he turned to three cars labeled —BOMB SQUAD—"You can go." THEY ALMOST EXPLODED MY BRIEFCASE! All joking aside, the police were not persecuting us, they were protecting the public.

ENJOYING OUR JUSTIFCATION   January 26

"Therefore, since we have been justified through faith, we have peace with God through our Lord Jesus Christ, through whom we have gained access by faith into this grace in which we now stand. And we boast in the hope of the glory of God." (Romans 5:1-2 NIV)

The doctrine of justification is very important. It brings to all of us a great measure of comfort and peace. It is sometimes said that Christians are saved by faith, by grace, by the Word of God. The technical meaning of justification comes from the court of law. The idea is that God, our Judge, declares us righteous—when we had not deserved it. Salvation is a gift. When we accept Jesus as our Savior and Lord by faith, God accepts us by grace because Jesus died for our sins!

Even humor can teach us. A man went to heaven. Saint Peter told him. "You can't get in unless you score 100; what have you done in life?" "Oh," the man said, "I attended church all my life." "Great," said Peter, "that will be four points, what else?" "I taught Sunday School for 40 years." "Wonderful, that will be another four points, what else?" "I gave half a million dollars to my church for missions." "Super," said Peter "that's another four points; what else?" "I was faithful to my wife, and a good parent to my children." "Marvelous, that's another four points." "What," the man blurted out, "At this rate I will never get in, but by the grace of God!" "That's it!" shouted Peter, "You understand, come on in!"

None of us deserves heaven (Romans 6:23). Only by the grace and mercy of God do we enter, after repenting of our sins and trusting Christ for salvation.

BECOMING LIKE CHILDREN   January 27

"At that time the disciples came to Jesus and asked, 'Who, then, is the greatest in the Kingdom of heaven?' He called a little child to him and placed the child among them. And he said, 'Truly I tell you, unless you change and become like little children, you will never enter the Kingdom of heaven.'" (Matthew 18:1-3 NIV)

Each of the Synoptic Gospels has a lesson on childlike humility, but only Matthew quotes Jesus as saying, "unless you change and become like little children, you will never enter the Kingdom of heaven." In the culture of Bible times, as well as in our day, children are the last and the least. They are the last to be consulted, and the least to be reckoned with. The followers of Jesus looked forward to doing manlike macho heroic deeds with Jesus, and could hardly imagine any greatness in becoming childlike!

Many of us remember our childhood experiences, at picnics or at school recesses. We chose up sides to play ball. The first to be chosen were the best pitchers and batters. Next came the best catchers, runners and fielders. Last of all were those who were left; and I found that extremely embarrassing! Yet in the Kingdom of heaven, according to Jesus, these are the greatest!

The disciples were dreaming of supernatural escapades, earthshattering achievements like walking on water, stilling the storms, healing the sick and raising the dead. They were hoping to merit the gold, silver and bronze in the Olympian finals of heaven. But Jesus used shock therapy and advocated a conversion—where they become like little children! This alone would meet the entrance requirements into the kingdom of heaven! Only the humble will be admitted.

LEARN FROM CHILDREN   January 28

"Therefore, whoever takes the lowly position of this child is greatest in the kingdom of heaven. And whoever welcomes one such child in my name welcomes me." (Matthew 18:4-5 NIV)

Jesus Christ, in his earthly life, displayed an amazing admiration of children. He even insisted that his adult followers must emulate the humble qualities of children! While in my Nebraska pastorate I learned of professor Dr. Paul Welter, who taught Educational Psychology at the University at Kearney. He wrote a delightful book, *Learning From Children*. He advocates that we view children as Master Teachers—our Spiritual Mentors. He practiced what he preached! At home he specialized in his role as Grandfather, at church he assisted with pre-kindergarten Sunday School, at the university he taught a large class entitled "Learning From Children."

Dr. Welter explains: "Young children model those traits which Jesus said are necessary to enter the kingdom of heaven. They are born free of those cultural restrictions and personal biases which are pressed upon us quite early in life. We are taught, for example, to compare ourselves with others, to be less than honest, and to be negative..."

Welter identified 22 childlike traits and devoted a chapter to each: humility, trust, honesty, optimism, courage, placing relationships over tasks, expressing love, caring, friendliness, sense of wonder, touch, laughter, sensitivity, forgiveness, mourning, ability to heal brokenness, moving, playing, singing, creativity, and the thirst for learning.

According to professor Welter, some children begin to lose their childlikeness in their second year, while others keep their childlike qualities into later childhood. Some adults never lose these characteristics at all. Some people in their 90's, still retain the childlike qualities of humor, courage, spontaneity and creativity. I highly recommend Paul Welter's book, *Learning From Children*.

TRAIN YOUR CHILDREN   January 29

"Train up a child in the way he should go: and when he is old, he will not depart from it." (Proverbs 22:6 NKJV)

Children at a very young age are exceedingly impressionable. This makes early training of utmost importance. Jesus taught that children have a quality of humility, which all Christians must have to reach heaven. Jesus also taught the importance of love and forgiveness. Paul Welter, in his book, *Learning From Children*, illustrates how easily children can forgive. He recalls the time when his two girls were age two and four: When big sister was disciplined for hurting little sister, big sister cried for her blanket (the special one that comforts her). I did not let her have it for a few minutes, so little sister, who had just been hurt by big sister went and brought her the blanket. What a beautiful quality this child displayed—instant spontaneous forgiveness.

Let me cite three examples of child training at churches. First, Dr Welter assisted with pre-kindergarten Sunday School at his church. He insisted that each nursery worker kneel or sit down eye-to-eye with each child several times each session. Secondly, recently a noted university professor was interviewed on radio. The host asked, "I heard that on Sundays you teach three year olds at your church; what do you tell them?" Answer: "I simply tell them three things: God made you, God loves you, and don't hit anyone!" Thirdly, in my third parish, my wife noticed that no nursery care was offered in this large church. She recruited ladies in their 50's, and provided nursery care so young mothers could worship undisturbed. At the same time the nursery staff became intimate friends with the moms, while lovingly caring for their kids. What a fruitful ministry for Christ!

CHALLENGE OF MISSIONS January 30

"But you will receive power when the Holy Spirit comes on you; and you will be my witnesses in Jerusalem, and in all Judea and Samaria, and to the ends of the earth. After he said this, he was taken up before their very eyes, and a cloud hid him from their sight." (Acts 1:8-9 NIV)

The challenge of worldwide missions comes directly from Jesus Christ our Lord, as he spoke his parting words at his Ascension. He placed upon his followers the obligation of carrying the good news of the Gospel to every living soul. The early pioneer missionaries sailed to pagan lands at the risk of their lives. They faced headhunters, snakes, diseases and other countless dangers! Yet their stories are filled with intrigue, excitement and miracles.

In my first parish, in Southern California, missionary J. Arthur Mouw held our congregation spellbound as he told of pioneer work among the Dyaks of Borneo. The Dyaks lived in Long Houses, five feet above ground, with 50 to 80 natives living in one house. He taught them Bible all day, and late into the night by candlelight. One night he fell asleep—exhausted—while he was still talking. When he awakened, he found scores of eyes focused on him, waiting to hear more! He was the first missionary to go to the Dyaks, and hundreds accepted the Gospel. As Mr. Mouw preached at our church that morning, he was scheduled to stop at 12:00 noon, but went 45 minutes overtime! Not one person left, or complained. He spoke with such anointing, such conviction, such power that everyone wanted to hear more!

My friends, these missionaries are the Real Heroes of the world. They deserve our financial support, encouragement, and above all, our daily prayers. Never forget that!

LEARNING FROM NATIVES   January 31

"While they were worshiping the Lord and fasting, the Holy Spirit said, 'Set apart for me Barnabas and Saul for the work to which I have called them.' So after they had fasted and prayed, they placed their hands on them and sent them off." (Acts 13:2-3 NIV)

At the church in Antioch, Barnabas and Saul [later called Paul] were commissioned to launch out on a missionary trip. Clearly, the Holy Spirit was leading them. Here is an ideal pattern: the Church endorsed them and sent them. This tends to guarantee financial assistance, prayer support and congregational interest. A faithful church will place a high priority on the mission budget, and secondly, on the training of new workers.

When J. Arthur Mouw, pioneer missionary from Borneo, spoke at our church, he made missions come alive. His stories fascinated the young and old alike! Hundreds of Dyaks embraced the Christian Gospel. One day Mouw took a native upstream 20 miles to another village. They went by canoe, but where the water was too shallow, they carried the boat. After several days of teaching they prepared to return home. That evening at the campfire, as they cooked supper, Mouw's convert said, "Why don't we pray for rain, so we don't need to carry our boat?" Mouw was tired, and short on faith—knowing it wasn't the rainy season. "Why don't you pray?" he replied. The Dyak prayed earnestly. That night it rained! The next day their boat floated all the way home!

What a lesson. When we win people to Christ, they can teach us a lot. Their zeal and childlike faith is so inspirational. They read the Bible stories and believe that God will answer prayer, even in our day. Their trust in God, builds our faith as well.

CONVERTS START TITHING February 1

"You are cursed with a curse, for you have robbed Me, even this whole nation. Bring all the tithes into the storehouse, that there may be food in My house, and prove Me now in this," says the Lord of Hosts, "If I will not open for you the windows of heaven and pour out for you such blessing that there will not be room enough to receive it." (Malachi 3:9-10 NKJV)

The tithing principle, giving ten percent to God, is stated often in the Bible. The Malachi passage is unique. There God invites his people to test Him—to see if he won't bless them in an abundant way! Jesus offered a similar promise (Luke 6:38) of a fourfold reward: "Give, and it will be given to you: good measure, pressed down, shaken together, and running over will be poured into your lap."

When missionary, J. Arthur Mouw, was teaching the Bible to his new Dyak converts in Borneo, the Lord urged him to teach tithing. Mouw objected, "These people are too poor!" As the urging persisted, he gave in. These new Christians started tithing. They brought chickens, eggs, corn and rice to the church. These items were traded for materials to put up a church building. As hundreds of Dyaks began tithing, immeasurable blessings descended, both spiritually and economically. As the years passed, people compared their crop yields, with those in other areas of Borneo, and the difference was striking!

Christians today need to realize that God still rewards faithful giving. My wife and I have tested God repeatedly. We've seen unexpected profit, unanticipated income, and surprised payouts. We've been shielded from hospital bills, car repairs and residential disasters. Above all, we have reaped spiritual blessings, too numerous to recount. God be praised!

PRAYER POWER & MISSIONS   February 2

"...Teacher, I brought you my son, who is possessed by a spirit that has robbed him of speech. Whenever it seizes him, it throws him to the ground. He foams at the mouth, gnashes his teeth and becomes rigid. I asked your disciples to drive out the spirit, but they could not....his disciples asked Him privately, 'Why couldn't we drive it out?' He replied, 'This kind can come out only by prayer.'" (Mark 9:17-18, 28-29 NIV)

Scholars like Peter Wagner and others have wrestled with the issue of prayer as it relates to the evangelism of the world. Can any zone be evangelized if the prayers of Christians haven't first bound the demonic powers in that territory? In many pagan cultures, demon-worship is practiced. The witch doctors have a stranglehold on the people—using curses, fortunetelling, and various miraculous activities to deceive and control families. The witch doctors become furiously angry when Christians, in Christ's name, command their special supernatural powers to be broken. Only prolonged persistent prayer will defeat such strongholds.

At our mission conference, J. Arthur Mouw, shared an experience from Borneo. After he won one group of Dyaks to Christ, he started up a certain river to reach another group. Suddenly, some invisible force grabbed him around the neck and started choking him. Immediately he turned around, and concluded that he could not go there—until more prayer had broken the demonic-power-hold on that region!

The average American church is thrilled when a member volunteers to become a career mission worker. However, one wonders whether the church understands the absolute necessity of undergirding the foreign missionary with daily earnest wholehearted prayer? Our prayers protect the missionary. Our prayers produce effective evangelism. But our lack of prayer will stifle the advance of the Gospel.

PRAYING OUT WORKERS   February 3

"When he saw the crowds, he had compassion on them, because they were harassed and helpless, like sheep without a shepherd. Then he said to his disciples, 'The harvest is plentiful but the workers are few. Ask the Lord of the harvest, therefore, to send out workers into his harvest field.'" (Matthew 9:36-38 NIV)

While I was a seminarian in Pasadena in 1955, Susan Joann and I drove to First Presbyterian Church of Hollywood one Sunday to attend Henrietta Mear's college class. How impressive: a class of 300. As a master teacher she exuded love and fostered a godly self-esteem. Students admired her as a counselor. She treated them as though they were the most important people she ever met! Her biographer claims that she prayed 400 young people into Christian service based on Matthew 9:38. One such person was Bill Bright of Campus Crusade. He said of Miss Mears that she thought, prayed, planned and loved supernaturally.

Dr. Henrietta Mears (1890-1963) was held in high esteem. Richard Halverson dubbed her as a "female Apostle Paul" and Lyle Schaller, a noted church analyst, thought her to be one of the most influential figures in American Christianity in her century. Her accomplishments stand as monuments to the power of prayer. She founded a retreat center called Forest Home, where two million people met her Lord and Savior.

Every church with a heart for missions and a burden for the lost, will be inspired by Miss Mears. Jesus urges us to pray that "the Lord of the Harvest" will send out harvesters. The key is not more demanding or more coaxing, but rather it is more praying. The successful church which sends a steady stream of workers to mission fields at home and abroad, will be the church that prays passionately.

LEARNING FROM MOTHER   February 4

"I am reminded of your sincere faith, which first lived in your grandmother Lois and in your mother Eunice and I am persuaded, now lives in you also....from infancy you have known the holy Scriptures, which are able to make you wise for salvation through faith in Christ Jesus." (2 Timothy 1:5 and 3:15 NIV)

The Apostle Paul writes to Timothy, his apparent convert, and for certain, his devoted associate, reminding him of his rare heritage. Paul gives high praise to Eunice and Lois, the mother and grandmother, who gave Timothy a thorough knowledge of Scripture. It could well be that his mother had led him to faith in Christ, before Paul ever came into the picture. Eunice and Lois are given special recognition for their spiritual parenting!

Earl Roe wrote, *Dream Big, The Henrietta Mears Story*. Miss Mears was known for her bold faith-packed prayer life. Her father was a banker and often traveled. But her mother was at home raising Henrietta. Each morning she withdrew to the bedroom to pray for an hour on her knees, with folded hands and lips moving. Henrietta idolized her and while still a preschooler, she made it her goal as well. She took an alarm clock to her own bedroom. With closed eyes she prayed for everything she could think of. Peeking at the clock, only one minute had passed. How could mother pray for an hour? Mother's praying was awesome and contagious!

While some women of necessity need to work, a stay-home mom has a unique opportunity to influence her own children. A mother can read Bible stories, sing songs, or play games. My wife says that a loving mother—by her very presence—teaches. Her reactions, her words, her work habits, her careful disciplining, all help to educate.

TAKE YOUR STAND   February 5

"I beseech you therefore brethren, by the mercies of God, that you present your bodies a living sacrifice, holy, acceptable to God, which is your reasonable service. And be not conformed to this world; but be transformed by the renewing of your mind, that you may prove what is that good, and acceptable, and perfect will of God." (Romans 12:1-2 NKJV)

The Bible declares that Christianity requires an open public declaration of our allegiance to God and His son Jesus Christ. Churches vary in how they handle this. The rural church we attended did not have an altar call on a typical Sunday morning. Nonetheless, during Revival Meetings we sometimes did. But the Gospel was clearly taught at home, in Sunday School and from the pulpit. We practiced Believer's Baptism. After a year of Catechism, I was baptized during my High School Sophomore year. The pastor asked, "Do you renounce the devil and all his works and declare the Lord to be your God?" I answered firmly, "Yes, I do." That was my first public stand in front of my church.

During a missionary conference at our church some 20 people went forward to commit their lives to God for service. I did not. The following year, in July, we had a community Youth for Christ meeting. The guest speaker gave a powerful message, urging youth to lay their lives on the altar for God, to go, to do, to be, whatever God wanted. I left my balcony seat, and walked down the aisle and stood with five others in total dedication to God! I was so filled with the Holy Spirit that I felt I was walking on air. At that point I didn't know if I should be a missionary, professor or a pastor?

GOD GIVES PROTECTION February 6

"Fear not, for I have redeemed you; I have called you by your name; You are Mine. When you pass through the waters, I will be with you; and through the rivers, they shall not overflow you. When you walk through the fire, you shall not be burned, nor shall the flame scorch you. For I am the Lord your God..." (Isaiah 43:1b-3a NKJV)

These comforting words were given to Israel through the prophet Isaiah. On many occasions God miraculously rescued his people: for example, Moses and Israel crossing the Red Sea, and Daniel's three friends protected in the fiery furnace! Every Christian alive today, can testify to the protecting hand of God in his or her life. God deserves our highest praise.

Seventy years ago, June 8, 1941 a tornado came roaring through our farming community in central Kansas, between Wichita and Emporia. The swirling winds cut a swath one quarter mile wide, traveling sixty miles an hour. Many farms were destroyed, and seven people were killed. It struck us on a Sunday night at 11:30 p.m. as we were asleep. All our buildings (the barns, silo, garage, hen house, grain elevator, and machine shed) were destroyed, except for the house. It was badly-stripped, with most windows blown in from the air pressure. My brother and I were sleeping upstairs in the southwest room. Red boards from our cow shed were found under our bed. Praise God for His Guardian Angels—my parents and their seven kids were all unharmed!

The next morning Dad looked out of the kitchen door, and gave one big sigh. Hundreds of people helped clean up. We put our tractors on steel wheels, because of nails. Dad rebuilt the whole farm. Later he testified, "After the tornado, I started farming for Jesus Christ."

OUR FINAL JOURNEY   February 7

"Precious in the sight of the Lord is the death of His faithful servants." (Psalm 116:15) "For to me, to live is Christ, and to die is gain...I am torn between two: I desire to depart and be with Christ, which is better by far." (Philippians 1:21, 23 NIV)

Christians live best, if they have reckoned with their own mortality. As we sometimes say—we always need to have our suitcase packed, ready to go in a moment, whether in death or in the Second Coming of Christ. We tend to live differently when we see this life as temporary.

Permit me to pay a tribute to my sister Frieda. She was a lifelong school teacher. She earned a Masters at Emporia State Teacher's College, and spent her final 20 years teaching in Leavenworth. She drove many miles to church at Lenexa, where she organized the monthly Friendship Luncheons. She was a 17-year cancer survivor, and transported many to support groups and cancer workshops. Over the years I often phoned Frieda and one day she broke the news, "I have Acute Leukemia, and my time might be short!" Promptly, she arranged her estate, and planned her funeral. After 60 days she was very ill. She phoned me to fly in. Two days later I was at her bedside at the K.U. Medical Center. After two blood transfusions, she was amazingly alert. We had a wonderful day—talking, praying and reading Scripture.

The next day by noon she was gone, at age 70. Frieda's meticulous planning was extremely helpful. She had chosen hymns, and a text (John 14). She requested the choir to sing the "Hallelujah Chorus," but that proved impossible. So my granddaughter, Sally, a high school piano student, played the "Hallelujah Chorus" by memory and won a thunderous applause!

START SERVING YOUNG February 8

"Command and teach these things. Don't let anyone look down on you because you are young, but set an example for the believers in speech, in conduct, in love, in faith and in purity. Until I come, devote yourself to the public reading of Scripture, to preaching and to teaching."
(1 Timothy 4:11-13 NIV)

Paul wrote to young Timothy that no criticism of his youthfulness should prevent him from being a full fledge example of Christian virtue. In the early 1950's, two of us Kansas farm fellows, barely older than 20, asked our parents for permission to go to the Ozarks to teach DVBS and to hold preaching meetings. My partner was a musician, playing both the piano and a trombone, while I was assigned to preach. We boarded a bus in Wichita and went to Alderson, Oklahoma, to the home of a lady from our church. She was a year-round mission worker, teaching Bible stories to the kids in the public schools of Eastern Oklahoma.

In the forenoon we taught Daily Vacation Bible School and in the evenings we conducted Revival Meetings. We stayed one week in each community, living inside the School Houses. We brought our own sleeping cots and food supplies. In one school I remember teaching the younger set, and my partner teaching the older ones. One day I was teaching a youngster the verse, "Rejoice in the Lord always, and again I say rejoice" (Philippians 4:4). He had a hard time saying the reference. So I explained: "Say fill, like fill a bottle. Say lip, like wash your lip, Say pin, like safety pins." [fill-lip-pins] The next morning I asked him to recite his verse. He said, "Rejoice in the Lord always, and again I say rejoice." "Where is it found?" He replied, "Clothes Pin 4:4!"

TRUSTING YOUR LORD   **February 9**

"Indeed, the very hairs of your head are all numbered. Don't be afraid; you are worth more than many sparrows....Do not be afraid, little flock, for your Father has been pleased to give you the kingdom." (Luke 12:7 and 32 NIV)

That summer in the early fifties, when the two of us, the farm lads, went to the Ozarks on a Christian service assignment, we spent the afternoons visiting homes. We invited the children to our morning Bible School, and invited the youth and adults to our evening Revival Meetings.

Our supervisors at Alderson must have sensed some fear in us, as we talked about sleeping in the school houses. So they told us a story. Two ladies working for the Go Ye Mission had stayed in a certain school. The door could be locked, but it had such a large hole, that they had pushed their suitcases through without opening the door! That night in the dark they heard prowlers going around the school looking for the entrance. The ladies prayed earnestly. God protected them. One man said, "This place is locked, let's go."

Here is our experience. One night a man yelled in our back window, "It's too early to sleep." We jumped up. My partner grabbed his trombone and stood behind the front door; I rushed to the window and saw a group of men walking home from the local saloon. One man approached our door. Just as he reached for the doorknob, I signaled, and my partner blasted his trombone like only a scared man could. The man froze, then slowly withdrew. The next day the man stopped by, "You sure scared the pants off of me!" God protected us night after night. And above all, he blessed our teaching and preaching that summer.

VICTORY THROUGH PRAYER February 10

"For God so loved the world, that he gave his one and only son, that whoever believes in him shall not perish, but have eternal life." (John 3:16 NIV)

In my first pastorate, I learned how prayer and evangelism fit together. My deacon led a neighbor lady to the Lord. She became an enthusiastic Christian. Soon she and her children began attending our church. One Sunday night, she and other new converts shared their testimonies, and followed the Lord in baptism. But her husband, Bill (not his real name) rarely appeared in church. He was an energetic business man who loved to golf on Sunday.

Bill's conversion became a prayer concern at our church. One day he was hospitalized, and I visited him. After a friendly chat, I asked him, "Bill, wouldn't you like to accept Christ as your Lord and Savior and join your wife at church?" "Pastor," he responded, "Do you think I should if I don't feel like it?" "Certainly not," I answered, "but be careful your feelings don't deceive you!" At church we made lists of people we hoped to reach. One Sunday 50 persons accepted lists for daily prayer. (I placed Bill's name on 20 lists!) On Easter Sunday—1966—I saw Bill in the audience. I preached my heart out. At the end, I gave an altar call. Praise God, Bill stepped forward! He became a dependable, faithful, hard-working church member.

WOW, what excitement when Bill became a Christian. People were pumped up with new faith! If Bill could be won, then others could be reached also. It is a beautiful event, when a pastor and his people work harmoniously in reaching the unchurched. Bill had an immediate support system. Those who had prayed for him, could now encourage, teach and mentor him.

ACKNOWLEDGE YOUR LORD   **February 11**

"Whoever acknowledges me before others, I will also acknowledge before my Father in heaven. But whoever disowns me before others, I will disown before my Father in heaven." (Matthew 10:32-33 NIV)

In evangelistic crusades, it is customary to invite persons to make an open declaration of their commitment. Billy Graham, in every altar call, stated that Jesus called people publicly. The open profession of faith undergirds one's assurance, and at the same time, becomes a witness to the observers.

In the summer of 1963, a Billy Graham Crusade came to the Los Angeles Coliseum. Our church supported the event with enthusiasm. We encouraged everyone to attend and several times even chartered a bus to take neighborhood friends to the meetings. I recall inviting a man to ride our bus one Sunday afternoon. I had made frequent house calls to befriend him, so I was delighted when he chose to come along. Yet he was jovial and talkative, coming and going, totally untouched by Mr. Graham's challenging Gospel message.

I had volunteered to be an advisor to the counselors. I attended training sessions. The Crusade lasted 23 days and I attended all but two. My responsibility was to interview those who came forward—after the counselor was finished—to see if their needs were met. Out of the hundreds who professed faith in Christ each day, I interviewed 51. It was thrilling. People came from many religious backgrounds. They were so sincere. Some said, "We never heard preaching like this before!" I also worked on a committee that tried to integrate these converts into churches. We found that those who came with a church group, were easier to assimilate, then those who came on their own. Converts need prompt encouragement and training. My friend, have you professed Christ openly?

ENJOY YOUR YOUTH   February 12

"Remember your Creator in the days of your youth, before the days of trouble come and the years approach when you will say, 'I find no pleasure in them.'" (Ecclesiastes 12:1 NIV)

All youth are fortunate if they have pleasant memories of their upbringing. Solomon, traditionally considered the author, urges all youth to remember their Creator. Here parental assistance is vital. Christian parents, who pour their lives into their children, will make it an enjoyable experience, while they pass on the baton of faith.

One summer, as a teenager, growing up on a farm in Kansas, my parents sent me to a Youth for Christ camp at Goddard. For fun, one afternoon, I went horseback riding. I assured the stable manager that I was an experienced rider. After I had ridden for some distance, I turned around. When the horse sensed he was homebound, he bolted forward—a real runaway—and I could not slow him down. Praying, I hung on for dear life! We covered the last mile in a few minutes. He turned full speed onto the highway. Luckily, no car was coming. I saw a hedge-row and turned the horse into the hedge. He came to a halt, right near the stable. I thanked God for a safe, but scary ride. WOW!

Each evening a speaker challenged us. Once I went forward. "Why did you come?" a young counselor asked. "I don't know if I'm willing to die for Christ?" I said. "Give me your Bible," he replied. So I handed him my sister's Bible. He thumbed through Philippians, and found a verse already marked (4:13) "I can do all things through Christ who strengthens me." As I reflected on this later, I thought, possibly it's harder to live for Christ than to die for Him!.

ELIMINATE YOUR RUBBISH   February 13

"Do not let any unwholesome talk come out of your mouth, but only what is helpful for building others up....And do not grieve the Holy Spirit of God, with whom you were sealed for the day of redemption. Get rid of all bitterness, rage and anger, brawling and slander, along with every form of malice. Be kind and compassionate to one another, forgiving each other, just as in Christ God forgave you." (Ephesians 4:29-32 NIV)

The Apostle Paul wrote to the Christians at Ephesus to clean up their lives, getting rid of all harmful language, all destructive attitudes, and all malicious activities. As Christians strive to become more Christlike, they need to take inventory periodically, to see where they are falling short. David, the psalmist, once prayed for God to search him, to see if there was any residual wickedness (Ps. 139:23-24)? Self-examination is essential!

Our oldest son lives in the San Francisco area. They bought a beautiful two-story cabin above Angel Camp on Highway four in the town of Arnold. At the elevation of 4000 feet the trees are gorgeous. Once a year, he is required to clean all pine cones, leaves, needles and broken limbs from around his house. We as grandparents love to help our son and his boys. With rakes, forks and wheelbarrows we fill a 12-foot trailer twice. We pick up any debris that could burn.

Paul admonishes us to have speech that is helpful and uplifting. Our feelings must be kindly compassionate, and our attitude needs to be one of forgiveness. In that way we resemble Jesus Christ! Years ago we sang the words of William Mackay: "Revive us again, fill each heart with thy love; May each soul be rekindled with fire from above!"

LANGUAGES OF LOVE   **February 14**

"Dear friends, let us love one another, for love comes from God. Everyone who loves has been born of God and knows God. Whoever does not love does not know God, because God is love. This is how God showed his love among us: He sent his one and only son into the world that we might live through him." (1 John 4:7-9 NIV)

We recently heard Jim Daly of Focus On The Family interview Gary Chapman, author of *Five Languages of Love*. This book has sold 6 million copies. Chapman lists five ways to express love. Each is important—but one may be primary. The discipline we use, should be shaped by a child's love preference.

TOUCH: At birth a baby is cuddled, held, kissed and loved. For some of us, this touching factor becomes the primary way of feeling loved, and of extending love, even in adulthood. Who doesn't appreciate a pat on the back?

WORD OF AFFIRMATION: For others, this is the prime way of feeling loved. Words of appreciation are so encouraging. When children and youth grow up with abundant affirmation, they will use this technique later, to show love to others.

ACTS OF SERVICE: Some of us notice how we feel loved when someone does special deeds to benefit us. This gives us an immediate clue that we show love when we perform services for others. This is a tangible way of loving!

QUALITY TIME: Psychologists have recommended intentional scheduling of quality time—parents with children, and husbands with wives. This is a powerful way of displaying love. Everyone appreciates this.

GIFTS: Yes, gifts can motivate children. Special tasks can be rewarded. A Dad can find a gorgeous stone or sea shell and his son will keep it in his drawer for years! Gifts need not be expensive.

JUSTIFIED THROUGH FAITH   February 15

"Therefore, having been justified by faith, we have peace with God through our Lord Jesus Christ." (Romans 5:1 NKJV)

In the doctrine of Justification, the Christian gets immediate "right standing" with God. In the doctrine of Sanctification the Christian is gradually transformed into the image of Jesus Christ. Let me explain Justification in a threefold way.

ACCEPTANCE: Through the merits of Jesus Christ, we are accepted by God, the moment we are converted. We accept Christ as He is and God accepts us as we are! Not that we deserve this favored status, but we are justified by faith. The righteousness of Jesus Christ is imputed to our account. Our salvation is not man-made or self-initiated. It is freely given by the sheer grace of God. It comes by divine initiative.

ACQUITAL: In justification, in a sense, we are not made righteous; we are declared righteous. The analogy comes from the court of law. When a criminal stands before a judge, the judge might choose to acquit him. He is forgiven, though in reality he is guilty. In salvation, our loving Heavenly Father acquits us, though as lost sinners we actually deserved His wrath. The best known Bible verse (John 3:16) states that God so loved us that He gave His son. Christ's death on the cross paid the penalty for our sins, so we could go free (Hebrews 2:9).

ADOPTION: Because of God's amazing grace and loving mercy, the Christian is adopted into God's family (John 1:12, Ephesians 1:5, I John 3:1-2). The Apostle John writes that God, "has lavished His love on us" in calling us His children—His sons and daughters. The Old Testament requires us to love God with all our heart; here is the proof that God loves us even more.

REALIZE YOUR SANCTIFICATION   February 16

"For this is the will of God, your sanctification: that you should abstain from sexual immorality." "Abstain from every form of evil. Now may the God of peace Himself sanctify you completely; and may your whole spirit, soul, and body be preserved blameless at the coming of our Lord Jesus Christ." (1 Thessalonians 4:3, 5:22-23 NKJV)

The doctrine of Justification speaks of our acceptance, forgiveness and sonship—all instantaneously granted to us by God, the moment we embrace Jesus Christ as our Lord and Savior. *The* doctrine of Sanctification, on the other hand, has an immediate blessing, but after that refers to the lifelong process of being conformed into the image of Jesus Christ.

The primary meaning of sanctification is to set something apart for holy use. In the Old Testament days the Israel people could sanctify their houses or fields for God's use. And especially the Levites frequently cleansed the temple of all defilement, by dedicating the altar, showbread table, and the vessels to God for His specific use (2 Chronicles 29: 15-18). In our days when we become believers, it is God's act to set us apart for holy living. God chooses us, not because we're so holy, but to make us holy. This is once and for all God's act.

The secondary meaning: sanctification is that process of becoming Christlike. This is man's part and a continuous responsibility. This is progressive. God expects His children to grow in holiness and purity, until they mature and attain to the fullness of Christ (Ephesians 4:13). The Holy Spirit indwells us and enables us to be victorious over our besetting sins. Our spiritual growth depends greatly on us (2 Peter 3:18). But sinless perfection is never fully realized until Jesus Christ returns and we receive our GLORIFICATION!

CONTROL YOUR TONGUE   February 17

"When we put bits into the mouths of horses to make them obey us, we can turn the whole animal....Likewise the tongue is a small part of the body, but it makes great boasts. Consider what a great forest is set on fire by a small spark....With the tongue we praise our Lord and Father, and with it we curse human beings, who have been made in God's likeness. Out of the same mouth come praise and cursing. My brothers and sisters, this should not be." (James 3:3, 5, 9-10 NIV)

It is imperative that we control our tongues. Words can soothe and comfort, or they can bite and sting. Any two people, including husbands and wives, can argue endlessly. It has been said, it takes two to fight, but only one to end it!

Some years ago we attended a Golden Wedding Anniversary. A nephew shared this joke: Frank and Maggie had a drag out argument, so they walked out to the porch and each sat in a favorite rocking chair. For a long time they rocked in total silence. Then suddenly a team of horses, pulling a wagon, passed by. "Look," said Maggie, "those two beautiful horses are walking in perfect harmony; why can't you and I harmonize that way?" "Well, well," retorted Frank, "we could, if we like them, had only one tongue between us!"

The Bible warns us that it is difficult to gain control of our tongues. Let me make several suggestions. First, we need to think before we speak. Secondly, we need to pray, asking God to help us. Thirdly, we need to apologize when we have lost it! A torrent of words is like a bag of feathers released in the wind. They can't be retrieved. The oftener we have to apologize, the faster we'll learn speech control!

LOVE YOUR NEIGHBOR   **February 18**

"Jesus replied: 'Love the Lord your God with all your heart and with all your soul and with all your mind. This is the first and greatest commandment. And the second is like it: Love your neighbor as yourself. All the Law and the Prophets hang on these two commandments.'" (Matthew 22:37-40 NIV)

Discrimination based on skin color, national origin, or religious persuasion is forbidden by the above text as given by our Lord Jesus Christ. Where we live, our immediate neighbors are Hispanic, Philippine, Caucasian and one is from Thailand. Nearby are African Americans and various Indians who wear their turbans. One Indian woman embraces my wife every time they meet on their morning walks. We enjoy this friendly neighborliness!

When I was 20 years old, in the early 1950's, I volunteered to teach DVBS in the Ozark Hills of Oklahoma. I boarded a bus at Wichita and as we crossed the state line, the bus driver ordered all blacks to the back. This was my first encounter with race prejudice. Eventually, I learned that throughout the South the whites and blacks—in many towns—had segregated cafes, restrooms, and drinking fountains. The Civil War, 90 years earlier, never solved the race issue.

In the early 1800's many blacks came to our country as slaves. While neither Christ nor Paul condemned slavery, yet the application of Christianity eventually outlawed it, first in England and next in America. In the Civil War (1860-1865) 600,000 men died! Historians say that this war was fought partly over slavery, partly over unifying our country. One thing is clear: WAR NEVER BREEDS LOVE! Though slaves were freed, yet Blacks were not granted equality for another century. The war spawned decades of hatred. Praise God, today in America in my world, the African American is loved as dearly as we love ourselves.

ENJOY YOUR RENEWALS   February 19

"After they prayed, the place where they were meeting was shaken. And they were all filled with the Holy Spirit and spoke the word of God boldly. All the believers were one in heart and mind. No one claimed that any of their possessions was their own, but they shared everything they had. With great power the apostles continued to testify to the resurrection of the Lord Jesus. And God's grace was so powerfully at work in them all." (Acts 4:31-33 NIV)

The Early Church assembled together and experienced a marvelous in-filling of grace and power. In my first pastorate in Southern California I attended the annual gatherings of the Revival Prayer Fellowship led by Armin Gesswein. One hundred of us pastors would meet in some mountain resort for several days for prayer and renewal. The Holy Spirit moved so mightily upon us, that I went on the strength of that for months. I was blessed!

One year Robert Munger was our guest speaker. Being a Presbyterian pastor from the San Francisco area, he shared how each Wednesday he went up in the mountains, above his church and prayed for each of his members. Normally I am very cautious about imitating others. But this time I felt the Lord speaking to me: "Albert, here is a pattern for you!" I went home and prayed weekly for my 200. Next, in my Kansas parish I prayed for 900. Later in my Nebraska church I prayed for 1,200. On a normal Friday, I set apart three hours to pray through the membership. Untold blessings came out of those prayer times! Praise be to God.

My dear friends, the Early Church had a mighty boldness and joy, as they were filled with the Holy Spirit. Through renewal retreats you can have the same. Don't miss it.

FRUITFUL IN OLD AGE   February 20

"The righteous shall flourish like a palm tree, He shall grow like a cedar in Lebanon. Those who are planted in the house of the Lord shall flourish in the courts of our God. They shall still bear fruit in old age; They shall be fresh and flourishing, to declare that the Lord is upright; He is my rock, and there is no unrighteousness in Him."
(Psalm 92:12-15 NKJV)

While some people dread the thought of aging, for the Christian the Golden Years can be fruitful, fulfilling and fun. Some people at 90 are still kind, caring, spontaneous, and courageous. Elderly saints can impart profound blessings via encouraging words and supportive prayers!

My parents both lived to be 94. When they approached 90, we children gathered at their Kansas farm to urge them to move into the nursing home in town—for balanced meals, for regulated medicines, and general care. For dad, it was a painful transition. In his last four years he appreciated when we read scripture and sang hymns. When we sang his favorite, "At the cross, at the cross, where I first saw the light, and the burden of my heart rolled away," he lit up with enthusiasm! Mother's adjustment was easier. However, she had a sore on her leg that gangrened. Some shrugged it off: "She has lived a good life!" But my sister and I gave a surgeon at Halstead permission to amputate her leg. Praise God, she lived another four fruitful years.

With the aging process comes an eventual loss of health. We become more vulnerable to any of a hundred ailments that plague humanity. Some sicknesses bring severe pain, but nothing is as sad as the loss of memory. Even at that, our sufferings are no comparison to the glory that awaits us in heaven (Romans 8:18)!

THE HOPE OF HEAVEN   February 21

---

*"And I heard a voice from heaven saying unto me, Write, Blessed are
the dead which die in the Lord from henceforth: Yes, says the Spirit,
that they may rest from their labors, and their works do follow them."
(Revelation 14:13 KJV)*

The followers of Jesus need have no fear of death. Those
who "die in the Lord" are promised the blessings of Heaven
with all its marvelous tranquility and stunning glory! No
doubt, the heavenly realm is so beautiful that the tongue can
scarce describe it.

Take my father-in-law, he lived with a gleam of heaven in
his eye. This South Dakota farmer was converted at age 28. He
once lost his farm, but not his faith. He counted his wealth each
morning, not by balancing his check book, but by naming each
child in prayer. The desire to please God through witness was
etched deeply in his soul. He was known to sing: "When I wake
with the blest in the mansions of rest, Will there be any stars
in my crown?" He retired early to give ten years to Christian
service. At age 88, his health began to fail. He was soon hospitalized. One day he asked his daughter-in-law, "Please pray
for me, I'm going home." So she prayed that the Lord would
undertake for him and bless him. Then he prayed, "Lord, take
care of Grandma, and send an angel to take me home!" She
stepped out of the room for a few minutes. When she returned,
he was gone.

For the funeral sermon I chose as my text—Rev. 14:13: Rendezvous with God, Rest from labor, and Reward for works.
The "reward-theme" as taught by Christ in the Gospels, has
permeated the consciousness of Christians down through the
years of history.

PRAYER AS A WITNESS   February 22

"...Daniel distinguished himself above the governors and satraps, because an excellent spirit was in him; and the king gave thought to setting him over the whole realm. So the governors and satraps sought to find some charge against Daniel...So [they] thronged before the king...'King Darius, Live forever!...make a firm decree, that whoever petitions any god or man for thirty days, except you, O king, shall be cast into the den of lions.'...Therefore King Darius signed the written decree. Now when Daniel knew that the writing was signed, he went home. And in his upper room, with his windows open toward Jerusalem, he knelt down...three times that day, and prayed...as was his custom...." (Daniel 6:3-4, 6-7, 9-10 NKJV)

Daniel's critics tricked the king, who was forced to place Daniel in the lion's den. King Darius, unable to sleep, fasted all night. He rose early and rushed to the lion's den. To his delight God had shut the lion's mouths and Daniel was safe. The courageous prayer-life of Daniel was a powerful witness to the King of the Medes and the Persians!

Let me share a memorable prayer experience of my grandson, Zachery Epp. For several years he played on the De Anza Force Soccer Club out of Cupertino, California. This elite team is coached by Jeff Baicher, a former pro-soccer player. As grandparents we attended their Southern California tournament, where in their semifinals they faced their archrivals, the San Juan Lightning team. They went into double overtime with the score two to two. Going into penalty kicks was next. Ten players took shots. Zach made the winning kick. He took the ball, dropped on one knee and bowed his head in prayer. He stood up and kicked the ball into the corner of the goal—right through the goalkeeper's hand. We were so proud of Zach's public prayer! "Dare to be a Daniel, Dare to stand alone!"

EXHIBIT TRUE GENTLENESS   **February 23**

"Rejoice in the Lord always. I will say it again, rejoice! Let your gentleness be evident to all. The Lord is near. Do not be anxious about anything, but in every situation, by prayer and petition, with thanksgiving, present your request to God. And the peace of God, which transcends all understanding, will guard your hearts and your minds in Christ Jesus." (Philippians 4:4-7 NIV)

Portraying a gentle spirit in everyday interactions with others, can be a forceful witness to the presence of Christ in our lives. And how we need it! When some event ruffles our feathers, we are prone to respond with a knee-jerk reaction—which does not resemble a Christlike spirit. I, for one, have to pray often for God's enablement to reflect a Christian gentleness!

In my third pastorate, in the Midwest, we initiated a new Sunday School class, teaching the Life of Christ. I volunteered to be the teacher for the first year. One Sunday, with 100 people present, I allowed time for sharing. A lady—I'll call her Molly— testified that recently her patience was severely tested. She took her four daughters shopping in a nearby town. The trip over was special. They enjoyed a very good spiritual talk! At the store, however, the shopping became trying and hectic. Molly almost lost it, until she remembered the nice talk en route. She feared that any harsh words, now, would erase the earlier benefits. So she whispered a prayer, asking God for strength. Praise God, she weathered the test!

My dear friends, let Molly's testimony encourage you. Remember you have two ears and one mouth—so give ample time for hearing, and be slow to speak. Here is a favorite proverb: "A gentle answer turns away wrath, but a harsh word stirs up anger" (Prov. 15:1).

ENCOURAGED BY SCRIPTURE   February 24

"But those who wait on the Lord shall renew their strength; they shall mount up with wings as eagles; they shall run and not be weary; they shall walk and not faint." (Isaiah 40:31 NKJV)

This magnificent passage assures us that Almighty God guarantees to help us Christians, if we utterly depend on Him. His victory is compared to the effortless soaring of an eagle, or the endurance capacity of a distance runner, or the tireless capability of a distance walker. Each metaphor speaks of God's strength given to us when we are tired, exhausted or weak. It is God's power that lifts us up, when we can't proceed another day! Let me repeat, the key is a complete reliance on God. He will not fail us. We need to ask Him for His help.

In one of my churches a lady shared this testimonial. We will call her Arlene. She was very anxious when her truck driver husband lost his job. (He had an accident and the other driver was killed). Arlene was a mother of three, and went to a nearby town to apply for a job. The company that hired her had a business of polishing and buffing used telephones. The work was tedious. She stood long hours. The work was hard on her back. One day when she thought she couldn't go on—she picked up the next phone. To her surprise, a Bible verse was painted on the phone. It was Philippians 4:13: "I can do all things through Christ who strengthens me." That verse gave her new strength to continue on!

The bottom line, my dear friends, is this: (1) Read your Bible, (2) Meditate on verses, and (3) Memorize key passages. Your mind, working like a computer, will pull up verses when needed.

FAITHFUL TO SPOUSE   February 25

"But for Adam no suitable helper was found. So the Lord God caused the man to fall into a deep sleep; and while he was sleeping, He took one of the man's ribs and then closed up the place with flesh. Then the Lord God made a woman from the rib He had taken out of the man, and He brought her to the man....That is why a man leaves his father and mother and is united to his wife, and they become one flesh." (Genesis 2:20-22, 24 NIV)

In the New Testament the Apostle Paul gives us a classic description (Eph. 5) of the wonderful relationship between husband and wife. When a man and a woman stand at the altar and pledge to be faithful to each other they become one. There is a mutual submission one to the other. The wife must respect the husband, and the husband must love his wife unreservedly.

Some years ago I attended a Golden Wedding Anniversary in a neighboring church. The pastor told a story on the honored couple. Years ago Herman and Millie attended a wedding and saw something they had never seen before. The couple took two candles and lit a large center candle; then they blew out the other two. "What does that mean?" Herman asked. "It must mean, no more old flames," replied Millie!

The Apostle Paul speaks of a profound mystery—the relationship between Christ and His church. Christ's extreme love, dying for His church becomes a striking pattern of the relationship between a husband and his wife. As the Christian is obligated to be faithful to Jesus Christ, so the wife is obligated to respect her husband and the husband is obligated to love his wife even unto death. What a challenge to every couple!

INTENTIONAL IN SPEAKING   February 26

"You are witnesses, and God also, how devoutly and justly and blame-lessly we behaved ourselves among you who believe; as you know how we exhorted, and comforted, and charged everyone of you, as a father does his own children, that you would have a walk worthy of God who calls you into His own kingdom and glory." (1 Thessalonians 2:10-12 NKJV) "And I, brethren, when I came to you, did not come with excellence of speech or of wisdom declaring to you the testimony of God. For I determined not to know anything among you except Jesus Christ and Him crucified." (1 Corinthians 2:1-2 NKJV)

Paul preached with compassionate love, and avoided flow-ery oratory. His goal was to be simple in his presentation, so that Christ and His gospel would be highlighted. It was all about Christ!

My second pastorate was in Kansas. I chose as my assistant a former missions executive. He was very knowledgeable, having traveled worldwide. He was an interesting dynamic preacher. He did, however, have one slight flaw—he occasionally went overtime. On self-examination he developed a unique remedy. As he started speaking he placed a cough drop in his mouth, and after 15 minutes he took a second one. When that was gone, he knew his 30 minutes was up. However, as the story goes, he was preaching in Canada, and he went on, and on, and on. Finally, he stopped and checked his cough drop. To his amazement he was sucking on a button!

In Acts 20, Paul and his entourage arrived at Troas and stayed seven days. After eating, Paul preached until midnight. A young man, Eutychus, fell asleep and dropped from the win-dow. He was dead. But Paul prayed over him, and continued preaching until daybreak. In the morning Eutychus was alive and well!

GOD'S BEAUTIFUL HANDIWORK   February 27

"The heavens declare the glory of God; the skies declare the work of His hands. Day after day they pour forth speech; night after night they reveal knowledge. They have no speech, they use no words, no sound is heard from them." (Psalm 19:1-3 NIV)

In all of creation, few scenes equal the beauty of a sunset, where the sun is setting in the West, and every cloud is gilded with gold and fiery red, where a gorgeous rainbow appears in the East. God's handiwork is awe-inspiring! And later a Full Moon peeks through the clouds. Our hearts vibrate with joy as we sing, "How Great Thou Art!"

Equally captivating are God's mountains, with rock formations, with waterfalls, and the giant Sequoia Redwoods. One such site is the Yosemite National Park, in the Sierra Nevada. Our first pastorate was in Southern California and each summer we took our three sons camping—some 350 miles north of LA—in Yosemite Valley. Those were memorable vacations! We hiked to the mountaintops to overlook the valley. We cooked dinner over the camp fire. We learned to chase off bears at night by banging and clanging cooking utensils. We filmed the waterfalls that dropped hundreds of feet into the valley below. We watched men jump from the cliff and float into the valley on their hang gliders. In short, the Yosemite scenery was breathtaking.

The Yosemite experience gave us a new admiration for God's creation. Our devotional times created a family togetherness— which we still recall with fondness. Two of our sons, later in their college days, accepted summer work at Yosemite in the Bike Shop. Taking time off from our busy schedules proved therapeutic for all of us. We all need times of rest and relaxation to be our best for God.

COMPASSIONATE IN BUSINESS   February 28

"Masters, give your servants what is just and fair, knowing that you also have a Master in heaven." *(Colossians 4:1 NKJV)* *"Servants, obey in all things your masters according to the flesh, not with eye-service, as men-pleasers, but in sincerity of heart, fearing God. And whatever you do, do it heartily, as to the Lord and not to men, knowing that from the Lord you will receive the reward of inheritance; for you serve the Lord Christ. But he who does wrong will be repaid for the wrong he has done, and there is no partiality."* *(Colossians 3:22-25 NKJV)*

Neither Christ nor the Apostle Paul made an attempt to abolish slavery, yet both insisted on an attitude of love and justice in the relationship between a master and his servant. This policy carries over to all business transactions: the employer and his worker, the lawyer and his client, or the landlord and his renter.

Forty-five years ago when we lived in Downey, California, we bought a few apartments. This year we had an agonizing decision. One renter, a widow age 82, was failing in health. She had paid rent faithfully for 20 years. Three times in 2010 she mailed her rent check twice, forgetting she had already paid. She still drove her car with no insurance or driver's license. One day she went to a neighbor 15 times, always asking the same thing. She was heartbroken when we contacted her daughter: "We will give you 30 days to find another place for your mother, since she needs help." Well, praise God, today she is in a rest home where her meds, food, and activities are all supervised.

In retrospect, as Christians, we tried to exercise prayerful compassion in keeping her rent low. However, we could not risk a tenant killing someone, while illegally driving a car!

EMPOWERED TO WITNESS   March 1

"But you will receive power when the Holy Spirit comes on you; and you will be my witnesses in Jerusalem, and in all Judea and Samaria, and to the ends of the earth. After He said this, He was taken up before their very eyes, and a cloud hid Him from their sight." (Acts 1:8-9 NIV)

Our Lord Jesus Christ promised Holy Spirit power to His followers moments before He ascended. This unique power would enable them to witness worldwide, at home and abroad. Here was the enormous mandate placed upon the church to share the Gospel story with every man and woman on earth. This continues to be the drumbeat for all missionary work—until Christ returns.

After pastoring churches for 40 years, in Los Angeles and in the Midwest, we retired to Bakersfield in 1996. The following year my wife and I were hired by Choice Books of Harrisonburg, Virginia to begin a Christian Book ministry in California. We were not permitted to sell books to any church or Christian Bookstore—we had to find secular markets. So we went to airports, Wal-Marts, hotels, hospitals, drug stores and truck stops. Soon our largest account was John Wayne Airport where we sold $5,000 worth every month. This was low-key evangelism—out in the world where the church needs to be!

Evangelism was our goal. Let me tell you about the Flying J Truck Stop at Ripon, north of Fresno. While delivering books, a trucker stopped us and thanked us. He had become a drunk—losing his job, his family, and all hope. He bought Dave Wilkerson's book from our rack, *Have You Felt Like Giving Up Lately?* He read it and accepted Christ! He started setting his life back together, with joy in his heart and victory in his daily life.

SHARING THE GOOD TIDINGS   March 2

"Then the angel said to them, 'Do not be afraid, for behold I bring you good tidings of great joy which will be to all people. For there is born to you this day in the city of David a Savior, who is Christ the Lord.'" (Luke 2:10-11 NKJV)

I once received a Christmas letter from my brother John in Hong Kong. He had gone to Asia with US government approval, to serve as a Pax Man under the Mennonite Central Committee (MCC), our relief agency. His job was to distribute food and clothes to thousands of poor needy students and orphans. His supervisors were Brethren-In-Christ mission workers, Norman and Eunice Wingert, who excelled at combining evangelism and social service!

At the Kwok Kwan Primary School, John met a Buddhist grandfather, who loved to hear children sing Christian songs, and enjoyed hearing John tell Bible stories. One day he confided that he wanted to become a Christian but he "didn't know the ceremony." So a Chinese Bible Teacher explained to him the way of salvation. It was none too soon, because a week later the grandfather suddenly died. The Buddhist family requested MCC to conduct a Christian service. After the funeral, it was truly a once-in-a-lifetime experience to accompany this procession, walking through the Wanchai slums led by an 18-piece band, playing "What a Friend We Have In Jesus" and "Nearer My God To Thee."

In Hong Kong John met a missionary named Ruth from South Dakota. They were married and for 40 years they worked in Hong Kong. During the last two decades, John pastored the English speaking Emmanuel Church, the very one he first attended when he came to Hong Kong. Meanwhile, Ruth pastored several Chinese speaking churches.

REFLECTING CHRIST'S LOVE   March 3

"A man with leprosy came and knelt before Him and said, 'Lord if you are willing, you can make me clean.' Jesus reached out his hand and touched the man. 'I am willing,' He said, 'Be clean!' Immediately he was cleansed of his leprosy....When evening came, many who were demon-possessed were brought to him, and he drove out the spirits with a word and healed all the sick. This was to fulfill what was spoken through the prophet Isaiah: He took up our infirmities and bore our diseases." (Matthew 8:2-3, 16-17 NIV)

The compassion of Jesus was awesome. After His ascension, this caring quality fell to His followers. What a task! When my brother John arrived in Hong Kong, as a PAX Man, the refugee problem was acute. Thousands had fled from the mainland crowding into Hong Kong, with no money, no food and no job. Everyday John delivered 3,000 school lunches in the MCC relief project.

As my brother joined hands with other Christians, to minister in Christ's name, he encountered poverty beyond description! CASE NO. 1: At one distribution center they handed a tin of meat to an elderly grandma. She took it and held it high in gratitude and said in Chinese, "THANK GOD." She was too poor to buy dentures. Yet she took every gift as a blessing from God. CASE NO. 2: A cancer victim, writhing in pain, lay on her charity hospital bed praying for death. Since she was fluent in English the MCC workers visited her often. She bemoaned her unhappy past life, but was told of Christ's love and forgiveness. She embraced the good news. On her own initiative she requested baptism before she died. A minister complied. Several days later she died with a heavenly smile on her face.

SOME DRAMATIC CONVERSION   March 4

"As he (Saul) neared Damascus on his journey, suddenly a light from heaven flashed around him. He fell to the ground and heard a voice say to him: 'Saul, Saul, why do you persecute me?' Who are you Lord? Saul asked. 'I am Jesus whom you are persecuting,' He replied. 'Now get up and go into the city and you will be told what you must do.'" (Acts 9:3-6 NIV)

A sudden flash of light dropped Saul to the ground. He had a stunning miraculous encounter with Jesus Christ. The very one he had been fiercely fighting against, Jesus Christ the Risen Lord, now met him head-on, "Saul, Saul, why do you persecute me?" In his travel case, Saul carried papers from Jewish authorities in Jerusalem, which gave him permission to arrest followers of Jesus, should he find some in the synagogues of Damascus. Saul came with evil intent—hoping to stamp out any advance of this new movement—"The People of The Way." Jesus instructed Saul to get up and enter the city, where further orders would be given him. In shock he arose and found himself blind. For three days he sat in utter darkness, neither eating or drinking. Then, in a vision, God spoke to a disciple named Ananias, and told him to go to the house of Judas and pray that Saul's vision would be restored. What a spectacular conversion!

Permit me to share a grand story in our day. A Muslim woman watching the Jesus Film on television was deeply moved. The film ended with Revelation 3:20, "Behold I stand at the door and knock...." Thinking of her house door, not the heart's door, she opened the front door. There stood Jesus! She believed and was saved, becoming a devoted follower of Jesus Christ.

SALVATION FOR EVERYONE   March 5

"For God so loved the world that he gave his only begotten son, that whosoever believeth in him should not perish but have everlasting life. For God sent not his Son into the world to condemn the world, but that the world through him might be saved." (John 3:16-17 KJV)

This salvation verse is a favorite of all and has probably been memorized by more people than any other! No verse highlights the loving mercy of our Heavenly Father better than John 3:16. This gracious invitation to eternal life needs to be heeded by every man and woman, and every boy and girl, on the face of the earth. Here is the foundation for the mission mandate of every church.

Ruth Veldcamp was a Christian Reformed missionary serving in Nigeria, Africa. As she was seeking to win people to Christ, she noticed that many Muslim leaders were linked to occult powers, often using witchcraft and sorcery. She enlisted 100 American Christians to pray daily for the binding of Satan and for the building of churches in Muslim communities. Eventually, she saw marvelous conversions among esteemed community leaders. How did many come to a belief in Christ? Not through the argumentation of theology, rather God communicated to many through visions and dreams!

This reminds us of the amazing conversion of Saul of Tarsus. His encounter with Jesus Christ turned him into the famous Apostle Paul—the greatest missionary of all times. Through his authorship of many of the New Testament books, he cast his shadow over much of the evangelistic outreach of the Early Church. His visitation, his letter writing, his extensive prayer life, and his use of associates to trouble-shoot on his behalf, has become a pattern for all of us on how to disciple our converts.

BILLY GRAHAM CRUSADE   **March 6**

"And He said unto them, 'Go into all the world and preach the gospel to every creature…' So then after the Lord had spoken unto them, He was received up into heaven, and sat on the right hand of God. And they went out and preached everywhere, the Lord working with them, and confirming the word through the accompanying signs."
(Mark 16:15, 19-20 NKJV)

Before His ascension, Christ commanded His followers to go and preach the gospel to all men everywhere. One of the most respected preachers of our day, Billy Graham, led a three week crusade in the Los Angeles Coliseum in 1963. I served as an advisor to the counselors. However, the 1949 LA tent crusade, the one that launched his evangelism, always fascinated me. There, certain celebrities were converted, namely Stuart Hamblin, as well as, Jim and Alice Vaus.

The conversion of Jim Vaus has long peaked my interest! He was a preacher's son. Already in college Jim tried to disprove the Bible. After two years he knew God was real and Jesus Christ was God's son—the Savior of men. Yet his life was unchanged. Slowly he was drawn into a world of crime: (1) As an expert in electronics, he used it in evil deeds. (2) Mickey Cohen, a gangland overlord, offered Jim big money to locate a microphone in his house. He did. (3) He became known as King of the wiretappers—once saving Cohen's life. (4) Next Jim built a wiretap teletypewriter, to delay horse racing results 90 seconds, to win all bets!

The night he was heading for St Louis, Jim and Alice drove by the Billy Graham LA tent. Out of curiosity they entered. As Billy Graham urged sinners to come forward, the Holy Spirit powerfully drew Jim and Alice to accept Christ, and be forgiven of all their sins. Praise God!

MAKING BIG RESTITUTION   March 7

"Then Zacchaeus stood, and said to the Lord, 'Look, Lord, I give half of my goods to the poor; and if I have taken anything from anyone by false accusation, I restore fourfold.' And Jesus said to him, 'Today salvation has come to this house.'" (Luke 19:8-9 NKJV)

The Old Testament clearly taught that giving to the poor was pleasing to God. And secondly, that stealing from others was to be repaid fourfold. In this way, this tax collector, Zacchaeus, showed true repentance for past sins, and a genuine change of heart as he became a follower of Christ. What a grand example.

As Jim Vaus knelt in the dirt and sawdust of the prayer tent, he pled with God to forgive him and to help him over the hurdles in the road ahead. How could he sever his connections with the crime syndicate? How could he change his life style? How could he make restitution to those he had harmed? Turning around is never easy, and for Jim it was very complicated. At that very time, his friend Andy was waiting for him to bring racing electronics to St Louis, and immediately! Any breaking of contracts brought severe threats from the crime syndicate!

He went to the Los Angeles District Attorney, and admitted that he had lied to a grand jury—putting an innocent policeman in jail! The judge gave him probation. He went to an electronic store and confessed shoplifting, requesting time to pay! Andy and three hoods stopped by his house to get racing-electronics. Jim declined and explained how God had changed his life and how he was making restitution. The men left, never to return. Amazingly, Jim put his house up for sale, to repay others. Jim had become a true Christian!

RIGHT LIVING REWARDED   March 8

"In mercy and truth atonement is provided for iniquity; and by the fear of the Lord one departs from evil. When a man's ways please the Lord, He makes even his enemies to be at peace with him. Better is a little with righteousness, than vast revenues without justice." (Proverbs 16:6-8 NKJV)

When Jim Vaus turned his life over to Christ, he trusted God for protection. Many of Jim's companions, while working for Mickey Cohen were murdered. Jim knew his risks. When the question arose, why Jim with his many violations, was not imprisoned, his answer was found in a proverb (Prov. 16:7). God richly rewarded Jim's spiritual commitment. The grace of God was big in his life!

The Vaus family had an urgent need, right off. How could Jim support his wife, Alice, and their four children? What can a reformed wiretapper do? Soon prisons, churches, schools, reformatories and army camps heard of his conversion and asked him to come tell his story. He built a reputation as a lecturer, and enough money came in to support his family. In the next eight years he logged over a million air miles.

One day Jim was lecturing in a Pennsylvania prison. A teen-age inmate, who was in for life for killing a policeman, asked Jim why he came into the prison to speak? He thought youth needed to hear him before they got into crime! Promptly, this lit a flame. Jim had heard of the crime-areas of New York City. He hurried to Manhattan, afire with a new idea. He asked the police—what is the worst area? They showed him 14 crime areas. One was in Harlem, one mile square, holding 190,000 inhabitants. It lay along the East River called Hell Gate, the police department's notorious 23rd Precinct. Here Jim hoped to start a work for God!

LAMBS AMONG WOLVES   **March 9**

"Then He said to them, 'The harvest truly is great...therefore pray the Lord of the harvest to send out laborers into His harvest....Go your way; behold, I send you out as lambs among wolves.'" *(Luke 10:2-3 NKJV)*

When Jim Vaus walked the streets of Harlem, pondering the idea of starting boy's clubs in this crime-ridden area, he was sickened by the stench, kicking dead rats into the gutter, and stepping over drunks. It was a tough choice. Starting a ministry in this dangerous Hell Gate area, would cost him the joy of being with Alice and four children in Los Angeles. The price was big; but Christ was calling!

He repaired an old store and moved in furniture. He fortified it with a second front wall, a heavy oak door and electronic surveillance. Then he announced his club was open for business. But not one soul came. He tried to meet some gang leaders. No luck. So he went to the local school—filled with 2,000 troubled kids. Jim appealed to the Dean of Discipline for help. He gave his testimony of finding Christ in a Los Angeles tent and his desire to share Christ with others.

Jim asked to host a school assembly. The school leaders treated him like a guest from outer space! What could really be his motivation? He was inspected by the school psychiatrist, then the school psychologist, and finally the school principal. To his joy they granted him permission to conduct an assembly. He unpacked his electronic gear—stuff that would make a man's hair stand on end. This had been tried and perfected in a hundred lectures. His show lasted 45 minutes. The youth liked it, and liked him! He ended with: "Come to my club and I'll teach you more."

GOD PROMISES SUCCESS   March 10

"Have I not commanded you? Be strong and courageous. Do not be afraid; do not be discouraged, for the Lord your God will be with you wherever you go." (Joshua 1:9 NIV)

God's word to Joshua, was fitting for Jim Vaus as well. When God calls, God also supplies. Going to Harlem was more dangerous than landing in darkest Africa. His school assembly was his entrée to the lives of these youth. They started coming to his counseling office, pouring out their stress and grievances. Jim went with them to the courthouse when trouble struck. He went to their homes to help with medical and dental needs. By winning their confidence, Jim won a chance to share the gospel. God blessed Jim's obedience in marvelous ways!

Gradually friends gave financial support to undergird this ministry. Community respect grew as Jim added summer camps, teen clubs and training sessions. He could accommodate only 150 at a time. A long waiting list developed! Jim was forced to organize as Youth Development Incorporated (YDI). That was how the cops in Harlem knew it. When Billy Graham stopped by, 123 gang leaders heard him preach. Over half accepted Christ! Jim followed up with three Bible classes, one on Sunday, and two during the week.

After six years, crime in the 23rd Precinct declined sharply, 40% in juvenile court, and gang killings dropped from 23 to ten per year. Of Vaus' first 12 club members, 11 were employed, two were married, one worked in a bank supervising 19 employees! But for the grace of God and Jim Vaus—All would have been in prison or living on welfare. The local detective, Lt. Cottell, gave Vaus high praise for preaching the Love of God by example. Instead of wild kids bent on self-destruction, the police were seeing young ladies and gentlemen emerging!

69

DISPLAYING ROTTEN FRUIT   March 11

"Make a tree good and its fruit will be good, or make a tree bad and its fruit will be bad, for a tree is recognized by its fruit. You brood of vipers, how can you who are evil say anything good? For the mouth speaks what the heart is full of. The good man brings good things out of the good stored up in him, and the evil man brings evil things out of the evil stored up in him." (Matthew 12:33-35 NIV)

In his discourse with the scribes and Pharisees, Jesus explained that no evil heart can produce good fruit! So in our day, no Bible teacher, deacon or pastor can be fruit-bearing with an evil heart. God cannot be fooled.

When I was about six years of age, my two older sisters and I attended a birthday party at a farm one mile from ours. We had strict orders to walk home. When I saw a car parked beside the road, I was afraid, so I asked a neighbor to take us home. Yes, I was blamed, and got a spanking. (I have long ago forgiven my dad; I chose not to explain things—he would have called me "chicken"). Soon that car appeared again as we came home from school. The man stepped out, zipped down his pants and exposed himself. At home we told mother. She jumped into our 1927 Chevrolet, and raced after him and got his license number. Dad phoned the County Sheriff. The car belonged to a minister in a town 10 miles away. So one Sunday we joined our parents to worship at that church. We children agreed—that's the man! What a hypocrite—evil on Wednesday, preaching on Sunday!

ASSISTING TOTAL STRANGERS   March 12

"Keep on loving each other as brothers and sisters. Do not forget to show hospitality to strangers, for by so doing some people have shown hospitality to angels without knowing it. Continue to remember those in prison as if you were together with them in prison, and those who are mistreated as if you yourselves were suffering." (Hebrews 13:1-3 NIV)

The Bible urges us to be gracious to all people, even to total strangers. I grew up on a Kansas farm in Depression days. We farmed the very land that my German speaking grandparents had purchased from the Santa Fe Railroad in 1876 when they migrated from West Prussia.

My god-fearing mother was always kind to a "tramp" who stopped in once or twice a year. He requested work in exchange for a meal. Mom enjoyed making a big breakfast: fried eggs, bacon, homemade bread with apple butter, pancakes with syrup, or corn bread with honey, and coffee. For work he usually chopped a pile of firewood, then he would come inside and eat a hearty meal. When he left Mom would give him a good send off with some cake, cookies and apples. He carried a sack on his back and often walked along the railroad track.

My father also displayed a Christian compassion through his visits to the Wichita Rescue Mission, and to the Eldorado jail. At the farm I recall a car slipping into the ditch. Even though we suspicioned that the man had stolen some items from our neighbor's tornado-ravaged farm, we harnessed a team of horses and pulled him out of the ditch and sent him on his way.

In 1961, when refugees were fleeing into Berlin, out of East Germany, my parents volunteered to serve under MCC for six months. Mother cooked meals and Dad did refugee counseling alongside Eastern European Mission workers.

GOD'S GREAT DELIVERANCE   March 13

"Therefore this is what the Lord says concerning the King of Assyria: He will not enter the city or shoot an arrow here….I will defend this city and save it, for my sake and for the sake of David my servant. That night the angel of the Lord went out and put to death a hundred and eighty-five thousand in the Assyrian camp. When the people got up the next morning—there were all the dead bodies! So Sennacherib king of Assyria broke camp and withdrew." (2 Kings 19:32-36 NIV)

Hezekiah, King of Judah, received a letter from Sennacherib that he planned to conquer Judah. So Hezekiah rushed to the house of the Lord, spread out the letter and prayed for deliverance. God answered in a dramatic fashion!

Some years ago, at the height of the war in Iraq, I volunteered to pray regularly for the conflict. I did not follow the pattern of many others who simply prayed for the safety of our men—I also prayed for Iraq: for a stable government, for safety of the medical workers, for the educators, for the business men, for the bankers, and for the oppressed women. I prayed for a sound solution.

About that time a recruiter persuaded my grandson, Josh, that the Marines had a good educational benefit package. So he enlisted. He had two tours in Iraq. Now I really had "skin in the game," and my prayers intensified. One day I reminded God of Hezekiah's prayer and of the divine intervention. Shortly after, the military sent extra troops, "THE SURGE," and the situation stabilized. This taught me again that the prayers of churches in America, and churches worldwide, are essential in accomplishing God's purposes. The most, and the least we can do is pray!

FORGIVENESS IS REQUIRED   March 14

"For if you forgive other people when they sin against you, your heavenly Father will also forgive you. But if you do not forgive others their sins, your Father will not forgive your sins." (Matthew 6:14-15 NIV)

The Bible is very clear—if we refuse to offer forgiveness to others, God will withhold forgiveness as well. Dr. Archibald Hart defines forgiveness as the act of surrendering my right to hurt you back.

Holding grudges is so easy, while initiating reconciliation can be so difficult. I recall an experience in my first parish. An elder and I tangled in a phone conversation. It was heated and abrasive. "I think I'll come over to clear this up," I fumed. "Yes, you better," he retorted. On the freeway I prayed for wisdom. I knew he was a godly brother, but I suspected his motives. He wanted me to take our youth to a different summer camp, and on top of that, he did not want our youth to interact with our downtown church where some were Hispanic and some Black! He called that "dangerous." Of course, I suspicioned prejudice!

He met me courteously and we talked. I raised basic issues. "Huh, I can see there will be no reconciliation here today," he rebutted. After more excruciating words, issues I did not want swept under the rug, I made two unconditional promises. "Brother, any time your name comes up in a conversation, I'll put in a good word for you. And secondly, whenever you enter my thoughts, I'll pray God's blessings on you." He arose and embraced me! For the next 20 years, until his death, he mailed us a Christmas greeting. Forgiveness is truly liberating. Basically, it is the genius of Christianity. God did it first. We follow his brilliant example!

FISHING WITH EXPECTATION   **March 15**

"When he had finished speaking, he said to Simon, 'Put out into deep water, and let down the nets for a catch.' Simon answered, 'Master, we've worked hard all night and haven't caught anything. But because you say so, I will let down the nets.' When they had done so, they caught such a large number of fish that their nets began to break. So they signaled their partners in the other boat to come and help them, and they came and filled both boats...." (Luke 5:4-7 NIV)

These expert fishermen had high hopes of a good catch, but went all night with no luck. In the morning Jesus sat in Simon's boat teaching people. *Then he* commanded Simon to go into deeper water and fish. They came up with such a huge catch the nets began to break and the two boats began to sink! The disciples were awe-struck by this miraculous catch!

Our oldest son lives in the San Francisco area and owns a cabin in Arnold, 60 miles east of Modesto. In a recent summer, we vacationed there a few days. One day we took our grandson Jordan up to Lake Alpine to fish. After several hours, he got tired and asked permission to go to the other side of the lake. About three hours later he showed up with a huge trout! At the Tackle Shop in Arnold, we entered it into the monthly contest (24 inches, and 4 ½ pounds). Yes, he had the biggest fish. His reward: a free Shakespeare Rod & Reel. How exciting!

The awesome catch of fish convinced the disciples that they should become devoted followers of Jesus. The fishing escapade with our grandson convinced us that relating to Grandkids is a good way to encourage them in our Christian faith.

WORK TO GLORIFY GOD   March 16

"Whatever you do, work at it with all you heart, as working for the Lord, not for human masters, since you know that you will receive an inheritance from the Lord as a reward. It is the Lord Christ you are serving. Anyone who does wrong will be repaid for their wrong, and there is no favoritism." (Colossians 3:23-25 NIV)

Paul urges all workers to please their masters in a God-fearing way. Therefore, whether we are in church work, or in the business world we need to do quality work. In reality, as Christians, we are all serving Jesus Christ.

In my first pastorate, in Southern California, I prayed earnestly about our financial needs and our future. Despite the comment of one banker—"What business does a pastor have in investing in real estate?"—I bought a fourplex. My dad, a Kansas farmer, gladly loaned me the down payment. And we own those apartments to this day.

On the pastor's day off, my wife and I often visited the apartments. Always there was something needing attention. We built a warm relationship with the tenants—they learned the names of our three boys. We did low-key evangelism by giving Christmas gifts and *Guideposts* magazines. One day a lady said, "I'm not in good health, I want your sons to inherit my fish aquarium. But more importantly, I want you to officiate at my funeral." I gave her my promise. The day came. At the funeral home I had the grand opportunity to share the Gospel with the entire neighborhood! I explained God's gracious love: His offer of forgiveness, eternal life, and a heavenly home, all through the death and resurrection of Jesus our Lord. To summarize: in both the spiritual realm and the secular, we do all for the glory of God!

BEREAVED BUT REDIRECTED   **March 17**

"Since my youth, God, you have taught me, and to this day I declare your marvelous deeds. Even when I am old and gray, do not forsake me, my God, till I declare your power to the next generation, your mighty acts to all who are to come." (Psalm 71:17-18 NIV)

When the elderly are widowed, they of course, feel lonely, or even helpless and useless. However, after a period of grieving, they begin to assess their future situation. Providing their health is good, they often visualize acts of service they can still render. Helping others is therapeutic!

Take for example our apartment renter who willed her fish aquarium to our sons. She was raised in an Episcopal home in Michigan. She married when barely 20 and moved with her husband to Southern California. After 38 happy years together, raising two children, her husband died and she was left to fend for herself. She sold her house and moved into the Downey apartment which we purchased. She really enjoyed reading, sewing, cooking and gardening. Above all, she overcame her widowhood loneliness by helping others.

At the Rancho Los Amigos Hospital of Downey she joined the volunteer service staff—often working three days per week. She shopped for patients, assisted with crafts, and served as a sponsor on field trips for some wheelchair patients. Two weeks before she died, we visited her at the Downey Community Hospital. With pride, she showed us the SERVICE PIN the Rancho Hospital had awarded her for her 4,600 hours of volunteer work! What a striking model for all seniors. Each of us can do something—like visiting, singing, praying, reading scripture, bringing cookies, giving rides to church, encouraging the pastor, and a host of other things. My friend, what are you doing for Jesus Christ?

PRAYING BEFORE EATING   **March 18**

"And he directed the people to sit down on the grass. Taking the five loaves and the two fish, and looking up to heaven, he gave thanks and broke the loaves. Then he gave them to the disciples and the disciples gave them to the people. They all ate and were satisfied, and the disciples picked up twelve basketfuls of broken pieces that were left over." (Matthew 14:19-20 NIV)

Here at the feeding of the 5,000, Jesus gave thanks, and after that, distributed the food to the people. I confess that I had not noticed that he prayed before they ate! But in the German culture of my upbringing, we always blessed the food before the meal, and thanked God after the meal. From my childhood days on our farm in Kansas, I recall the humorous story we often told. A man announced that on his farm some never bowed their heads and prayed before eating. So the response was "Really, who was it?" Answer, "the pigs!"

My mother was a poet, and she crafted several Table Graces. Here is one:

The cattle on a thousand hills, The sparrows in the tree,
Are constant in thy watch care Lord, Are daily fed by Thee
And we who are Thy children, Now raise our voice in praise
For food, clothes and shelter, All through our lifelong days.

Today, whether we are at home or in a restaurant, it is our family custom to pray before we eat—showing thanks to God, and being a witness to others.

GOD DESERVES LOYALTY   March 19

"...The Lord your God is testing you to find out whether you love him with all your heart and with all your soul. It is the Lord your God you must follow, and him you must revere. Keep his commands and obey him; serve him and hold fast to him." (Deuteronomy 13:3-4 NIV)

Here God warns the Israelites not to be influenced by impostors. When a prophet or a dreamer performs some miracle, and commands them to follow a new god, they should not respond. They should eliminate such deceivers from the land! The Lord God deserves their undivided loyalty. He brought them out of Egypt in a mighty miraculous demonstration.

When our youngest son, Nathan, was in junior high, I sometimes played basketball with him, on the driveway in front of our house. One day we played "horse" and later took turns driving to the basket. I viewed my activity as properly fulfilling my responsibility as a father. Suddenly he startled me, "Dad, pay attention!" WOW! True, I had watched the cars go by on First Street, I had waved a neighbor in her yard, and I had talked with a couple who sauntered by on their daily stroll. But my son wanted my total concentration!

I can visualize my Heavenly Father saying, "My child, please pay attention." And certainly, we as Christians owe him our undivided loyalty. Why? First, because he created us, and secondly, because he redeemed us through the work and merits of Jesus Christ. Everything we enjoy—our sins forgiven, our daily guidance, our abundant provisions, our prospect of heaven, and our promise of the Second Coming of Jesus Christ—we owe to God. Over the years our family always prayed before meals. Sometimes we asked ourselves, "Were you actually thinking of God?" He wants our undivided!

TRAGICALLY LOSING FAITH   March 20

"Then you will call on me and come and pray to me, and I will listen to you. You will seek me and find me when you seek me with all your heart. I will be found by you, declares the Lord...." *(Jeremiah 29:12-14 NIV)*

In my first pastorate, we heard the amazing news that the 70 year old senior pastor of the nearby South Gate Chapel had experienced a conversion! Some months later we invited him for dinner, and scheduled him to share his life story at our Sunday evening service.

To a packed church, Dr. Ray Jarman, told of his childhood in Kansas City. His parents were devoted members of a Disciples of Christ Church. When he chose to become a minister, his parents sent him to their denominational university in Missouri. The school was teaching an "enlightened" theology coming from the University of Chicago. One day a prof disowned the "Virgin Birth." Ray asked, "If you reject one part of the Bible, how can you believe any of it?" The professor threatened to expel him. But by year's end, Ray endorsed "Higher Criticism" with its denial of the divinity of Jesus Christ.

In his first pastorate in Bowling Green, a dying woman asked him to tell her about heaven. Concealing his unbelief, he read John 14. His self-talk was "you hypocrite, you better resign!" He tested the idea with a pastor in Kansas City. He said, "No, we need you. Soon nobody will believe the Bible. Latch onto some great idea and preach it!" Jarman determined to do just that. Next he jumped at the chance to take a church in Michigan, so he could do graduate studies in Chicago, with famous teachers in that environment of Liberalism. Sadly, he began to doubt the tenants of Christianity.

STRUGGLES WITH FAITH   March 21

"The fool says in his heart, 'There is no God.' They are corrupt, their deeds are vile; there is no one who does good. The Lord looks down from heaven on all mankind to see if there are any who understand, any who seek God. All have turned away, all have become corrupt; there is no one who does good, not even one." (Psalm 14:1-3 NIV)

Dr Jarman arrived in Chicago, already having lost his faith. He was eager to learn from these "world-renowned" teachers. They taught that angels and demons are human creations to explain good and evil; holding that only verifiable truth is believable; that modernism extracts the best from all world religions and formulates a beautiful syncretistic philosophy— the wave of the future!

In 1942, the Jarmans moved to Huntington Park, California. Though he believed nothing supernatural, he was a popular speaker, quoting long Bible passages by memory, and conducting many weddings and funerals. His wife, Grace, remained a strong Bible believer and worried over Ray's radical leanings. She raised their children; he counseled his parishioners.

Eventually, Dr. Jarman noticed that his "Re-make Yourself" theology was powerless to change people. He kept searching "in dangerous waters" as he later called it. From a smorgasbord of religious ideas he dabbled in Yoga, astrology, spiritualism, Christian Science, hypnotism, and even reincarnation. But nothing compared to his Menlo Park experiment! He paid doctors $500 for a religious-LSD experience. He saw God at the top of a jewel-studded ladder, but he himself kept helplessly sliding down toward Hell, where the devil was tormenting people familiar to him. It was horrifying! A psychologist escorted him home, 400 miles. It took days to recover. His religious search left him confused and dissatisfied.

RINGING HEAVENLY BELLS   **March 22**

"Therefore if anyone is in Christ, the new creation has come; the old has gone, the new is here. All this is from God, who reconciled us to himself through Christ and gave us the ministry of reconciliation."
(2 Corinthians 5: 17-18 NIV)

In the South Gate Chapel, where Dr. Ray Jarman was minister, two people were key to his conversion. One was Shannon, a 14-year member. He asked Jarman about the deity of Christ. "Jesus was no more divine than we are," quipped Jarman, "History has mountaintop figures like Lincoln, Shakespeare and Jesus. Some seize upon that quality." Shannon was shocked. At a Full Gospel Business Men's Rally in Phoenix, Shannon accepted Christ and was baptized in the Holy Spirit. Back home he began carrying his Bible. Jarman despised Bible toters.

The other key person was Carmen, Jarman's secretary. She had a dream of a white bird, dying to protect her chicks. Her metaphysician was baffled. Then accidentally, she heard Gospel Radio, and understood the death of Christ! On her knees, she felt great love as she wept, worshiped and accepted her Christ. What a shock—Jarman's closest aid began reading her Bible. Daily doctrinal debates ensued.

One day Jarman surprised Carmen, "I wish I could be born-again. It's no use, I'm too old." That evening, March 28, 1966, Shannon appeared at Jarman's apartment. "Ray, you must approach God as a helpless child. Just accept Jesus." "Shannon, I want Him," said Jarman. As Jarman knelt, God showed him his sin—deceiving thousands in 52 years of preaching. An avalanche of agony crushed him. Suddenly, he felt a glorious peace. In a vision Christ appeared and touched him. He knew he was born-again. He used to think Bible believers were unenlightened, yet when he arose from his knees, he knew the Bible was true.

ALTAR-CALL COMMITMENT   **March 23**

"Therefore, if you are offering your gift at the altar and there remember that your brother or sister has something against you, leave your gift there in front of the altar. First go and be reconciled to them, then come and offer your gift." *(Matthew 5:23-24 NIV)*

Jesus taught that giving money or doing service, was not as important as living harmoniously with our brothers and sisters. Some years ago, two neighboring churches in Minnesota invited me to come as a Bible Teacher for some old-fashioned renewal meetings. I vividly recall one Monday night. My topic centered on "facilitating caring in the church," enabling people to liberate each other through confession and forgiveness.

At the end I devised an altar-call to bless the whole church, where the Holy Spirit had freedom to move. I asked any concerned person to rise and speak, after which Pastor John or Pastor Joe would pray. The response was beautiful. A sixth grade lad, sitting between Mom and Dad, stood and requested prayer for victory in his life. Pastor Joe prayed for him. Next, a lady gifted with a singing ministry, spoke of the criticism she gets when she sings at other churches. Two ladies arose and asked forgiveness for their critical spirit and prayed for her. Next, an elder confessed his lack of caring. The response etched most deeply in my memory, came from a 60 year old member. He spoke with a trembling voice: "Please pray for our family. Since my parents died, our family is caught in a terrible inheritance squabble. It's a disgrace!" Pastor John offered that prayer.

Pastors and church leaders have a special duty, admittedly difficult, to alleviate the friction areas of the church. The Bible concept of the church being one body is helpful. Any injury in the body, sends shock waves of pain to the rest of the body.

PARABLE OF FAITHFULNESS   **March 24**

"For the kingdom of heaven is like a man traveling to a far country, who called his own servants and delivered his goods to them. And to one he gave five talents, to another two, and to another one, to each according to his own ability; and immediately he went on a journey." (Matthew 25:14-15 NKJV)

This morning at our church our pastor continued his summer series on the parables of Jesus, using as his text Matthew 25:14-30. A business man entrusted money to three men, to each a different amount, based on their skills and abilities. (A talent was roughly a thousand dollars). The first two men worked hard and doubled the net worth of the trust, while the third man was a total failure, burying his talent in the ground. The underlying theme of the sermon was one of "accountability." God has entrusted to each of us Time, Talents, and Treasure.

Our pastor used his Uncle Larry as an example of utter faithfulness. He pastored a small Virginia church for 20 years. He worked hard meeting the needs of adults and relating to youth in sports. Once he stated, "When I jump making a basketball layup, I wish I could continue upward into the presence of God!" Several months later, at age 49, he died of a heart attack playing basketball. At his funeral there was standing room only in the little church, and at the cemetery there was not room enough for all the cars! He was so loved by all the folks he had led to Christ!

In Christ's parable about the day of reckoning, the first two men got the master's praise, "Well done, good and faithful servant! You were faithful over a few things, I make you ruler over many things. Enter into the joy of your Lord."

EDUCATION IS A PRIVILEGE   March 25

"I will open my mouth with a parable, I will utter hidden things, things from of old—things we have heard and known, things our ancestors have told us. We will not hide them from their descendants; we will tell the next generation the praiseworthy deeds of the Lord, his power, and the wonders he has done." (Psalm 78:2-4 NIV)

The Old Testament is emphatic that fathers are responsible to offer proper instructions to their children—to teach them to appreciate the praiseworthy acts and wonders of their Almighty God. God, in history, has been gracious to us all!

My father insisted that a college education was a privilege, not a right. He enabled each of his eight children to graduate from Bible College. But he himself never had that opportunity, though he craved it dearly. When he graduated from grade eight, he was forced to stay home and farm. At age 19 he got one year of high school—that was the extent of his formal training. My father often belittled graduation gifts. Why reward kids who enjoyed such a privilege? Interestingly enough, my parents gave us each a good watch when we graduated from high school; but the gift was given at Christmas time, so it did not appear like a reward for graduating! Going to school was a privilege, not a right—so dad thought.

My parents were devoted Christians. We had regular Bible reading and prayer in our home. We were raised in weekly Sunday School and Church Worship, as well as Daily Vacation Bible School (half day Bible lessons, half day German lessons). We attended many Community Revival Meetings, Missionary Conferences and Evangelistic Tent Crusades. I was genuinely inspired by many of the guest speakers who spoke with such fervor and who held the audience spellbound.

A PRE-EVANGELISM WITNESS   March 26

"With great power the apostles continued to testify to the resurrection of the Lord Jesus, and God's grace was so powerfully at work in them all, that there were no needy persons among them. For from time to time those who owned lands or houses sold them, brought the money from the sales and put it at the apostle's feet, and it was distributed to anyone who had need." (Acts 4:33-35 NIV)

As the revival fires burned in the Early Church, the apostles gave a powerful witness to their community. While the opposition was fierce, the apostles continued their evangelism with unabated boldness, showing no fear!

In church history the Moravian Revival, in August of 1727, likewise had a powerful impact on the world. This spiritual awakening fell on the German estate of Count Nicholaus von Zinzendorf and melted and motivated a group in a dramatic way. The result was twofold—it spawned a 100-year prayer meeting, and secondly, it unified the village of Herrnhut with one goal: worldwide evangelism! This group had a major affect on the life of John Wesley. Wesley went from England to America to witness to the American Indians. On the ship ride, they encountered a severe storm. Wesley feared for his life. He saw a group of Moravians on the ship who prayed and sang, showing no anxiety! Wesley asked a Moravian brother, "How is it that you show no fear?" Answer: "Don't you have the witness in your heart that you are a child of God" (Romans 8:16)? Wesley could not answer.

This is an example of "Pre-Evangelism." Our questions, or our testimony, can be used of God to produce spiritual hunger. Wesley went to America to share the gospel, but lacked assurance of salvation. Later on, this Moravian witness led to his conversion!

JOHN WESLEY'S CONVERSION   March 27

"Now, Lord, consider their threats and enable your servants to speak your word with great boldness. Stretch out your hand to heal and perform signs and wonders through the name of your holy servant Jesus. After they prayed, the place where they were meeting was shaken. And they were all filled with the Holy Spirit and spoke the word of God boldly." (Acts 4:29-31 NIV)

Without fail, kingdom advance stems from strong praying. The church goes forward on its knees. As the Early Church shook the religious establishment by her vigorous praying, so also the Moravian Revival, inspired by Count Zinzendorf using round-the-clock praying, developed a worldwide missionary enterprise that worked hard, winning souls in many countries.

John Wesley was a trophy of Moravian evangelism. According to Peter Boehler, on April 26, 1738, Wesley came weeping, requesting prayer as a "poor brokenhearted sinner." Later on May 24, at a Moravian small group meeting at Aldersgate, Wesley's heart was "strangely warmed." He writes, "I felt I did trust in Christ, Christ alone for salvation, and an assurance was given me that he had taken away my sins, even mine, and saved me from the law of sin and death."

John Wesley became a fiery evangelist. His converts met in "bands" of six or more, confessing faults to each other, and praying for each other, according to James 5:16. Membership in his groups required six month probation periods, for growth and nurture. He became the founder of the Methodist Church. At the time of his death in 1791, Europe had 72,000 Methodists and America had 57,000.

Friends, you may be struggling with assurance of salvation, like Wesley. I did as a teenager. What joyful relief when assurance came! Don't wait until death to find out. Claim it today (1 John 5:13-15)!

TEACHING WORK ETHICS   March 28

"I went past the field of the sluggard, past the vineyard of someone who has no sense; thorns had come up everywhere, the ground was covered with weeds, and the stone wall was in ruins. I applied my heart to what I observed and learned a lesson from what I saw: A little sleep, a little slumber, a little folding of the hands to rest—and poverty will come on you like a thief and scarcity like an armed man." (Proverbs 24:30-34 NIV)

Solomon went past a field covered with thorns and weeds. He thought to himself: "That lazy jerk, if he doesn't clean the field and raise a good crop, poverty will overtake him!" From my upbringing on a Kansas farm, I recall how well we knew which farmers usually kept a clean field. Some men hired teenagers to walk the milo and soybeans, to pull every cocklebur and chop every sunflower.

In 1970, when I was working on my doctorate at Fuller Seminary, in between pastorates, we lived in Glendora, California. A neighbor confronted me with a proposal—I have a four acre lot on the next street and I would like to hire you and your boys to pull all the weeds. My sons age 13, 10, and 8 all agreed. We had a great time! One huge weed, the boys could not pull. I grabbed it, gave a big pull and when it came out, I fell flat on my back. The boys roared with laughter. I also remember the profound lesson I taught them—"the whole earth is hanging on the other end of this weed!"

My sons still laugh about this job assignment. For me as a dad, it allowed me to teach a work ethic—when we commit, we work to the finish!

ARRIVING HOME IN HEAVEN   March 29

"Yea, though I walk through the valley of the shadow of death, I will fear no evil; For You are with me; Your rod and Your staff, they comfort me." (Psalm 23:4 NKJV) "Precious in the sight of the Lord is the death of His saints." (Psalm 116:15 NKJV)

My sister Martha Epp, age 81, went to be with the Lord on October 21, 2010. The Wichita doctors had sent her to the Kansas University Medical Center to replace two heart valves. Unexpectedly, after surgery she suffered a severe stroke. She had expected to come home with better health. We were in Nebraska at the time visiting family; so we stayed another week to attend her funeral at the Emmaus Mennonite Church of Whitewater, Kansas—her home church.

Martha was a career missionary nurse, serving in Africa from 1956 to 1986, under the Sudan Interior Mission. Because of the political turmoil she rotated back and forth from Ethiopia to Sudan several times. She worked at hospitals, orphanages and various outpatient clinics. While in Ethiopia, she was selected to be the private nurse of the Empress, wife of Emperor Haile Selassie. Her final term in Ethiopia had her serving in the famine relief project.

Most of her final 15 years were spent in Wichita, teaching international Arabian women Bible studies and language classes. Already as a child she aspired to be a missionary lady, and to her dying day she was faithful to that vision. In her last decade she faced health problems due to what her doctors called congenital heart failure. Yet she never gave up. Her motto seemed to be: "...Be steadfast, unmoveable, always abounding in the work of the Lord, forasmuch as you know that your labor is not in vain in the Lord" (1 Corinthians 15:58).

FACING HOSTILITY WITH LOVE   March 30

"Blessed are you when people insult you, persecute you and falsely say all kinds of evil against you because of me. Rejoice and be glad, because great is your reward in heaven, for in the same way they persecuted the prophets who were before you." (Matthew 5:11-12 NIV)

Jesus Christ our Lord spoke blessings on His followers who experience hatred and false accusations. Confronting such enemies with love and care brings great rewards. I have experienced that in numerous pastoral encounters.

In our first pastorate in the Los Angeles area, one member on the roster (we'll call him Willie) had not attended for years. On a visit to his home in Paramount, I found his wife studying with Jehovah Witnesses. She gladly accepted my offer for some home Bible studies. One day I had the joy of leading her to faith in Christ. However, her health declined and I visited her in the Long Beach Hospital the day she died.

Willie turned bitter—to God, the church and the pastor. He hired a stranger to conduct the funeral. At times I visited Willie at his service station in Lakewood. After years of boycotting the church, the Elders asked: "Is this membership meaningful to you, or should we drop it?" He retorted, "Who are you to play God? Hassle me and I'll transfer membership back to Newton, Kansas, where I was baptized as a teen, shortly before my army tour!" With time his name was erased. In the meantime, I left that church and pursued a doctorate in Pasadena, and next I accepted a call to a church in the Midwest—never dreaming that I would ever meet Willie again. But God had a marvelous surprise in store for me. All my loving care paid off!

A PRODIGAL COMES HOME   March 31

"When he came to his senses, he said, 'How many of my father's hired servants have food to spare, and here I am starving to death! I will set out and go back to my father and say to him: Father I have sinned against heaven and against you. I am no longer worthy to be called your son; make me like one of your hired servants.' So he got up and went to his father. But while he was still a long way off, his father saw him and was filled with compassion for him; he ran to his son, threw his arms around him and kissed him." (Luke 15:17-20 NIV)

In 1971 we accepted a call from a 900-member parish in Newton, Kansas. Imagine our surprise—wife and I were invited to Ramada Inn one Sunday evening to have coffee with Willie and his new wife, a childhood sweetheart. The moment we sat down, Willie began: "Pastor, I apologize for the way I treated you in L.A. I have long admired you two for attending my wife's funeral after I intentionally snubbed you! According to Steps Five and Nine of Alcoholics Anonymous I'm making amends wherever possible."

"Willie, I never held a grudge." I said, "but thanks for your apology; We warmly forgive. But Willie, how did you get to Kansas?" "It was this way," he replied, "I was a helpless alcoholic. California authorities sent me by train to my cousin's farm to dry out. The A.A. group from Newton came out twice a week to bring me to their meetings. That's how I got help."

Eventually, Willie bought a large home, three blocks from our church and began taking in alcoholics. We raised money and built a wooden privacy fence for him.

WILLIE'S GRAND RECOVERY   April 1

"As they traveled along the road, they came to some water and the eunuch said, 'Look, here is water. What can stand in the way of me being baptized?' And he gave orders to stop the chariot. Then both Philip and the eunuch went down into the water and Philip baptized him." (Acts 8:36-38 NIV)

One Sunday I preached on the Prodigal (Lk. 15). Barely home the phone rang. It was Willie. "Pastor, I heard you on radio. I'd like a cassette. That's my story. The first year in AA, I was so bitter I refused to say 'God' in the 12 steps of AA." Just as the eunuch took a voluntary step with Philip, so Willie took big steps with me.

Later Willie gingerly asked, "Can wife and I take Communion at your church? The last time I took communion was 38 years ago at this church when I was baptized." My response was, "If you believe in Jesus Christ—his death and resurrection for you, and desire to live for him, you are welcome." Some months later Willie cautiously asked a bigger question: "Can wife and I join your church again? You know my background— my ungodly life in the army, my past divorce, and my derelict alcoholic spree? Remember, Pastor, I ask no special favors!" With great joy I responded, "Willie, we are a hospital for sinners, not a holy club for saints. As you join us in serving Christ, we'll join hands with you in helping the alcoholics!"

So on a Sunday, April 7, Willie and Sue joined our church, some 17 years after I started praying for Willie in California. Going the Second-Mile had paid off beyond our wildest dreams. Friends, your fervent prayers are always heard. Keep praying and leave the outcome to God. He is not willing that any should perish.

MY CLASS SONG SUBMISSION   April 2

"Praise the Lord. How good it is to sing praises to our God, how pleasant and fitting to praise him!...He heals the brokenhearted and binds up their wounds....Sing to the Lord with grateful praise; make music to our God on the harp." (Psalm 147:1, 3, 7 NIV)

In 1953 I graduated from Grace Bible Institute (now Grace University) in Omaha. Class members were asked to enter a class-song contest. Mine was chosen! I was then 21 years of age and engaged to be married (July 31) to my college sweetheart. We were enrolled to continue studies at Wheaton College that fall. We felt assuredly that God was calling us into full-time Christian service.

MY CLASS SONG ENTRY, 1953

Once the clutch of death's dominion, held our hearts ensnared to sin,
Filling breast with pangs of sorrow, till the Savior entered in.
Ne'er before such peace was sheltered, in that lone and contrite heart.
Now God's Son, our precious Savior, bids all foes and fears depart.

Seal dear Lord our consecration, set apart for service free.
Take each act and thought and motive, make it purely one for Thee.
Send us forth to regions yonder, where men grope in endless night.
Holy Spirit cleanse and fill us, to reflect the Gospel Light.

When life's fleeting days have vanished, Lord we'll stand before your throne.
By your grace and endless mercy, let us not stand there alone.
Fill our hands with blood-washed trophies, yes the souls from sin set free.
There to glorify thee ever, as we give them Lord to thee.

BUILD EACH OTHER UP   April 3

"But you, beloved, building yourselves up on your most holy faith, praying in the Holy Spirit, keep yourselves in the love of God, looking for the mercy of our Lord Jesus Christ unto eternal life. And on some have compassion, making a distinction; but others save with fear, pulling them out of the fire, hating even the garment defiled by the flesh." (Jude 1:20-23 NKJV)

The scriptures encourage us to reach people for Christ and then work zealously to build them up in the faith. I recall a member coming to me in my third parish and complaining, "You preach evangelistically. We're not pagan, we're all on the church roll." Obviously, he forgot that Jesus told a story of a shepherd leaving his 100, in order to seek one lost sheep!

My special burden was for the young husbands who were irregular in worship. Some lacked salvation assurance. Some did not tithe, showing little enthusiasm for the church. Some lacked the ability to teach their own children spiritual truths. They needed nurture and mentoring.

My wife and I developed covenant groups, 12 men at a time, and opened our home for this discipling. We zeroed in on prayer, Bible study, writing our pilgrimage of faith and reading important growth books. In ten years we discipled 128 men at our home. This demonstrated that we were approachable and touchable, "keeping ourselves in the love of God."

The church is not called to successfulness but to faithfulness. My wife and I felt that every effort we invested in discipling was richly repaid. Even seven nonmembers took our course, and four later joined our church. From this experience we learned the value of covenant groups and the potential they hold in building healthy, mature and effective saints for Christ!

DISCOVERING GOD'S WILL · April 4

"My son, do not forget my law. But let your heart keep my commands; For length of days and long life and peace they will add to you....Trust in the Lord with all your heart, and lean not on your own understanding; In all your ways acknowledge Him, and He shall direct your paths." (Proverbs 3:1-2, 5-6 NKJV)

As a teenager, many years ago, I stood on these verses, when I was seeking God's will for my life. And over the years I have come back to this passage frequently when facing major decisions. This promise has given me great comfort.

In my second pastorate, my sons were teenagers, also grappling with their future occupations. Their Youth Pastor helped them navigate through the myriad choices. To start out, the Pastor urged them to write down what they have learned so far: (1) I made good grades in math; (2) My aptitude test pointed to business skills; (3) My English teacher liked my debating achievements; (4) My Aunt Susie thought I showed compassion and could be a pastor or counselor; (5) My Uncle Bill thought I'd make a good farmer or rancher. Then the Youth Pastor asked my sons—"What do you think?"

In counseling with youth, our Youth Pastor always ended with the question, "What do your parents think?" And, invariably, the teen would say, "I never thought of asking them!" YET WHO WOULD KNOW THE STRENGTHS AND WEAKNESSES OF A CHILD BETTER THAN THE PARENT? Opinions of others are helpful. In my men's Gift Discernment classes—if a man said "My spiritual gift is teaching," but if no peer agreed, then surely it wasn't. Beyond the counsel of others, and spiritual gift discernment, the bottom line is—What is God's will for me (Prov. 3:6)?

MAKING DIFFICULT CHOICES   April 5

"If anyone wants to do His will, he shall know concerning the doctrine, whether it is from God or whether I speak on My own authority." (*John 7:17 NKJV*)

When Jesus Christ walked on earth, His credentials were often questioned. He claimed to be the promised Messiah, the Son of God. He asserted that anyone who really wanted to know the will of God, could receive that assurance.

I grew up on a farm in Kansas. I had to decide whether I wanted to become a farmer. In my high school days I made an unreserved pledge to God, that I was willing to fulfill His purpose for me whatever that was. One day I was working with my dad at the north farm, and I told him that I felt God was calling me into Christian Service, whether foreign missions, Christian educational work, or pastoring a church—I didn't know. Step by step God led me into the pastoral ministry.

Our youngest son graduated from Westmont College, and looked forward to getting medical training. One year he attended Intervarsity's Urbana Conference. He had one question, "In God's eyes, is a Medical doctor as valuable as a Christian worker?" He was assured—YES. He graduated from Medical School in Iowa, and entered a six-year Surgery Residency at Loma Linda University Medical Center. Today he is a surgeon in Indiana.

One of our grandsons recently quizzed me: "How do you discern the will of God?" He is in college and aspires to be a Park Director or a Forest Ranger. I said that a moving car is easier to steer than a stalled car. For guidance you have your Bible, your church, your family, and your friends. Follow their best advice and depend on God to lead you.

BLESSINGS OF BELONGINGNESS   April 6

"If we say we have fellowship with Him, and walk in darkness, we lie and do not practice the truth. But if we walk in the light as He is in the light, we have fellowship with one another, and the blood of Jesus Christ cleanses us from all sin." (1 John 1:6-7 NKJV)

Christianity brings with it a marvelous blessing: fellowship with Jesus Christ, and a togetherness with all saints worldwide. Christ's death in our behalf endears us to Him eternally. And our common belongingness in the Gospel, binds us in love to all Christians. Meeting a stranger in the airport—a Christian—can be as heartwarming as the best family reunion ever!

The author, John Drescher, a good friend of mine, wrote a book outlining the needs of children. One of those needs was the feeling of belonging. He relates a story out of the *New York Times*. A small boy was riding a downtown bus, huddled against a lady in a gray suit. His dirty shoes touched another lady, who promptly asked the first lady to have her boy get his feet off the seat. The lady in gray responded, "He's not my boy, I never saw him before." The lad squirmed, "I'm sorry, I didn't mean to." The ladies found out that the boy's parents were both dead. He lived with Aunt Clara, but was often shipped by bus to Aunt Mildred. Now, the ladies in full sympathy told him he was very young to be shifted around. "Oh I don't mind," he said, "but I get lonesome sometimes. So when I see someone that I think I would like to belong to, I sit real close and snuggle up. Again I pretended to belong, and I forgot about my dirty feet."

NET-WORKING WITH GRANDSONS   April 7

"In the same way, you who are younger, submit yourselves to your elders. All of you, clothe yourselves with humility toward one another, because God opposes the proud but gives grace to the humble."
(1 Peter 5:5 NIV)

Our college-age grandson, Jordan, living in San Jose frequently phones us. He loves to talk to Grandpa and Grandma; and we love to talk with him. He is a fine committed Christian fellow. Several weeks ago he phoned and asked if he could come down for a couple days. He hoped to bring his high school aged brother Zachery along. And, of course, he wanted to go fishing! We responded—"Yes, be sure to come and bring Zach along."

Last week they came. Grandma had spent a whole day baking caramel rolls and banana nut bread, and cooking string bean soup, meat loaf, and beef stroganoff, and making peach jello. THE BOYS COME TO EAT! On Tuesday, we drove 50 miles up the Kern River Canyon to fish at Lake Isabella. We caught two trout (18 inch and 13 inch). It was too hot and too late for the best fishing—but it was fun!

In our spare time we played games (BOGGLE, the word game, SKIP-BO, the card game, and RUMMIKUB, the numbers game). When left to themselves, the boys watched Channel #61 "Animal-Planet," featuring outdoor wildlife. Jordan enjoys hunting and fishing. He aspires to become a Forest Ranger.

As grandparents we love our role of being examples, in clean speech and loving deeds. We love Christ and like to model it. We pray often. We like to listen to the concerns of our grandchildren. I read to Jordan and Zach a story I recently wrote about a man I had led to Christ, after praying for him 17 years!

MOTHER TERESA'S SELF-GIVING   April 8

"Learn to do right, seek justice. Defend the oppressed. Take up the cause of the fatherless, plead the case of the widow." (Isaiah 1:17 NIV)

The Prophet Isaiah urged his people to plead the case for the oppressed: orphans and widows. No one embodies that concern better than Mother Teresa! At age 20, Agnes Bojaxhiu of Yugoslavia left an Irish convent to join the "Loreta Sisters" of Calcutta. For sixteen years Mother Teresa taught geography to well-to-do girls. In 1946, on a train ride in the Himalayas, she heard God calling her to serve the poorest of the poor. This started an incredible venture!

In 1952, as monsoon rains drenched Calcutta, Mother Teresa stumbled over an old lady lying in a pool of water. Her toes were chewed off by rats. She was scarcely breathing. Mother Teresa carried the lady to a hospital. They refused her. So she started for the next hospital; but the victim died in her arms. The next day she stormed the Municipal offices regarding the dying. They offered a house and Mother Teresa founded the Nirmal Hriday—a home for dying destitutes. Soon a hundred indigent folk, cot by cot, lined the rooms. By 1985, Mother Teresa had 285 such homes worldwide.

Truly the Christian's symbol is a cloak of humility, an apron of service—deeds done in Jesus' name. To follow Christ is to love the last, the lowest and the least. A newsman observed Mother Teresa's daily routine among the sick and the suffering. "I wouldn't accept your job for a million dollars," he concluded. "I wouldn't either," said Mother Teresa, founder of the "Missionaries of Charity." Here is one of the great Heroes of the world—a ministry that is worthy of emulation—being Christ's heart, hands and feet in our generation.

SERVE: LOWEST, LAST & LEAST   April 9

"Then the righteous will answer Him, saying, 'Lord, when did we see You hungry and feed You, or thirsty and give You drink? When did we see You a stranger and take You in, or naked and clothe You? Or when did we see You sick, or in prison, and come to You?' And the King will answer and say to them, 'Assuredly, I say to you, inasmuch as you did it to one of the least of these, My brethren, you did it to Me.'" (Matthew 25:37-40 NKJV)

Here is the classical passage which states categorically that the kindness we show to the last and the least, is actually showing kindness to Jesus Christ! What a challenge. Jesus even said that a cup of cold water, given in His name, will be rewarded. The rewards handed out in eternity will surprise us all!

The life of Mother Teresa shines as a beacon, to lead us all to deeper faithfulness. A man photographed workers on the day Sadhana, a high caste girl, started working at Nirmal Hriday. Her first task was to clean up a man reeking with sores, gangrened and maggot-filled. Suddenly she fled. "You have lost a worker," quipped the reporter. Mother Teresa went to chat with Sadhana. Soon Sadhana returned to her task. When completed, the reporter quizzed her, "What did Mother Teresa tell you?" "She told me to do it for Jesus," said Sadhana, "I have been touching Christ's body for the last three hours!"

How do we become the faithful church? Believers today want to make a "spiritual-commitment" and then walk away scot-free; but alas we are forever obligated. Jesus is Lord! He modeled leadership and humble service. Never forget, the aimless church like leached out salt, is useless!

APPROPRIATE THE POSITIVE   April 10

"Whatever city you enter, and they receive you, eat such things as they set before you. And heal the sick who are there, and say to them, 'The Kingdom of God has come near to you.' But whatever city you enter, and they do not receive you, go out into it's street and say, 'The very dust of your city which clings to us we wipe off against you. Nevertheless know this, that the kingdom of God has come near you.'" (Luke 10:8-11 NKJV)

Jesus prepared His disciples for both acceptance and rejection. This would shield them from discouragement. The unreceptive hosts were to be warned—to be reminded of Sodom. Shake the dust off your feet and go on. The emphasis is on the positive. Find the receptive, stay there, eat their food, bless them and heal their sick. Teach that God's kingdom is near.

What a lesson! A seminary professor once advised me, "Al, watch for the cream that comes to the top. Work especially with people responsive to your kind of ministry." Great Idea! Why focus eyes on the disgruntled; they will derail your priorities.

In my third parish, sensing a need, I started discipleship groups at my house for young men in their 30's. It worked great! I briefed my deacon-elders, but not the church as a whole. I didn't want my men scrutinized. So some accused me of secret meetings. When confronted, I said, "Anyone can join my next group." A second concern was our Sunday School attendance—dropping from 800 to 500 over the years. My superintendent and I, announced a new class to start in the balcony. Some leaders said, "No one will join!" We mailed out 400 invitations and 125 enrolled. Our weekly attendance was raised to 600 for several years!

CALCULATING DISCIPLESHIP COSTS   April 11

"Suppose one of you wants to build a tower. Won't he first sit down and estimate the cost to see if he has enough money?... For if he lays the foundation and is not able to finish it, everyone who sees it will ridicule him, saying, 'This person began to build and wasn't able to finish.'" (Luke 14:28-30 NIV)

Jesus borrowed cost-effectiveness ideas from the business world to bring home a discipleship lesson. Builders of towers calculate cost. Planning is linked to job-completion, asserts Jesus, and protects the builder from public ridicule.

A fascinating example of counting the cost while planning a Christian lifestyle, comes from a university law student in Brazil. He belonged to a wealthy family of industrialists who had no reputation for integrity. Jim Petersen, a Navigator worker of dogged persistence met each week with Sergio for Bible study at a lovely spot overlooking the city. Gradually, Sergio moved from agnosticism to faith, and by graduation time was quite mature as a Christian disciple.

In graduation week Sergio made two decisions—to put God first, and to be transparently honest! Back home he opened a law office. One day he attended a farm auction—a sale to collect taxes. Sergio bought the farm. All saw him as a wealthy opportunist, but this Christian lawyer shocked his town! He gave the land deed back to the farmer, and suggested the farmer repay as he could. Sergio acted out of grace to the farmer, just as God had once acted out of grace to him. What a beautiful story. Sergio counted the cost of being a compassionate Christian, and unselfishly helped a brother in need. This is what Jesus meant. To live a Christ-honoring life, we must count the cost and pay the price.

SELFISH RENUNCIATION DECLARED   April 12

"If anyone comes to me and does not hate...even his own life—cannot be my disciple....In the same way, those of you who do not give up everything cannot be my disciple." (Luke 14:26 & 33 NIV)

A professor of mine, George Ladd, laid the theology bare. Denial of self means the renunciation of one's own will, so the Kingdom of God will become the all important concern of life. The cross means the death of self, of personal ambition, and of self-centered purpose. One is to desire alone the rule of God. In brief, our one and only passion is to please God. Here is discipleship in radical form, surrendering what one is and what one does. This is the acid test of the Kingdom, it spells out beyond doubt who is Lord!

Another professor of mine, Archibald Hart laid the psychology bare. We must not deny the part of the self called the ego, the "I" or "ME." This part of me is who I am. It is the I who lives in Christ and Christ lives in me. It makes no sense to speak of denying this part of me. It was worthy enough for Christ to die for and save, so it must be given liberty to become what he wants it to be. Dr. Hart explains that selfish preoccupation with my own self-aggrandizement on the one hand and self-disparagement on the other are two extremes of dealing with myself that will only produce unhappiness. Joy and wholeness will be ours as we yield our lower nature to the control of Jesus, claim our spiritual inheritance as his heir, and assertively work to do his will. It is in the yielding, and the unselfish spirit-filled living that true happiness will be ours.

HIGH COST OF FAITHFULNESS   April 13

"Blessed are you when they revile and persecute you, and say all kinds of evil against you falsely for My sake. Rejoice and be exceedingly glad, for great is your reward in heaven, for so they persecuted the prophets who were before you." (Matthew 5:11-12 NKJV)

Jesus gave us the forewarning that some who become Christians will pay the supreme price for following Him. That is true today in many countries. In this devotional today we pay tribute to a Dutch family who laid their lives on the line for Jesus Christ in World War II.

The fateful day was February 28, 1944. The German Gestapo stormed the home of a peaceful Dutch watchmaker and accused them of sheltering Jewish refugees. True, they had a secret hiding place where hundreds of Jews had been escaping capture. Father ten Boom, and daughters Betsy and Corrie were loaded into a truck, with others, and hauled 200 miles to the Hague, the Gestapo Dutch headquarters, at the federal penitentiary. One by one the prisoners were questioned. Abruptly, the head interrogator noticed Father ten Boom. "That old man—did he have to be arrested?" They led Father to his desk. The Gestapo chief said, "I'd like to send you home, old fellow; I'll take your word—promise me you will cause no more trouble." Father stood erect and answered calmly, "If I go home today, tomorrow I will open my door to any man in need who knocks!" The kindness drained from the Nazi's face. He yelled, "Get back in line—Schnell!"

That was "cross-bearing" in the purest form—serving Jesus as Lord, and humans as brothers and sisters, with a total disregard for one's life and safety. (Father ten Boom soon died in prison).

FORGIVING ENEMIES IS REQUIRED   April 14

"Bless those who persecute you; bless and do not curse....Do not repay anyone evil for evil. Be careful to do what is right in the eyes of everyone....Do not take revenge my dear friends but leave room for God's wrath, for it is written, 'It is mine to avenge; I will repay,' says the Lord....Do not be overcome by evil, but overcome evil with good." (Romans 12:14, 17, 19, 21 NIV)

Corrie ten Boom miraculously escaped death in the Nazi prison, where her father and sister died. Years later Corrie came face to face with the very guard that undressed women, and daily helped choose victims for the gas chambers. Corrie told of her enormous struggle to practice forgiveness, at a meeting I attended.

In my first pastorate we invited Dr. James Graham from Taiwan, Presbyterian leader to speak in my pulpit. He is the Mission Executive who after the Boxer Rebellion, where 100 missionaries and family members were killed in the Shansi Province of China, returned to see if it was now "safe"? Late at night the executioner of these Christians came to him, "How can I atone for my sin?" He was deeply shaken; many Christians had died singing praises to Jesus!

Graham knew that this man had killed many of his close friends. Suppressing his rage, Graham explained the gospel: "Your sins are great—Very great. But God's mercy is even greater. Jesus is God's son who came to earth to die for sinners like you. I too am a sinner. Because Jesus died for you, God can forgive you." That night, the missionary brought a murderer to Christ, who like Saul (Acts 8:1) had the blood of Christians on his hands! Dr. Graham knew that the Bible demanded forgiveness, and he offered the Chinese man our glorious gospel!

DESIRED QUALITY OF HUMBLENESS   April 15

"...God resists the proud, but gives grace to the humble. Therefore submit to God. Resist the devil, and he will flee from you....Humble yourselves in the sight of the Lord, and He will lift you up." (James 4:6-7, 10 NKJV)

In the ministry of Jesus He often spoke of the importance of humility in our relationship with others. His own life portrayed that quality. God rewards those who show a humble spirit.

Two of our sons graduated from Westmont College of Santa Barbara. At that time Dr. Myron Augsburger, President of the Christian College Coalition spoke in chapel and I ordered a cassette. He gave this example of humility. In Madras, India, after preaching at St. George Anglican Church he walked with Pastor Azariah to Cathedral Road, a street lined with beggars and lepers. The pastor pointed to a man: "You must meet him. He is an umbrella repairman and shoe cobbler. His eight year old son is blind. His wife is dead. His two daughters board at a school. Some days he gets 20 rupees for his livelihood."

Once Pastor Azariah went to the cobbler with a proposal: "We have raised 100 rupees for you. We want you to have a platform one foot above the street where you can sit and have a shelter from the hot sun." Gazing intently he retorted, "No thanks, just as soon as you lift me one foot above the sidewalk, my friends will no longer sit along side me and talk." Augsburger challenged the students to serve humbly, on the level of the people, and not arrogantly, one foot above the rest. Jesus taught that greatness stems from lowly service, not from regimenting, manipulating or ruling. Friends, what a lesson for all of us. Humble service in Christ's name is paramount.

JESUS ORDERED FOOTWASHING   April 16

"Now that I your Lord and Teacher, have washed your feet, you also should wash one another's feet. I have set you an example that you should do as I have done for you." (John 13:14-15 NIV)

In Christ's day footwashing was part of the culture. In our day some Mennonite and some Brethren churches still practice footwashing, as part of their service of communion. It is a high form of humble service. (In Bible days people normally wore sandals, and their feet got dirty from the dusty road. It was an act of hospitality to wash a guest's feet when they entered the house).

In 1987, on the campus of Union Biblical Seminary of Pune, India, Esther Augsburger made a nine-foot sculpture of Jesus washing a disciple's feet. A Muslim army officer quizzed her, "But you Christians claim that Jesus is God. God would never have stooped down and washed a person's feet." She replied, "We believe that God came to us in Jesus, in self-giving love, forgiving us and accepting us as his own, and that he did express this love by washing the disciple's feet." The man stood in silence. Pondering this thought, he shook his head in amazement and walked away.

To Jesus the last, the least, and the lowest are the greatest in His kingdom. This is mind-boggling, a total reversal of human standards. As disciples of Jesus we are salt, we are light, we are love, we are childlike and we are servants. There it is—we flavor society, illuminating the way. We are neighbors to those in need, being spontaneously transparent. And finally we do the most menial deeds. Like Jesus we give our lives in service for God (Matthew 20:28).

PRACTICING HARVEST STRATEGY   April 17

"When he saw the crowds, he had compassion on them, because they were harassed and helpless, like sheep without a shepherd. Then he said to his disciples, 'The harvest is plentiful but the workers are few. Ask the Lord of the harvest, therefore, to send out workers into his harvest field.'" (Matthew 9:36-38 NIV)

Jesus told us that no one comes to God, unless he or she is providentially drawn in. That is to say, as we seek to lead people to Christ, it is God who prepares and softens hearts. This has significant implications for our evangelism strategy.

Church Growth theorists remind us that "receptivity" to the Gospel worldwide is providential. At times, missionaries should concentrate on the hearts God has prepared. An agrarian analogy might help. If a farmer has two combines and two fields, he doesn't send one to the ripe field and one to the green field. He sends both to harvest the ripe grain. Donald McGavran claims that the people, the Yorubas, were once "receptive." However, Christians generally were too preoccupied with perfecting their saints. So Muslims stepped in and won three million converts without even providing education, medicine, or the emancipation of women. It's simply a case of people being winnable at a given time and someone responding to their search for truth.

In *Gentle Persuasion*, Joseph Aldrich states, that the Great Commission (Mt. 28:16f) provides our methodology for evangelism. It is not "winning decisions" but "making disciples" (bringing them to Christ, folding them into the church, and deploying them in redemptive service). Aldrich insists that of converts who remain faithful to the church, 80 per cent were won by friends. Of those who later drop out, 70 per cent were led to Christ by strangers! So friendship is the prelude to enduring fellowship.

A CONVERT FAILS AGAIN — April 18

"Then Peter came to Him and said, 'Lord, how often shall my brother sin against me, and I forgive him? Up to seven times?' Jesus said to him, 'I do not say to you, up to seven times, but up to seventy times seven.'" (Matthew 18:21-22 NKJV)

Early in my ministry, three brothers started riding our church bus to Sunday School. After Hilda, our Church Visitor, contacted the home, the mother began coming also. To our joy, she made a profession of faith in Christ and affiliated through baptism. As for her husband, Jimmy—that was another story. He was in prison. Apparently, he had a record of alcoholism and forgery.

When Jimmy was released, men from our church befriended him. They took him to Christian Businessmen's meetings and eventually led him to Christ. He found local Alcoholics Anonymous meetings helpful. More than once I joined him for encouragement. On a day in August he followed the Lord in baptism and joined our church. It was thrilling to see the whole family grow in Christ.

One day Jimmy came to me with a heavy heart: "Pastor, I'm in trouble. I found a personalized check book and forged four checks at lumberyards where I get my construction materials. I know they are after me. I should not have done it. But now it is too late." We bowed in prayer, asking God to forgive. We asked God for wisdom on how to proceed. In a matter of days he was arrested and charged. He was released on his own recognizance awaiting the date of trial. For me it was a learning experience. I knew he had violated his own conscience, tarnished the reputation of our church, and disappointed his Lord and Savior Jesus Christ!

ACCOUNTABILITY AND RESTORATION   April 19

"Brethren, if a man is overtaken in any trespass, you who are spiritual restore such a one in a spirit of gentleness, considering yourself lest you also be tempted." (Galatians 6:1-2 NKJV)

As a young pastor, my goal was to be forgiving and redemptive. After a long conversation with Jimmy, I confronted my church board: "Jimmy is willing to go with me to each lumberyard and apologize and I would like to pay the bill each time with a church check." The big concern was the size of the debt. The answer: $2,000 (figure adjusted for inflation). Our leaders "lost their false teeth!" "Pastor, do you trust an alcoholic? Once a paperhanger, always a paperhanger!"

I explained our once-in-a-lifetime opportunity to encourage this fledgling Christian—being redemptive and Christlike—teaching him accountability, showing the court that churches care, and showing the family our willingness to help. Was his failure a reason for abandoning him? With caution the board reached full consensus.

Jimmy and I went to each lumberyard—four times he apologized and I wrote a check. The church told Jimmy that their help was a symbol of love, but membership entails accountability, and he would need to reimburse the church. This he did bit by bit. Jimmy's lawyer postponed the trial until the lawyer was fully paid! On court day, we drove to the Los Angeles County Court, where Jimmy's case was rushed through. We were deeply disappointed that the lawyer never mentioned Jimmy's restitution, nor his church support group. The judge sentenced him to six months at the prison work camp at Saugus. There Jimmy assisted the chaplain and experienced good spiritual growth! Soon he was back home worshiping with our congregation. He repaid every cent of his monetary debt. Praise God, the rest of his life he remained alcohol-free and forgery-free!

CONGREGATION: VAST ASSIMILATION   April 20

"And they sang a new song: You are worthy to take the scroll and to open its seals, because you were slain, and with your blood you purchased for God persons from every tribe, and language and people and nation. You have made them to be a kingdom and priests to serve our God, and they will reign on the earth." (Revelation 5:9-10 NIV)

In the church we currently attend, the majority of the members are white, though we work hard to welcome every Black, Hispanic or Chinese person who enters our door. Jesus died for all, and we hope to offer his salvation to every single person!

In his monumental work, *Understanding Church Growth*, Donald McGavron spelled out his vision of multiplying the churches and incorporating converts as reliable members. His writings were a great impetus to worldwide evangelism. One of his claims drew universal attention, namely, that people prefer "to become Christians without crossing racial, linguistic, or class barriers." This idea sparked many heated debates. Some of my pastoral friends devoted much energy to prove that they could integrate people of all races into one harmonious happy fellowship. They succeeded with varying success.

No church easily incorporates everybody. In my Kansas pastorate, in the decade of the 70's, local people sponsored 15 Chinese-speaking Vietnamese refugees. We supplied housing, and found jobs. Sunday worship had little meaning to them since English was not their language. So we engaged a missionary, home from Hong Kong, fluent in Cantonese, to teach weekly Bible lessons at our house. The refugees loved it. On the final night all 15 accepted Christ! A few were baptized at our church, but eventually all moved to Vietnamese communities, apparently seeking a Vietnamese church. We tried our best to minister to them while in our town.

WORLD NOT WORTHY   April 21

"Women received back their dead, raised to life again, others were tortured, refusing to be released, so that they might gain an even better resurrection....They went about in sheepskins and goatskins, destitute, persecuted and mistreated—the world was not worthy of them. They wandered in deserts and mountains, and living in caves and holes in the ground." (Hebrews 11:35, 37-38 NIV)

Jesus Christ our Lord spoke candidly about the sufferings and persecutions which the church would encounter down through history. Many of our forefathers migrated to America in search of religious freedom. They found it here. They could worship according to the dictates of their conscience. They got permission to propagate the gospel at home and abroad. We pray this freedom will continue!

In our day international concern is growing over an American, Pastor Saeed, being held hostage in Evin Prison in Iran. Being tortured, he's denied any medical care. Some 550,000 people worldwide have signed a petition to free him. The American Center for Law and Justice (ACLJ) with Chief Counsel Jay Sekulow, has asked our Secretary of State, John Kerry, to request Saeed's release. He has. Also Sekulow has asked people to write supporting letters to the imprisoned pastor. Already 20,000 have. That's historic! Iran officials insist—no release unless he denies his faith in Jesus Christ. Many are praying for Pastor Saeed.

Here is a neat story from Holland. In 1551 Menno Simons ordained Leenaert Bouwens, a dynamic speaker, as Bishop. Leenaert's wife objected, the risk looked too big. In a letter of loving tenderness, Menno recited the urgency of the work, pleading with her to trust God. Leenaert kept a list of all he baptized—all 10,252. He died in Hoorn, Holland in 1582—amazingly—of natural causes! Finally, my friends, who are the heroes in your Heritage? Never forget their sacrifices.

SHOW LOVE, SPEAK TRUTH   April 22

"You were taught, with regard to your former way of life, to put off your old self, which is being corrupted by its deceitful desires; to be made new in the attitude of your minds, and to put on the new self, created to be like God in true righteousness and holiness. Therefore each of you must put off falsehood and speak truthfully to your neighbor, for we are all members of one body." (Ephesians 4:22-25 NIV)

I have long felt that all forgiveness grows out of a healthy mature Biblical love. Alas, many unchurched people view the church as uncaring, unloving and unforgiving. Some will turn their back on the church, believing it is hypocritical for churches to preach love, while they exhibit rancor and division.

Several decades ago, a plane ride from Los Angeles to Portland, Oregon landed me in the middle of a heated church squabble. As a district rep I was joined by a denominational leader from the east. Together we conducted a preaching mission in the evenings. Daytime hours were filled with prayer, interviews, and reconciliation-talk. Since slander and gossip were cheap, we held people accountable. We discounted hearsay and required people to speak for themselves. We verified each accusation and discovered a hopelessly entangled skein. The pastor of this 325-member church had walked out with 50 parishioners in a protest move. As we went from charge to countercharge, members were laying on each other special conditions for forgiveness. Soon we knew we could never unravel things this side of eternity!

There I learned one superb lesson: unconditional love with no strings attached is an absolute prerequisite for healing, harmony and happiness. Making the score even, tit for tat, never satisfies an unloving, unforgiving soul. Remember, our new self is created to be like God: righteous, truthful and loving.

INSTRUCTING EACH GENERATION   April 23

"He decreed statutes for Jacob and established the law in Israel, which he commanded our ancestors to teach their children, so the next generation would know them, even the children yet to be born, and they in turn would tell their children. Then they would put their trust in God and would not forget his deeds but would keep his commands." (Psalm 78:5-7 NIV)

One hallmark of a healthy fruit-bearing church is a solid educational program. Christ's Great Commission calls for it: "...teaching them to obey everything I have commanded you...." (Mt. 28:20). But alas this tends to be the weakest area in most churches.

If I was a cartoonist I would draw four frames entitled, "The Church's Worst Nightmare," depicting a Saturday night phone call by the SS Superintendent. **Scene #1:** "Hi, is this Mary? We've got a small crisis at First Church. We need a teacher, of course, no big deal. I've phoned 37 folks and all are busy. The young Couples class, that's the one I'm talking about. The enrollment is 65; but don't worry, last month the attendance averaged 17. The job is easy." **Scene #2:** "Oh, you don't think you can? Your schedule is tight? Your summer is planned?" **Scene #3:** "Say, Mary, last week I taught the class with no preparation. No Sweat. All went great. They are big talkers. Mary, how about 60 days? Last week we barely looked at the lesson and we were off into a grand discussion." **Scene #4:** "Did I hear, YES! Oh, thanks Mary. That's eight Sundays, WOW. One thing more, Mary, can you start tomorrow morning at ten?"

Good education requires commitment, yet our shortcut fast-food microwave generation simply lacks the will, patience, and the "stick-to-itiveness" that this spiritual task requires. How about you—Can you help your church?

DILIGENTLY TEACH CHILDREN   April 24

"These commandments that I give you today are to be on your hearts. Impress them on your children. Talk about them when you sit at home and when you walk along the road, when you lie down and when you get up. Tie them as symbols on your hands, and bind them on your foreheads. Write them on the doorframes of your houses and on your gates." (Deuteronomy 6:6-9 NIV)

Carolyn Eklin and Peter Benson did a monumental three year study, comparing the Southern Baptist Convention with five mainline denominations. These bodies had 35,000,000 members. They found that in most churches, Christian education was a "tired enterprise," out of touch with youth and adult needs.

Their conclusion was that Christian Education was clouded with four myths. **Myth #1:** It is for children. Proof is in the percentage of people participating: children 60, junior high 52, senior high 35, and adults 28. **Myth #2:** Good teaching only transfers information. NO! It also aids in decision making and learning in the crucible of experience. **Myth #3:** Teaching does not require training. SADLY, only half of the churches offer annual classes in effective teaching methods. **Myth #4:** Christian education is peripheral and not really at the hub-of-energy for all that the church does.

Furthermore, they found that faith-maturity was best enhanced by "family religiousness." For example, a child and mom conversing about God, or a boy and his dad talking about faith, or a home having family devotions, or a family making a meal for the sick, or making a Christmas package for the poor. These activities profoundly impact children! And at the church, Christian education builds faith and loyalty, developing a commitment that thwarts dropout and inactivity. All in all, the potential of solid Christian education is profound!

ARE CHILDREN BORN SINLESS?   April 25

He went on, "What comes out of a person is what defiles him. For it is from within, out of a person's heart, that evil thoughts come—sexual immorality, theft, murder, adultery, greed, malice, deceit, lewdness, envy, slander, arrogance, and folly. All these evils come from inside and defile a person." (Mark 7:20-22 NIV)

Jesus taught that a born-again experience was necessitated by our inherent sinfulness. On top of our human birth, we need a spiritual birth (John 1:11-13). In this God takes up residence in our hearts as we receive Jesus as Lord and Savior. This is a faith-commitment that transforms us to be more Christlike, and it enables us to live victoriously over sin and evil.

My wife has devoted many years to a nursery ministry with babies and toddlers. She tells me that no children need lessons on how to practice evil. A selfish streak appears in the earliest stage of development. Inherently, kids know how to scream, hit, bite, and kick! And children, age three to five, very naturally lie and cheat to escape the awful embarrassment of losing face or losing a game. She says that the inherent sinfulness of human nature is unarguable.

We believe that Christ died for children as well as for adults. If children die before reaching the age of accountability, many of us believe that they will be saved. Where children are reared in a Christian home, their knowledge of Christ dying for them may be learned so gradually that they cannot pinpoint the exact time they first believed. After all, they never resisted the added truth. However, by the time they reach junior high years, they should be able to affirm that they have repented of sin, accepted God's gift of salvation, and desire to live for Christ the rest of their lives.

CHRIST'S LIFE AND TEACHINGS   April 26

"From this time many of his disciples turned back and no longer fol-
lowed him. 'You do not want to leave too, do you?' Jesus asked the
Twelve. Simon Peter answered him, 'Lord, to whom shall we go? You
have the words of eternal life. We have come to believe and know that
you are the Holy One of God.'" (John 6:66-69 NIV)

The Apostle's Creed, a powerful affirmation of the great
truths of Christianity, jumps from the birth of Jesus to the trial
and crucifixion, bypassing the life and teachings of Jesus. (The
creed first appeared under that title in about A. D. 390 and
was used only in the Western Churches). Since some churches
today quote this creed in their weekly liturgy, this omission is
unfortunate.

The Incarnation, seen from a discipleship point of view,
needs to accent the life and teachings of Jesus, as well as his
birth, death and resurrection. Jesus emphasized disciple-mak-
ing (Matthew 28) with instructions to go worldwide, to baptize
publicly in the name of the triune God, and to implement sound
educational methods, "...teaching them to obey everything I
have commanded you." This is called "practicing Christology
from below," where the church uses the life and teachings of
Jesus for discerning crucial issues in our day.

The Jesus-way-of-life as reflected in the Gospels is part of
God's unfolding revelation of himself. Jesus Christ is the climax to a progressive kind of revelation beginning in the Old
Testament. The Jesus-event is a watershed. Everything in the
Bible points forward to him, or back to him. As an evangelical,
I believe that the Gospels and Epistles are equally authorita-
tive. Both were written by followers of Jesus—remember Jesus
wrote no book. While the teachings of Jesus are very important, the epistles of Romans and Hebrews place Christ in the
clearest theological perspective. Praise God for the Bible!

USE YOUR SPIRITUAL GIFT   April 27

"Each of you should use whatever gift you have received to serve others, as faithful stewards of God's grace in its various forms." (1 Peter 4:10 NIV)

The subject of "Spiritual Gifting" is of supreme importance in the life of any church. While we appreciate mass evangelism, like Billy Graham's, and church evangelism where pastors win most people to Christ, we cannot be content with that. A full-orbed biblical evangelism requires that every believer is a witness. Yes, the Great Commission (Matt. 28:16-20) is binding on all of us.

However, it is important that I clarify this. While we all must participate in winning people, only some of us have the specific gift of evangelism (Eph. 4:11). I have heard the Church Growth scholar, C. Peter Wagner, assert that in a healthy church about ten percent might have this gift. So as these lay-evangelists bring in new converts, the rest of us have crucial roles to fill as well.

Believers with the gift of hospitality can invite the converts to their home, or take them out for dinner, or invite them to a ball game. Those with the gift of teaching can invite them to their class, or lead them to a new-member class that may be most helpful. Others with the gift of service can volunteer to help converts move into a new house, or offer to bring meals to the home when someone has surgery, or offer to baby-sit when there is a special need.

There are other spiritual gifts as well. But the point we are making is—when each one in the church is using his or her spiritual gift, then all needs will be met. Each member needs to identify his or her gifting, and then look for opportunities to serve. My friend, are you using your gifts to serve Christ?

UNDERSTANDING SPIRITUAL GIFTS   April 28

"There are different kinds of gifts, but the same Spirit distributes them. There are different kinds of service, but the same Lord. There are different kinds of working, but in all of them and in everyone it is the same God at work. Now to each one the manifestation of the Spirit is given for the common good....All these are the work of one and the same Spirit, and he distributes them to each one, just as he determines." (1 Corinthians 12:4-7, 11 NIV)

The above text states that (1) each one receives a spiritual gifting, (2) the gifts are given for the common good in the church, and (3) the Holy Spirit determines which gift to place on each believer. So it is clear—we don't need to whip up an emotional surge to get certain gifts. The Spirit dishes them out as he wills!

The question naturally arises—how do my natural abilities fit in with my spiritual gifts. It seems natural to start with one's own abilities and assume that one's spiritual gifts will fairly well resemble them. At times that is true, but not always. While in Bible College, a colleague of mine, with a serious speech impediment, came along to street meetings, and witnessed with fluent speech seeking to win a person to Christ. He obviously had the gift of evangelism. In the school dorm he could not speak without stuttering. Take another area: teaching. Normally if a person has no interest or aptitude in teaching, we never say he has the gift of teaching. When we work in the area of our gifting, it comes with ease, enjoyment, and supernatural endurance. We don't tire quickly.

My friend, what is your spiritual gift? Have you identified it? Usually you need a class or small group to assist you. With their help and God's confidence, you can find your niche in your church.

TEACHING GIFT DISCERNMENT   April 29

"So Christ himself gave the apostles, the prophets, the evangelists, the pastors and teachers to equip his people for works of service, so that the body of Christ may be built up until we all reach unity in the faith and in the knowledge of the Son of God and become mature, attaining to the whole measure of the fullness of Christ." (Ephesians 4:11-13 NIV)

Why were spiritual gifts given to the Church? The text above gives us a summary answer: (1) to prepare Christians for works of service, (2) to build up the body of Christ, (3) to reach unity in faith and knowledge of Christ, and (4) to attain maturity by achieving full Christlikeness.

In my third pastorate, while I was leading a Wednesday All Church prayer meeting, with 50-75 folks in attendance, I asked how many did not know what their spiritual gifts were? Three hands shot up. The first one was a lady named Alice, a hard worker in the church. I said, "Lets identify Alice's gifts right now." One person suggested the gift of Teaching, she has taught Sunday School for 20 years. Another offered Encouragement, she has invited his family over for a meal and offered some timely advice. The third idea was Service, she is a hard worker in the women's service projects. The fourth thought was Hospitality, she often opens her home to others. Finally, I turned to her husband, Ted. "Tell me," I said, "what are her two key gifts?" Without hesitation he answered, "Teaching and Service!"

I have offered this story from real life, to demonstrate how easy it is to pinpoint spiritual gifts. First, decide which gifts you might have, then ask a class or group to agree or disagree. You will feel greatly affirmed.

DEPLOYING SPIRITUAL GIFTS   April 30

"We have different gifts, according to the grace given to each of us. If your gift is prophesying, then prophesy in accordance with your faith. If it is serving, then serve; if it is teaching, then teach; if it is encouraging, then give encouragement; if it is giving, then give generously; if it is to lead, do it diligently; if it is to show mercy, do it cheerfully." (Romans 12:6-8 NIV)

Three biblical passages list 20 gifts (Rom. 12:3-8, 1 Cor. 12:1-31, Eph. 4:7-13). Three other texts add these: celibacy, hospitality and martyrdom. For those interested in Spiritual Gifts, it is imperative to give careful study to biblical gift passages. Without this, gift-discernment is confusing.

In one pastorate I discipled twelve men at my house annually. Each time we devoted numerous sessions to gift-discernment. Peter Wagner's book, *Your Spiritual Gifts Can Help Your Church Grow*, was required reading. Each disciple was asked to state what he thought his gift was. Then the group would offer their affirmation or disagreement. This narrowed down the possibilities. We always suggested that the first naming of a gift should be tentative, since later you might change your mind, or possibly God may give you a different gift. Try these steps:

1. Explore ideas: study gifts, learn their function.
2. Experiment with gifts. Which don't you have?
3. Examine your feelings. God's gifts bring joy.
4. Evaluate effectiveness. Do you affect others?
5. Expect confirmation. Do you get affirmation?

From my experience with groups, it appears that for every one with a leadership gift, at least ten named service, mercy or helps.

HOLY SPIRIT EMPOWERMENT May 1

"But you will receive power when the Holy Spirit comes on you; and you will be my witnesses in Jerusalem, and in all Judea and Samaria, and to the ends of the earth." (Acts 1:8 NIV)

Before his ascension, Jesus told his followers that they would be baptized with the Holy Spirit. At Pentecost and following, many times the book of Acts says that they were filled with the Holy Spirit; we will name six occasions.

1. **FILLED FOR EVANGELISM.** The first filling came on the Day of Pentecost, where the disciples declared the Gospel of Christ with mighty power. The result—3,000 souls were converted and joined the Apostolic Church! (2:4)
2. **FILLED FOR DEFENSE.** Peter and John were jailed, teaching the resurrection. Peter was filled with the Holy Spirit when he gave his strong defense. (4:8)
3. **FILLED FOR BOLDNESS.** The disciples healed a cripple; the Jews were irate. After praying, the place shook and all were filled with the Holy Spirit. (4:31)
4. **FILLED FOR ASSURANCE.** When Saul of Tarsus had a miraculous conversion Ananias was sent to lay hands on him; and he was Holy Spirit-filled! (9:17)
5. **FILLED FOR REBUKE.** Saul and Barnabas were sent on a missionary trip; they came in Cyprus to Paphos, there a sorcerer named Elymas opposed them, but Saul, filled with the Holy Spirit, soundly rebuked him! (13:9-11)
6. **FILLED FOR ENCOURAGEMENT.** After Paul and Barnabas were expelled at Antioch, the disciples were filled with joy and with the Holy Spirit. (13:52)

What a lesson for the churches of our day. OH, TO BE FILLED WITH THE HOLY SPIRIT AS THE EARLY CHURCH WAS! The Bible promises renewal when we repent, when we pray, when we yield, when we seek the will of God. Amen

NEHEMIAH'S LEADERSHIP STYLE   May 2

"Then I said to them, 'You see the trouble we are in: Jerusalem lies in ruins, and its gates have been burned with fire. Come let us rebuild the wall of Jerusalem, and we will no longer be in disgrace. I also told them about the gracious hand of my God upon me and what the king had said to me.' They replied, 'Let us start rebuilding.' So they began this good work." (Nehemiah 2:17-18 NIV)

Today in our morning worship, the sermon centered on the book of Nehemiah, which highlights lessons in prayer, sacrifice, and tenacity. The person, Nehemiah, held a high wealthy position with Artaxerxes, King of Persia. He was the chosen cupbearer. As an exile in Persia, in 445 B.C., Nehemiah, begged permission to rebuild the walls of Jerusalem, and rally the Jews as a nation. The king granted the request. Nehemiah's work mirrored five leadership traits.

1. **Moral character.** Nehemiah willingly sacrificed luxury, to tackle a huge and monumental job, rebuilding Jerusalem, restoring God's national reputation.
2. **Confront conflict.** Nehemiah met opposition from Non-Jewish neighbors. He wisely protected his workers, and rebuilt the wall against all odds!
3. **Keep composure.** Nehemiah was a man of prayer. He ignored threats, and continued to work, assured that God was guiding him and granting success.
4. **Stay focused.** As opposition intensified, Nehemiah ordered half of his men to work as armed guards, and half as wall builders—working night and day.
5. **Stay humble.** After rebuilding the walls and restoring the gates, Nehemiah invited Ezra to come teach the JEWISH LAW, to affect a SPIRITUAL REVIVAL!

Nehemiah becomes a role model for every Christian leader. The practice of honesty and truthfulness pays great rewards. Humbly taking every conflict and major decision to God in prayer brings peace of heart and blessings from God.

GOD'S AMAZING CHALLENGE   May 3

"Bring the whole tithe into the storehouse, that there may be food in my house. Test me in this, says the Lord Almighty, and see if I will not throw open the flood-gates of heaven and pour out so much blessing that they will not have room enough to store it." (Malachi 3:10 NIV)

This amazing text challenges us to tithe (giving ten percent) to the house of God and God will take notice. In fact, he will open the floodgates of heaven and pour out an overwhelming blessing. My wife and I have tested the Lord on this, time and again, and found this promise to be true.

Early in our marriage we accepted a pastorate in Downey, California. One day I drove to the Veterans Hospital in West Los Angeles to minister to a critically ill man. On the way home I stopped at a red light and a car crashed into me from the rear. I jumped out to assess the damage. Here was a lady sobbing, with her face in her hands. "My husband is divorcing me," she said, "and this is the second accident I have had this week."

Immediately I saw a purpose in this mishap—God wanted me to witness and offer comfort. I shared with her how God loves her, and how Christ came to provide salvation for us, and how he wants to carry our hurts. Momentarily, a police came and wrote up the accident. Her insurance fixed my car promptly. Because of my whip lash, I refused to sign off. A week later her insurance agent said, "We'll give you $150, if you sign off." By then my neck felt better, and I signed. That is exactly how God placed extra money in our pocket, while we were tithing and had some bills to pay. My friend, are you trusting God with your finances?

COPING WITH COMPASSION   May 4

"Let your conversation be always full of grace, seasoned with salt, so that you may know how to answer everyone." (Colossians 4:6 NIV)

The task of child training tests the patience of adults, requiring understanding, compassion and tolerance. In smaller churches children often are part of each worship. In larger churches pastors typically insist on all infants being kept in a nursery, so that no children can disturb the worshipers.

While attending Fuller Theological Seminary some decades ago, my Professor of Apologetics, Dr. Wilbur M. Smith, announced that he was scheduled to give the address at the Dedication of a new church sanctuary in the suburb of Downey. My wife and I decided to attend. The sanctuary was filled to capacity with about 600 in attendance. The stained glass windows portrayed beautiful biblical themes. The choir, in their new robes, inspired every one. Above the choir loft was another stained glass window, a gorgeous portrait of Jesus Christ, as captain at the helm of a ship. After the usual preliminaries, Dr Smith was introduced. While his sermon was eloquent, and his manner erudite, I don't remember the content of his talk. But as a seminarian, I vividly recall a happening—when a child in the audience started crying. He paused and said, "When a child cries, I have two suggestions: carry him out, or hand the baby to the ushers!" Then he continued his address.

Wife and I knew that the Smiths had no children, and that he typically demanded absolute attention. But this became a learning moment for me, the student. Wife and I discussed this at length. What would I do someday? We agreed that it was probably best to keep talking. People quite automatically look around at the crying child, and the parents quite spontaneously step out.

GUIDING CHILDREN'S BEHAVIOR   May 5

"Wives, submit yourselves to your husbands as is fitting in the Lord. Husbands, love your wives and do not be harsh with them. Children, obey your parents in everything, for this pleases the Lord. Fathers, do not embitter your children, or they will become discouraged." (Colossians 3:18-21 NIV)

Unguided children are not happy. They actually appreciate some regulation or structure. They tend to follow in the paths taken by their parents. They are indeed fortunate if they have both a loving father and a loving mother. But parents need to realize that the strongest influence to shape the behavior of their children is not their words, but their silent lifestyle and daily behavior which they model in the presence of their children.

My wife and I raised three boys. All are Christians, all graduated from college, and all are raising their families in churches—in California, Nebraska and Indiana. We are normally in contact with them each week. All three were born during the seventeen years we lived in Southern California. We remember a time, in their upbringing, when we were utterly frustrated. Our oldest son, Steven, when about eight years old, perpetually teased and hit his brothers, and often picked fights with our neighbor boy. He refused to shape up. No discipline seemed to help. Finally, in desperation, my wife drove him 12 miles to the Los Angeles skid row. "Look at these bums," she said, "if you don't start behaving, you will end up like one of them!"

Today our sons make us proud. One is a Computer Programmer, one a Certified Public Accountant, and one a Surgeon. Every deed of love, and every hour of prayer has been richly rewarded. God has blessed our children and grandchildren. They are the objects of our daily prayers.

SPIRITUAL GIFT: ENCOURAGEMENT   May 6

"News of this reached the church in Jerusalem, and they sent Barnabas to Antioch. When he arrived and saw what the grace of God had done, he was glad and encouraged them all to remain true to the Lord with all their hearts. He was a good man, full of the Holy Spirit and faith, and a great number of people were brought to the Lord." (Acts 11:22-24 NIV)

In Acts, Barnabas was a noted "Encourager." Once as we were discerning gifts, Harry felt he had the Gift of Encouragement (Romans 12:8). The group agreed. At age 25 Harry had accepted Christ, right when low markets and cattle losses brought his farm extra stress. His spiritual decision transformed his attitude.

One night he had a dramatic dream—the ceiling opened and a heavenly light shone in! After that he had a burning desire to rise early and read the Bible. He began to use scripture to encourage others. Now at age 37, Harry was affirmed by eleven of his peers. His reality test was: (1) it brought him joy, (2) it blessed others, and (3) it was clearly a supernatural gift.

Four years later tragedy struck. In January he was forced to make farm sale, and in March his wife died of cancer, leaving him with five children to raise. He said Christians literally carried him forward on wings of prayer. With each trial his sensitivity to others increased. At a funeral, he gave the widow a verse of hope (Jeremiah 29:11). She called it a "great comfort." Later a friend asked for prayer. Her daughter, after an accident, faced a manslaughter charge. Harry gave them a scripture (Matthew 10:18-20) and alleviated their fears! My friend, if you have the Gift of Encouragement, use it. It will bless countless people.

SPIRITUAL GIFT: SERVICE   May 7

"Whatever you do, work at it with all your heart, as working for the Lord, not for human masters, since you know that you will receive an inheritance from the Lord as a reward. It is the Lord Christ you are serving." (Colossians 3:23-24 NIV)

In any church, a host of people have the Spiritual Gift of Service. One such person was my parishioner named Fernando. At age 40, he recalls four assignments he fulfilled for Mennonite Disaster Service—MDS for short. Two were flood cleanup in Arkansas and Texas. The third was house building in Nicaragua. The fourth was home repair after Hurricane Hugo (1990) in St. Croix.

Five weeks in St. Croix demanded sacrifice—losing several thousand dollars from work, and farming out three teenagers. Fernando stood on God's promise (Phil. 4:19). A lady offered to move into their home to care for the children! Fernando decided that swapping Nebraska blizzards for the warm sea breezes of the Virgin Islands was hardly a sacrifice when MDS pays transportation, food and lodging! So on January 10 he and his wife were airborne to St. Croix.

The island's 84 square miles were utterly devastated. Many roofs were tarp-covered. Fernando, a contractor, expected to do roofing, but the MDS director assigned him to be the estimator, appraising needs in 60 homes. People provided materials, MDS the labor. In each home Fernando shared his testimony. After listening to their plight, he shared how he once had cancer surgery. Friends drove him 60 miles, 40 days straight, for radiation treatments. For months he could not work. Now it was his turn to help others. Fernando called this service trip to St. Croix a mountaintop experience. As to sacrifice, Christ taught that God's shovel is bigger than ours (Luke 6:38).

DEMONSTRATION OF LOVE   May 8

"Dear friends, since God so loved us, we also ought to love one another. No one has ever seen God; but if we love one another, God lives in us and his love is made complete in us." (1 John 4:11-12 NIV)

When my wife and I go to the Department of Motor Vehicles to secure a new drivers license, we always laugh at our portraits. Hers looks so good and mine looks so austere. Mine would qualify for the list of fugitives posted in the local Post Office. The lady snapping the photo never said, "Now smile, I want a good photo." She took it before I was ready, and that may be intentional. I have learned that identity is easier to spot from a neutral face than a smiling face. State officials need to detect identity theft, and so protect us all.

Jesus specified that a Christian can be identified, "By this all will know that you are my disciples, if you have love for one another" (John 13:35). Love can be expressed in a hundred ways. Last Sunday afternoon, my wife suggested that we visit a certain shut-in couple, absent from church for health reasons. I phoned, "Can we come over at 4:00?" Their answer, "Yes, we would love that!" We drove the six miles and were welcomed with hugs! We updated church events, asked about their children, and asked about their health needs. The visit was delightful. Normally, we limit our sick calls to ten minutes; but this visit lasted an hour. Before leaving I read Psalm 34:1-9 and offered a prayer of blessing.

My friend, what deed of love can you do today: phone, bake, mow lawns, or visit? Even a cup of water, in Christ's name, will be rewarded.

RESTORATION ON EXHIBIT   May 9

"Therefore, since we are surrounded by such a great cloud of witnesses, let us throw off everything that hinders, and the sin that so easily entangles, and let us run with perseverance the race marked out for us, fixing our eyes on Jesus, the pioneer and perfecter of our faith. For the joy set before him he endured the cross, scorning its shame, and sat down at the right hand of the throne of God." (Hebrews 12:1-2 NIV)

Today was "Restoration" day at our MAN-UP Saturday breakfast. By request some 15 of us displayed our custom or vintage cars; mine was a restored 1947 Chevy Fleetline the one my dad, a Kansas farmer, bought after WW2, when I was 16. Today my car has AM/FM radio with CD, air-conditioning, 350 Chevy V8 engine, and seat belts. The color is the original indigo blue. The car is a beauty!

As we sat around tables in the open air parking lot, our speaker read the above text and spoke on Spiritual Restoration. First, we throw off all hindrances of pride and self-sufficiency and embrace Jesus as Lord and Savior. In conversion we receive forgiveness, sonship, and a new nature. This is Positional Restoration. Next we need Experiential Restoration. This means advancing, growing and maturing. We confess all entangling sins (1 John 1:9). We enjoy the filling of the Holy Spirit. We increase Bible study and prayer. We go to Sunday Worship. We join a Small Accountability Group for mutual encouragement. Finally, we expect Ultimate Restoration in Glory, being totally restored in Christ's image. We shall be like him; we shall see him as he is!

My friend, as we race toward glory, let's be faithful: loving God, sharing Christ, anticipating our glorious Restoration.

SPIRITUAL GIFT OF GIVING   May 10

"Remember this: Whoever sows sparingly will also reap sparingly, and whoever sows generously will also reap generously. Each of you should give what you have decided in your heart to give, not reluctantly or under compulsion, for God loves a cheerful giver." (2 Corinthians 9:6-7 NIV)

In one of my pastorates, a farmer told me of his stewardship concepts and how they broadened with time. While working hard to enlarge his operation, he learned that managing time and land was no more crucial than cultivating caring relationships with people and with God. His expansion goals as a farmer met repeated setbacks for 15 years. God taught him patience! Once he wanted to buy, but his wife feared indebtedness. Once he bid $1,900 an acre, but withdrew his offer when a young farmer started bidding. In the meantime he taught Sunday School for 15 years, and served as treasurer for his Churches' Tenth Man Program.

Unexpectedly, on March 1, 1985, he experienced the highlight of his career. He attended a land auction at the County Court House. His banker warned him not to bid on this half section, due to weed problems and water scarcity. The previous two farmers had gone under! What a shock—bidding started at $400 per acre. He saw no "big farmer" in the crowd. To him the land was worth over $200,000. He started bidding. Finally, at $173,820 the auctioneer shouted, "SOLD—316 acres sold as one unit!" WOW, he got it for $550 an acre. He renovated the land and dug two new wells. For the first three years the corn averaged 155 bushels per acre. He was overwhelmed. He and his wife had always tithed, but now due to no high debt, or high interest, they gave the Lord an extra $20,000.

SPIRITUAL GIFT OF EVANGELISM   May 11

"In the same way, faith by itself, if it is not accompanied by action, is dead. But someone will say, 'You have faith; I have deeds.' Show me your faith without deeds, and I will show you my faith by my deeds.... As the body without the spirit is dead, so faith without deeds is dead."
(James 2:17-18, 26 NIV)

In my third parish, Al and Nadean shared this story with me. For 15 years they volunteered at the local women's prison. Theirs was a low-key friendship evangelism, more like seed-planting than apple-picking. Their spiritual gifts of teaching, showing mercy and hospitality have been a helpful asset in evangelism.

God led them marvelously. Each disappointment forced them to choose between becoming bitter or becoming better. Three events especially shaped their lives: (1) As newly weds, they gave two years to Cross Cultural Voluntary Service on Chicago's south-side where they saw poverty, unemployment, rent-gouging, and discrimination of all sorts, (2) The birth of their son was heart-rending. As a brain damaged baby, he never once smiled, and died at age four, (3) A Lay Witness Mission came to the church. The upshot was that they started a Young Adult Bible study at their farmhouse. The group grew to 35. In James 2 they read that faith without works is dead, so they started a prison ministry.

The conversion of Sheri is a thrilling story. Her upbringing was tough, her mother was an alcoholic and her dad committed suicide. In high school she used drugs, and later was jailed for selling drugs. In prison she accepted Christ! Today she and her husband help Al and Nadean each week, as inmate after inmate is being introduced to Jesus Christ. Each prisoner is precious, needing unconditional love!

SPIRITUAL GIFT OF TEACHING   May 12

"Meanwhile a Jew named Apollos, a native of Alexandria, came to Ephesus. He was a learned man, with thorough knowledge of the Scriptures....though he knew only the baptism of John. He began to speak boldly in the synagogue. When Priscilla and Aquila heard him, they invited him to their home and explained to him the way of God more adequately." (Acts 18:24-25b, 26 NIV)

The Gift of Teaching is mentioned in three primary lists of spiritual gifts (Rom. 12, 1 Cor. 12, and Eph. 4). Priscilla and Aquila clearly had this gift, and used it with Apollos. I know a lady, whom I call Patricia, who used her teaching gift effectively in small groups.

Patricia grew up on a ranch in Washington state. She met her husband at Bible College, and after marriage settled into his home community. She joined a discipleship support group and noticed how fast it knit together via a prayer bond. She saw how sharing exposed person's needs. Above all, the participation dynamic was far superior to anything in the typical Sunday School class. So with enthusiasm she discipled 25 ladies in three years.

Patricia learned from Karen Mains that "painful memories" will impact us forcefully. If not resolved, resentments turn into bitterness. Patricia jotted down all her hurtful events. She brought the list to Jesus, and prayed for release from pain. With this insight she challenges each group: "It's your choice—hold on and grow bitter, or release and get peace." Later from Norm Wright she added the technique of placing Jesus in a chair opposite her, pouring out her list to Him. Christ is loving, accepting and forgiving. He helps release all anger. Finally the list is burned in the fireplace! Patricia loves discipleship groups. They offer beautiful spiritual growth!

THE JOY OF RESTITUTION   May 13

"If your brother or sister sins against you, go and point out their fault, just between the two of you. If they listen to you, you have won them over." (Matthew 18:15 NIV)

In Anabaptist theology few scripture passages received more attention than the words of Christ on confronting a brother who has hurt you (Matthew 18:15-20). Here is true accountability. The Great Physician wanted no sick-festering relationships among his disciples. Silent suffering is not always therapeutic. Our Lord prescribed an effective confronting technique to resolve matters!

Yes, Christ gave advice on what to do when we are "sinned against." But the Bible also teaches us that we need to repent and make restitution voluntarily when we have harmed someone, or have disobeyed a parent's rule (Acts 17:30-31). To a generation devoid of the sense of God's righteousness and holiness, the subject of "clearing conscience" surely smacks of an overly scrupulous attitude. But when properly understood, it ties in closely with mental health; it assures a healthy feeling of self-worth.

As a teenager I felt the agony of confession and the joy of release! Not till I surrendered unconditionally to Jesus Christ did I have the guts to own up to my own shortcomings. Here is my experience: in high school I drove my dad's car six miles to school, and he gave me a 30 mile an hour speed limit. That made sense on the dirt road and gravel road, but when I drove on pavement I liked to rev it up to 50. It was difficult to face my dad and make a confession, but I did. His response: "maybe I can raise it to 35!" At least my conscience was cleared. My friends, prompt restitution pays off and offers peace of heart.

INSPIRING MUTUAL ASSISTANCE   May 14

*"Let us hold unswervingly to the hope we profess, for he who prom-
ised is faithful. And let us consider how we may spur one another
on toward love and good deeds, not giving up meeting together,
as some are in the habit of doing, but encouraging one another—
and all the more as you see the Day approaching." (Hebrews
10:23-25 NIV)*

The Bible urges Christians to assemble regularly, in order to
increase their love for one another, and to motivate each other
in their practice of good deeds. This togetherness was so beautifully demonstrated in the Early Church (Acts 2-4). It gave a
powerful witness to a hostile world!

In my third pastorate, where I discipled 12 men each year,
an elderly couple came to my office: "We don't like what we
see—those weekly group meetings at your house. No previous pastor had such a job description!" I responded that our
groups met at 6:00 a.m., or 9:00 p.m. and didn't conflict with
anything. In fact, these groups minister to each other, and save
me hours of counseling time. They disagreed: "You should visit
each home." Later as I reviewed this advice—I knew I could
visit 500 homes, shoot the breeze over coffee and cookies, and
end with prayer, but little spiritual growth would occur.

By contrast, in one of my Discipleship groups, an urgent
prayer request was placed on the Prayer Page, "Fellows, please
pray for me this week. My brother and I are in a serious dispute
over the use of our pickup. I hope to initiate a reconciliation!"
The next week he reported, "Mark a PTL, the problem is
solved." It happened repeatedly, when one man shared deeply,
others gained courage to share deeply as well.

PAYING TRIBUTE TO PEOPLE   **May 15**

"I commend to you our sister Phoebe, a deacon in the church in Cenchrea. I ask you to receive her in the Lord in a way worthy of his people and to give her any help she may need from you, for she has been the benefactor of many people, including me. Greet Priscilla and Aquila, my co-workers in Christ Jesus. They risked their lives for me...." (Romans 16:1-4 NIV)

At the end of Romans, the Apostle Paul greets some 26 friends, of whom possibly nine are women. He gives special tribute to Phoebe and Priscilla, both of whom were very dear to him. Paul's example inspires us to give credit to significant people. I'll mention several.

The first is my mother who lived 90 years on the Kansas farm her parents bought in 1876, having migrated from Poland. I owe to her my physical life and spiritual life. At her knee I learned Bible stories. Prayer was key at our house: before meals, at evening family devotions, and Mother met regularly with other women to pray for their children's salvation. She insisted on all-around clean ethical living, with no swearing. Her favorite verse was : "Abstain from all appearance of evil" (1 Thes. 5:22). As a cook she knew my favorite food was New Years Fritters!

The second is my wife, I can't say enough good about her. She is my inspiration, not a "lazy bone" in her. She is God's gift to me—a good housekeeper, a careful spender, a super cook, and a devoted yard worker. In my 40 years of preaching, she praised my sermons. Now in retirement she partners in my prayer time. She is in constant communication with grandchildren! My friend, who are the spiritual trailblazers you need to thank?

SALUTING HARD WORKERS   May 16

"Greet Mary, who worked very hard for you…Greet Tryphena and Tryphosa, those women who work hard in the Lord. Greet my dear friend Persis, another woman who has worked very hard in the Lord." (Romans 16:6, 12 NIV)

In the early verses of Romans 16 Paul praises Phoebe and Priscilla for their spiritual zeal. In the above text he acknowledges the very hard work of other women as well. Paul gives these ladies a well deserved credit. (By the way, would not Tryphena and Tryphosa be cute names for twin girls?) In this devotional, I want to salute two other women who were significant in my past.

The first is my Aunt Helen Ruth. She hosted many of our family gatherings, being the housekeeper for Grandpa on his Kansas farm. When I was about four, a huge rooster chased me and my aunt consoled me. Later at age five, I went there for vacation. Sleeping on the porch, one morning my bed was wet. I told my aunt, "It must have rained in!" She smiled knowingly. She took special interest in our schooling and eventual occupations. When one of us went into mission work, she was the first to offer encouragement.

The second lady was my high school typing teacher. Attending a Christian Academy, my toughest course was typing and I was in danger of flunking. On the final exam, I knew the passing score. I self-graded my paper—I had just passed. Then I saw another error. I decided not to count it. That summer I felt so convicted, I wrote the teacher a confession. She sent back a tender note of forgiveness, letting the passing grade stand. My friends, never hesitate to make things right, it will give you peace of heart.

SOLOMON'S WISEST WARNING   May 17

"Wine is a mocker, intoxicating drink arouses brawling, and whoever is led astray by it is not wise." (Proverbs 20:1 NKJV)

Solomon's warning is so apropos for our generation. In Solomon's day only the wealthy had access to large quantities of intoxicating drinks. In our day any common worker, with his weekly check in his pocket, can walk into a drug store and buy a big case of liquor. A friend of mine recently attended a Baby Christening at church and then went to the home to celebrate. Many were drinking and a quarrel developed over the chairs. A young man whipped out a knife and stabbed my friend in the abdomen—miraculously missing vital organs! Hearing about this, I went to the man's house and prayed for his healing.

Recently a couple we knew, attended a late night company party. Homebound, being intoxicated, they hit a tree. The man crawled out through the windshield, but the wife was trapped under the dash and burned to death. We attended the funeral. This beautiful young mother tragically lost her life!

Not long ago, TV News carried an article on college students abusing liquor. No university president wants this advertised; it may cut down enrollment. However, hundreds of students have died in binge drinking, and from the use of drugs. This is such a fearful trend.

Dr. Anderson Spickard Jr., author of *Dying For A Drink* (Thomas Nelson, 2005), is a professor of medicine and psychiatry at Vanderbilt University Medical Center. His book is claimed by some experts to be the best faith-based book written on alcoholism. I recommend it. His third chapter (pages 11-19): "Who is at Risk?" is priceless! My friends, I urge you to read this book, cover to cover. It offers you amazing insight!

LIMITING CHRISTIAN LIBERTY   May 18

"Do not destroy the work of God for the sake of food. All food is clean, but it is wrong for a person to eat anything that causes someone else to stumble. It is better not to eat meat or drink wine or to do anything else that will cause your brother or sister to fall. So whatever you believe about these things keep between yourself and God. Blessed is the one who does not condemn himself by what he approves." (Romans 14:20-22 NIV)

In our culture food is no ethical issue, but the drinking of wine is. In America some 120,000,000 folks drink alcoholic beverages. The serious implications of this is spelled out in Dr. Anderson Spickard's book, *Dying For A Drink*. I'll list some.

1. Alcoholism is the single greatest cause of domestic violence in our country. Just imagine the turmoil in thousands of our homes. Families tend to tell no one for seven years. And after that wait two years before taking action.
2. Children leaving home to escape an alcoholic parent, have a four times greater risk of developing alcoholism, than children of nondrinking parents. The prime key is not environment, it is the genetic factor.
3. Health wise, heavy drinking destroys brain cells and damages the liver.
4. Substance abuse accounts for more than half of all suicides, experts say.
5. Out of every ten social drinkers, one becomes an uncontrollable alcoholic.

Friends, your example is powerful. You might choose to limit your liberty in order to influence your children positively. Also you might be "an enabler" if you continue to cover up for others. Don't be a stumbling block. "Blessed is the man who does not condemn himself by what he approves." Let us all pray earnestly for wisdom—to be a testimony for Jesus.

INTERPRETING BIBLE STORIES   May 19

"Therefore do not be foolish, but understand what the Lord's will is. Do not get drunk on wine, which leads to debauchery. Instead, be filled with the Spirit, speaking to one another with psalms, hymns, and songs from the Spirit. Sing and make music from your heart to the Lord, always giving thanks to God the Father for everything, in the name of our Lord Jesus Christ." (Ephesians 5:17-20 NIV)

The Bible a hundred times over condemns drunkenness (Galatians 5:19-21). Yet in our day many drink to intoxication and laugh about it. This is especially true of those who don't limit their drinking to mealtime. At drinking parties many drink so much that the sick alcoholics cannot be identified.

Many Christians justify their imbibing with, "Well, Jesus turned water into wine" (John 2). That is true, Jesus helped the wedding celebrate. Remember, Jesus never came to change the social structure, he came to die for the sins of the world. A case in point: Neither Jesus nor Paul condemned slavery, yet today the whole Western World disapproves it, due to the influence of Christianity. The issue of imbibing alcohol is similar. The world has changed. Alcoholism is costly in the working world, the health area, and family security.

Think of the invention of the car and the gun. Today, in the USA, someone is killed by a drunk driver every 24 minutes. Mental health leaders report that half of all suicides stem from substance abuse—some use a gun, some a drug. If Jesus lived on earth today, what would he say? Dr. Anderson Spickard Jr., author of *Dying For A Drink*, gives us all a challenge: If addiction is in our Family Tree (parent, uncle, sibling, or children) there are compelling reasons to give abstinence a serious consideration!

THE ROAD TO RECOVERY   May 20

"When Jesus came down from the mountainside, large crowds followed him. A man with leprosy came and knelt before him, and said, 'Lord if you are willing you can make me clean.' Jesus reached out his hand and touched the man. 'I am willing,' he said, 'Be clean.' Immediately he was cleansed of his leprosy." (Matthew 8:1-3 NIV)

A sick man, a leper, came to Jesus and pled for healing. Jesus touched him and healed him. In the same way Jesus touches many alcoholics and miraculously heals them. In a discipleship group I had a recovering alcoholic. He was 47 years old; I'll call him Bill.

Bill was born in Iowa, and raised in California. His parents always had liquor in the house. As a teenager he started to sneak drinks. His dad didn't care. By the time he was a senior he drank a lot. He had a four year stint in the Air Force, and more drinking. Back home he got married, but sadly "drank his marriage to death." Bill followed his dad to Oregon, working as a mechanic. There he met a Nebraska gal, fell in love, and was married. Eventually, they moved to Nebraska to assist his wife's dad.

Bill went to his wife's pastor for help, joining the church. After a mishap, he was jailed. In desperation he prayed, and promised his wife he'd go to Alcoholics Anonymous. With a constant graving for liquor, he saw his choices: return to booze, prison and death or surrender to God. He decided to try God. One night at home he prayed fervently, "God, please take my obsession for drink away; God it's all yours." God healed him! Joining my group he said, "I'm grateful to be a Christian. By God's grace I'm liquor-free!"

MISHAPS IN GOD'S PLAN   May 21

"In the year that King Uzziah died, I saw the Lord, high and lifted up, seated on a throne, and the train of his robe filled the temple… 'Woe is me,' I cried, 'I am ruined! For I am a man of unclean lips, and I live among a people of unclean lips, and my eyes have seen the King, the Lord Almighty.'" (Isaiah 6:1, 5 NIV)

Isaiah reports that he saw God Almighty and felt totally unworthy and sinful. Then a seraph flew to him, touched his mouth with a live coal, and offered forgiveness. Next the Lord asked who might be His special messenger. Isaiah said, "Send me." The prophet knew the precise time of this call—when King Uzziah died! So often in the providence of God, some tragedy, or even death becomes the precise marker when God speaks.

I once attended a Pastor's Conference at Harrisonburg, Virginia. When we divided into groups to share our Life Stories, a pastor from Lancaster, PA told how he had been in business, had a family, and continually resisted the call of God. Then at age 30 he volunteered for ministry. He remembers the exact time—it was when his four year old daughter died!

By birth I'm a farm boy. When I was nine years old, a tornado struck our Kansas farm at nighttime. Our house stood, but was badly stripped. Gone was the silo, the horse barn, the cattle barn, the grain elevator, the hen house, the garage and the machine shed. The next morning dad opened the kitchen door and saw the devastation and sighed, "Oh My!" Later he testified that that was the very time he started farming for God, June 8, 1941! Friends, always remember, no event escapes the notice of God.

SETTING KINGDOM PRIORITIES   May 22

"Therefore I say to you, do not worry about your life, what you will eat or what you will drink; nor about your body, what you will put on. Is not life more than food and the body more than clothing?.... For after all these things the Gentiles seek. For your heavenly Father knows that you need all these things. But seek first the kingdom of God and His righteousness, and all these things shall be added to you." (Matthew 6:25, 32-33 NKJV)

Jesus urged His followers to seek first the Kingdom of God. This is extremely important. When parents drop church attendance from once a week, to once a month, you can bet your bottom dollar, the children and grandchildren will never attend at all. Parental example is powerful! It has often been said—the church is always one generation away from extinction.

We fill our lives so full—family trips, hunting trips, fishing trips, golfing trips, bowling trips, skiing trips, vacation trips, swimming trips, football trips, basketball trips, volleyball trips and any kind of pleasure trip. Of course, good leisure is very wholesome, but Christian priorities are absolutely essential. In any church, a whole decade can pass with little happening for God—none entering Christian service or missionary careers, and none serving locally at Rescue Missions, Soup Kitchens, or opposing Abortion Clinics.

What does it take to follow through for God, generation after generation? It takes shining examples of dedication, discipleship and mission work. People need to be taught to pray. Blessed is the church where the senior pastor leads a church-wide weekly prayer meeting—upholding their missionaries, the sick, the needy and the churches' outreach. I did it for ten years in a church with 1,200 members. My friends, is your church "seeking first the kingdom of God and His righteousness?"

LIVING RIGHTEOUS LIVES   May 23

"For the grace of God has appeared that offers salvation to all people. It teaches us to say 'No' to ungodliness and worldly passions, and to live self-controlled, upright and godly lives in this present age, while we wait for the blessed hope—the appearing of the glory of our great God and Savior, Jesus Christ..."(Titus 2:11-13 NIV)

The Bible lays great emphasis on the need of converts to Christianity, to lay off the old robes of ungodliness, and put on new robes of righteousness. Jesus died for our sins and delivers us from the penalty and power of sin. Holy godly living is expected of every follower of Jesus Christ.

This was a major concern of my forebearers, the Anabaptists of the Reformation. They sought to restore New Testament Christianity—a church free from state control, having freedom of religion, practicing Believer's Baptism and exercising Church Discipline. But it was against the law to be an Anabaptist in Catholic regions, Lutheran regions and Reformed regions. These three regions all practiced Infant Baptism. So every person was both a member of the church and member of the state. Severe persecution ensued. Some 5,000 Anabaptists died as martyrs between A.D. 1525 and 1560. While the Anabaptists owed a big debt to Martin Luther for his teaching of "justification by faith," they observed so much ungodly living in all three regions. Churches had many unregenerated undisciplined folks.

Praise God, the sufferings of the Anabaptists have borne rich fruit. Their belief in the separation of church and state is a firm principle of American democracy, their doctrine of believer's baptism is widely held, and their emphasis on total discipleship is an integral part of the church's message. Protestantism owes them a great debt of gratitude.

GOD'S HAND IN HISTORY   May 24

*"Have confidence in your leaders and submit to their authority,
because they keep watch over you as those who must give an account.
Do this so that their work will be a joy, not a burden, for that would
be of no benefit to you. Pray for us. We are sure that we have a
clear conscience and desire to live honorably in every way." (Hebrews
13:17-18 NIV)*

Let's look at our national history. In graduate school I took
a course on "Religion in Early America." We leaned heavily
on Franklin Littell's superb book, *From State Church to Plural-
ism.* America never was a Christian nation, except in a nominal
sense. The time of the founding fathers was no age of Christian
virtue, free enterprise, nor "states rights." Ethically speaking,
promiscuity, materialism and racialism were rampant. The
churches struggled to evangelize the throngs.

George Washington, and most Puritans, attempted to establish a state church, after the pattern of Europe, thinking that no
nation could be strong without it. Fortunately, people moved
West so fast that the state lost it's grip. The Methodist Cir-
cuit-Riding preachers and Baptist horseback evangelists did a
fantastic job of evangelizing the frontier. Littell asserts, even
crass evangelism is far better than enforcing religion with the
sword! It was a great day for Revivalism.

The American scene looked more like the Anabaptists of
the Reformation than the main reformers, Luther and Calvin.
Here was freedom of religion, separation of church and state,
and often the practice of Believers Baptism. From 1800 to 1950
more people were swept into the church, than any place else
ever! On the positive side by 1950, 60% were church members,
while in 1800 only 5 percent. Negatively, strict church standards did decline. Friends, we need to be on our knees, thanking
God for our freedoms, and praying we won't lose them!

THE INDESCRIBABLE JOY   May 25

"It is good to praise the Lord and make music to your name, O Most High, proclaiming your love in the morning and your faithfulness at night....For you make me glad by your deeds, O Lord; I sing for joy at the works your hands have done." (Psalm 92:1-2, 4 NIV)

The above text formed the basis for the meditation at the memorial service for Dr. Norman Rempel, 65, at Fresno, CA. He graduated from Grace Bible Institute, where he met his wife. His educational career was launched at his alma mater, teaching Bible and Philosophy. After graduate studies, he was hired by Fresno Pacific University to teach, and eventually become school Registrar. In his last years he succumbed to multiple sclerosis. Yet in his working years, and final suffering years, he never complained! He had an amazing joyful disposition. So on his tribute folder was a large colored smiling photo with these words above his name: "Indescribable Joy!"

When tributes from the audience were elicited, I accepted the mike. "I'm Albert Epp. On June 8, 1957 I attended the funeral of Elizabeth Rempel at Downey, CA. In fact, I officiated. I was 25, fresh out of seminary, conducting my first funeral. This widow left three children—Erwin 13, Norman 11, and Barbara 9. The children chose their favorite uncle and aunt, farmers in Montana, to be their new parents. All these years we have followed them with interest and prayers."

At the luncheon, I visited with Erwin. He is retired, living with wife and children at Harrisonburg, Virginia, following a notable missionary career. And Barbara is married to an ambitious Kansas farmer who uses a 16-row planter and a 30 foot Gleaner combine! They attend my home church near Whitewater. This funeral was truly an inspiration!

THE TRAVELER'S PSALM   May 26

*"I will lift up my eyes to the hills—From whence comes my help?
My help comes from the Lord, who made heaven and earth. He will
not allow your foot to be moved; He who keeps you will not slumber.
Behold He who keeps Israel shall neither slumber nor sleep." (Psalm
121:1-4 NKJV)*

This was called the Traveler's Psalm long before Super highways, Jet Air travel, or Amtrack trains. The Psalmist lived in
days of foot travel. His dangers were real. He feared attacks
by thieves, desert heat and illnesses. In childhood I remember
Pastor Kaufman driving his 1935 Chevy. Prior to trips he read
Psalm 121. Once home, his sermon contained travel anecdotes.
I liked that!

The Psalmist didn't worship mountains like pagans did. He
worshiped Jehovah, the creator. What an affirmation: "My help
comes from the Lord." At age 15, in my baptismal ceremony,
my pastor asked, "Do you renounce the devil and all his works
and declare the Lord to be your God?" I firmly said, "YES!"
WE ARE KEPT IN GOD'S PROVIDENCE (121:3-4) "He
will not allow your foot to slip" and secondly, God promised
Israel He would not slumber or sleep. So day and night God
watches over His own!

In America today, sports endanger many lives. Football
games have the risk of head concussions, auto racing can be
fatal, and a week ago in the NCAA semi-finals, Kevin Ware,
a Louisville Cardinal broke his leg on the basketball court. I
watched the game! It was gruesome—his bone was sticking
out! He was sent to the hospital for surgery. A week later, in
the Final Four at Atlanta, Louisville played the Wichita State
Shockers, and Kevin Ware was in the audience on crutches.
With the doctor's help and our prayers to God, he is doing fine!

146

PSALM 121 PROTECTION   May 27

"The Lord is your keeper; The Lord is your shade at your right hand. The sun shall not strike you by day, nor the moon by night. The Lord shall preserve you from all evil; He shall preserve your soul. The Lord shall preserve your going out and your coming in from this time forth, and even forevermore." (Psalm 121:5-8 NKJV)

WE ARE KEPT IN HIS PROTECTION (Psalm 121: 5-6) "The Lord is your keeper" This scripture promises that God will be our shade and the sun will not smite us. In periodic heat waves, with temperatures above 100, some protection is appreciated. In agricultural areas: peach orchards, grape vineyards, and wheat fields, tractors usually have cabs or umbrellas to protect the workers from sun damage. In Jonah 4:8, Jonah was overcome by heat. Even moon rays can be harmful in some regions.

At the Bethel Deaconess Hospital, Newton, KS where I was born, some nurses were ordained as lifelong Deaconess Sisters. (They agreed never to marry). One was named Sister Zipporah. When she was too sick to talk, she often pointed to a Psalm 121 wall motto, "My help comes from the Lord."

WE ARE KEPT BY DIVINE PRESERVATION (Psalm 121:7-8) "The Lord is my keeper" The keeping power of God is again accented. Lawyers, when drawing up documents often add a statement to cover any imaginable crisis. The Psalmist includes a blanket coverage. God keeps our comings and goings. God keeps His eye on us from birth to death. When my father-in-law, Joe M. Walter was 78, he underwent major surgery in Wichita, KS. When he was critically sick, we told him that all children had been phoned for prayer. He was upset. He was heaven-bound! But he recovered and lived another nine good years.

ONE WAY TO HEAVEN   May 28

"Jesus answered, 'I am the way and the truth and the life. No one comes to the Father except through me.'" (John 14:6 NIV) "Salvation is found in no one else, for there is no other name under heaven given to mankind by which we must be saved." (Acts 4:12 NIV)

Both Christ and the early apostles taught there is only one way to heaven. Jesus called it the "Narrow Way" which leads to life, in contrast to the "Broad Way" that leads to destruction (Matthew 7:13-14).

Recently, I heard TBN-television interviewing Franklin Graham. The first question was expected—how is your father, Billy Graham, doing these days? His answer went about like this: "My dad is over 90, and is doing fairly well. He still holds the same conviction he did 60 years ago when he started his crusades, that Jesus Christ is the only way to salvation. He died for our sins and arose again from the dead, and through faith in him we have salvation!"

The popular secular view is that a just God must be very tolerant. Surely there are as many ways as there are religions. There is some good in every religion, they say. So the ideal is a syncretism, blending the best ideas from each and making one ideal Master-Religion! All that counts is sincerity. But we counter, if we accidentally take poison, thinking it's medicine, we will sincerely die.

The noted Kenneth Scott Latourette, the author of the seven volume *A History of The Expansion of Christianity*, wrote: "If Christians in the Christian era would not have insisted that Jesus is the only way, and would have merged with other religions and syncretism, there would be no Christianity in the world today." Friends, staying true to the Bible, is our only Saving Hope.

THE IMPERATIVE OF PRAYER   May 29

"They said to me. 'Those who survived the exile and are back in the province are in great trouble and disgrace. The wall of Jerusalem is broken down, and its gates have been burned with fire.' When I heard these things, I sat down and wept. For some days I mourned and fasted and prayed before the God of heaven." (Nehemiah 1:3-4 NIV)

Prayer seems to precede any spiritual Awakening or Revival. In Nehemiah's case, he wept and prayed, before getting up courage to ask the King of Persia for approval to go to Jerusalem and repair the city. His prayer was one of utter repentance, asking God to forgive his people for their sins and their rebellion against God's Covenant. Nehemiah wanted God's glory restored in the life of Israel. Later as Nehemiah's crew started building the wall, he resorted to prayer when the enemies threatened them (4:4-5, 9). Upon completion, Nehemiah and Ezra read the Book of the Law to the people and spiritual renewal ensued.

In America the Great Awakening of 1858-1859 was fueled by swarms of people praying everywhere. In Kalamazoo, Michigan an ecumenical prayer meeting was called, ranging from Baptists to Episcopalians. At the first meeting a request was read, "A praying wife requests prayer for her unconverted husband." Suddenly a man arose, "I am that man. I have a praying wife. This request must be for me. I want you to pray for me." Seven men in turn and in tears stood up: "I think that was my wife. I need your prayers!" The power of God fell mightily on the group. Before long nearly 500 people were converted. In two years, in America, two million converts were swept into the churches. Friends, please join us in fervently praying for another Great Awakening in America!

ALWAYS PRAISING GOD   May 30

"Rejoice in the Lord always. I will say it again: Rejoice! Let your gentleness be evident to all." (Philippians 4:4-5 NIV)

The Apostle Paul was a remarkable man. He had faced imprisonment, stonings, whippings and persecutions of all kinds, yet he urged his followers to "Rejoice in the Lord always!" He felt anxiety was unnecessary, since he could bring every concern to God—who anticipated his requests. And he promised this outcome: a transcendent peace that floods the heart and mind (Phil. 4:6-7).

Between my first and second pastorates, I carved out two years to go back to school and earn a doctorate. I borrowed $5,000 and my wife went to work to buy groceries. One of my professors was renowned. His library had 25,000 volumes. His memory was remarkable and his lectures inspiring. I enjoyed him. One day my wife was working in the Intensive Care of a Catholic Hospital. She noticed the town of her patient—Do you know Professor So and So? "Yes, he's my neighbor. But he's very unfriendly. He walks his dog and never says hello to anyone. He doesn't know we exist. He looks as grouchy as his dog!!" Apparently, he had not memorized Paul's motto.

By contrast I recall an acquaintance who was also a professor. He exemplified the very cheerful disposition the Apostle Paul urged us all to model. He also, like Paul, encountered severe trials and adversity. Yet he was never known to complain. When his children griped about things, he typically replied, "Do you want to be grumpy or joyful, it's your choice." Clearly his motto was, "Rejoice in the Lord always." My friend, are you a joyful, gentle, smiling Christian? Nothing pleases God more than finding his children reflecting a Christlike spirit!

UNQUALIFIED PRAISE TO GOD   **May 31**

"I will bless the Lord at all times; His praise shall continually be in my mouth. My soul shall make its boast in the Lord; the humble shall hear of it and be glad. Oh, magnify the Lord with me, and let us exalt His name together." (Psalm 34:1-3 NKJV)

On a late night talk show, a lady posed a question: "If God is omnipotent, why does He permit wicked men to hurt innocent people?" The emcee reminded her that God cannot be blamed for the mess man makes. But she persisted, "If God is all powerful, why doesn't God prevent such suffering?" Let's ponder this—were man a mere puppet, he would lose his volition. If God's integrity is questioned over man's abuse of power, storms and diseases pose a bigger problem: West Coast earthquakes, Midwest tornadoes, East Coast hurricanes—all beyond man's control! As we affirm the sovereignty of God, we don't deny the free will of man, nor the Satanic realm of evil, where God gives the devil some leeway. I reaffirm, GOD IS SOVEREIGN! In Christ, there is absolute power for the Christian over sin, flesh and the devil (James 4:7-8).

HERE THE PSALMIST SPEAKS OF UNQUALIFIED PRAISE TO OUR SOVEREIGN LORD

First: Continual Praise (34:1) "His praise shall continually be in my mouth." Under all circumstances we give praise to God. He alone sees purpose in each event. We won't know that purpose until we reach the pearly gates!

Second: Contagious Praise (34:2) "The humble shall hear of it and be glad." As we praise God consistently, people will be blessed! Our praise will inspire others.

Third: Corporate Praise (34:3) "O magnify the Lord with me." We invite the whole church to come join us. Corporate praise will motivate every believer!

UNRESERVED PETITION TO GOD   June 1

"I sought the Lord and he answered me; he delivered me from all my fears. Those who look to him are radiant; their faces are never covered with shame. This poor man called, and the Lord heard him; He saved him out of all his troubles. The angel of the Lord encamps around those who fear him, and he delivers them." (Psalm 34:4-7 NIV)

1. **Unreserved Petition: Ernestly** (34:4) "I sought the Lord and he answered me." Tradition says that David fled from Saul but was captured by the Philistines and brought to King Abimelech. In fear, David acted crazy, saliva running from his mouth, while he prayed! He escaped, the king expelled him as "insane."

2. **Unreserved Petition: Deliverance** (34:5-6) "saved...out of all his troubles." David had a deliverance from fear, shame, and troubles. Jesus also has a deliverance ministry. His churches can bring deliverance to captives in God's power. Nelson Litwiller speaking at Hesston College told of a disturbed lady in a hospital. He discerned her problem and in Christ's name asked for deliverance. She was healed.

3. **Unreserved Petition: Angels help** (34:7) "The angel of the Lord encamps around those who fear Him..." Guardian angels are for real, surrounding God's children. I read a story in *Guideposts*, a lightning storm started a fire near Reno, Nevada. At 4:45 p.m. the wind shifted and a fire wall came toward the home of Joe Stevenson. He fled praying, "Lord, I place my house in your hands." Friends had binoculars and formed a prayer circle. The next morning three houses were gone, three damaged, but Joe's was untouched! Three persons had seen someone wetting his roof. Strange—Joe had no ladder nor water pressure! Joe concludes that an angel protected them (Heb.13:2).

UNFLINCHING PROCLAMATION   June 2

"Taste and see that the Lord is good; blessed is the one who takes refuge in Him. Fear the Lord, you his holy people, for those who fear him lack nothing. The lions may grow weak and hungry, but those who seek the Lord lack no good thing. Come, my children, listen to me; I will teach you the fear of the Lord." (Psalm 34:8-11 NIV)

Bishop Niles wrote that evangelism is one beggar telling another beggar where to find food. You wives have many cookbooks. You share your good recipes because you like them. The Psalmist shares his recipe for a happy life. Here it is: TRY GOD, TASTE HIS WAYS, THANK GOD, TEACH OTHERS. This is the path to satisfaction.

Here is a fascinating story. Lew Wallace was a literary genius, a close friend of Robert Ingersol, the noted skeptic. They covenanted to research Christianity and then jointly write a book to destroy the myth of Christianity. For two years, Wallace studied in leading libraries of Europe. While writing his second chapter he fell on his knees. The evidence of the deity of Christ was overwhelming! He started serving Christ. He wrote the great novel on the time of Christ—*Ben Hur*.

The Psalmist urges us to teach our children. Matthew Henry's great historic commentary states: "...David was a famous musician, soldier and statesman, but he did not say to his children, I will teach you to play upon the harp, or to handle a sword, or I will teach you the rules of state policy; but I will teach you the fear of the Lord, which is better than all arts and sciences..." David tells the children the benefits of living for God. Friends, truly it's the most satisfying life on earth!

BIBLE: VALUABLE TREASURE   June 3

"Your word I have hidden in my heart, that I might not sin against You....Your word is a lamp to my feet and a light to my path." (Psalm 119:11, 105 NKJV)

For years, Paul Harvey was our favorite newscaster. He shared this remarkable story: In Cleveland, Ohio, a 60 year old lady inherited three million dollars at the death of her father. She invited a nephew and niece to live with her in their college days. She had one requirement—to read a chapter in the Bible each evening. Both youth were not too enthused, but felt that possibly some day this wealthy aunt might leave them a reward.

Very unexpectedly, the aunt died. In due time her lawyer called people together to read her will. One million went to various charities, and the second million went to a certain relative. Then a thousand went to a house maid, and a lesser amount went to a list of others. By now the hopeful nephew and niece were becoming frantic. Finally, the lawyer opened a white letter written in the aunt's own handwriting: "To my nephew and niece, I leave these two boxes." Each box contained a beautiful Bible, exquisitely bound. The pair was greatly disappointed.

The next day the nephew packed his clothing and left town. The niece soon followed. The boxes containing the Bibles were placed into storage. Some thirty years passed, and in 1950, to be exact, a certain lady was going through items in the storage room and came across two boxes. She lifted each Bible out of the box and carefully leafed through them. To her amazement, interspersed between the pages was money—much money— $800,000.00! Sadly the pair had been rightful owners of this for 30 years and hadn't known it. But more tragically, they viewed the Bible as irrelevant!

PRACTICE GOD'S PRESENCE   June 4

"Restore to me the joy of Your salvation, and uphold me with Your generous spirit. Then I will teach transgressors Your ways, and sinners shall be converted to You." (Psalm 51:12-13 NKJV)

As you know we are living after the historic coming of Christ to earth: to live among us, to teach us and supremely to die for us. His teachings inspire us. He promised to meet our needs (Matthew 6:33). His death rescued us, offering us the assurance of salvation (John 3:16). Before He ascended He promised us His Presence forever (Matthew 28:18-20). What gives us more joy than the fact that God's presence is with us!

When Nicholas Herman entered a monastery in Paris, he chose a unique phrase as his goal in life: "Practicing God's Presence." He was converted at the age of 18, and for his remaining 62 years, he lived strictly and solely for the glory of God. His conversations are recorded in *THE PRACTICE OF THE PRESENCE OF GOD*. The subtitle of his book is "the best rule of a holy life." He writes about his own attempt to enjoy God's presence every moment!

While I was in seminary my wife and I lived at an apartment complex, where we had free housing in exchange for maintenance work. One of the residents was a cancer surgeon at the City of Hope. I invited him to attend a Men's Bible Study in Altadena, in the home of a prominent business man. Each week 75 or more folks met to hear another surgeon lecture on the Bible. He came with me and on the third visit, he accepted Christ! Later he told me, "Now it is so different, as I perform surgery, I feel God is right by my side." Yes, God's presence is a marvelous blessing!

PATHWAY TO BLESSING   June 5

"Then Jesus, being filled with the Holy Spirit, returned from the Jordan and was led by the Spirit into the wilderness, being tempted for forty days by the devil...Then Jesus returned in the power of the Spirit to Galilee, and news of Him went out through all the surrounding region." (Luke 4:1-2, 14 NKJV)

General William Booth once predicted: "The chief danger of the 20th century will be religion without the Holy Spirit, Christianity without Christ, forgiveness without repentance and heaven without hell." Luke, the beloved physician (Col.4:14) wrote both the Gospel and Acts. He stressed the role of the Holy Spirit. Christ models the pathway to blessing. First comes blessing, then testing, then power.

BLESSING: The baptism of Jesus in the Jordan was a glorious event. God's voice from heaven spoke: "This is My Beloved Son" and the Holy Spirit descended on Him in the form of a Dove. When youth accept Christ, baptism follows. Parents will exclaim: "Son, we are thrilled to see you take a public stand for Jesus!"

TESTING: The Holy Spirit took Jesus to be tempted by the devil. During three temptations, twice the devil said, "If you are the Son of God." The first attack: "Make this stone into bread and eat." The second: "Worship me and become successful." The third: "Jump off the temple and get a spectacular following." Quoting scripture, Jesus overcame! We too will be tested after every victory.

POWER: Jesus returned empowered in the Spirit, showing compassion to the Samaritans, tax collectors, women, lepers, prostitutes, and the poor. Those Jewish society rejected, Jesus accepted with open arms. Christian Missionary Alliance Churches once moved into towns, selecting the worst derelicts and transforming them by God's grace! Every church today, bathed in prayer and filled with the Holy Spirit, needs to impact its community—winning souls and discipling them.

THE PERIL OF UNFORGIVENESS   June 6

"When Joseph's brothers saw that their father was dead, they said, 'What if Joseph holds a grudge against us and pays us back for all the wrongs we did to him?'...But Joseph said to them, 'Don't be afraid. Am I in the place of God? You intended to harm me, but God intended it for good to accomplish what is now being done, the saving of many lives. So then don't be afraid. I will provide for you and your children.' And he reassured them and spoke kindly to them." (Genesis 50:15, 19-21 NIV)

Joseph was a champion of forgiveness, after his brothers wickedly sold him into slavery. As a man of God, he interpreted the king's dream and was exalted to second in command over all of Egypt—to store grain in seven prosperous years and to sell grain in seven famine years. God enabled Joseph to offer forgiveness.

The story is told of twin brothers jointly owning a store. One day a man bought an item and the dollar was placed on the cash register. Then the brother walked the customer to the door. Returning, the money was gone. He accused his brother of stealing, which he vehemently denied. Distrust and anger grew, until they built a center partition and formed two stores. They didn't speak together for 20 years.

One day a stranger entered. "Twenty years ago I was unemployed and penniless. I got off a box car, sneaked into your store and grabbed money off your cash register. I was raised in a Christian home and taught not to steal. I am here to pay you!" The brother started weeping, "Please tell my brother next door." He did. As tears flowed, the two brothers were reconciled! Friends, carrying a grudge is unnecessary and often costly! Forgiving is priceless!

FIGHT THE GOOD FIGHT   June 7

"I have fought the good fight, I have finished the race, I have kept the faith. Now there is in store for me the crown of righteousness which the Lord, the righteous judge, will award to me on that day..." *(2 Timothy 4:7-8a NIV)*

Paul, the great apostle, was ready to graduate from earth to glory. He gave a brilliant valedictorian speech, his last words of his 60 some years on earth. His audience was his associate, Timothy, age 30 to 35. In him Paul had utmost confidence because he loved Paul's converts dearly (Phil. 2:20).

MILITARY IMAGERY "FIGHT THE FIGHT" Christ spoke of the cosmic battle between the Kingdom of God and the Kingdom of Satan. Paul picks up the same theme in his first letter to Timothy (6:12-13), using Christ's witness before Pontius Pilate as a model. Now five years later, Paul's own testimonial is "I have fought the good fight." Paul endeavored to do his very best for Christ.

ATHLETIC METAPHOR "FINISH THE RACE" Paul, though chained to a guard in a dirty dungeon, confidently spoke of finishing God's grueling race, reaching the finish line. He was heaven-bound. Last week we got word that our grandson Hans, in Nebraska, went to state in Cross Country. Out of 100 runners he came in seventh. He had a great run!

STEWARDSHIP METAPHOR "KEEP THE FAITH" The Apostle was faithful in guarding the Gospel entrusted to him—protecting the church from error and propagating the truth broadly. Not long ago, I was asked to speak at my brother-in-law's funeral. He was a 40-year missionary, serving the Ashanica Indians in the jungles of Peru. His passion was providing Ashanica Bibles and hymnals for 60 churches with 4,000 believers. I chose this text: he fought, finished and kept the faith and earned his crown!

AGREEMENT VIA COVENANT   June 8

"After David had finished talking with Saul, Jonathan became one in spirit with David, and he loved him as himself....And Jonathan made a covenant with David...Jonathan took off the robe he was wearing and gave it to David, along with his tunic, and even his sword, his bow and his belt." (1 Samuel 18:1, 3-4 NIV)

David and Jonathan built a beautiful covenant relationship, and renewed it again later (23:18). Years earlier God made an historic covenant with Abram (Genesis 15:1-21), wherein He promised his descendants the land from the River of Egypt to the River Euphrates—replacing ten groups of people. In our day we have a kind of covenant agreement when we join a church and pledge our loyalty. A notable example is the marriage vow, an unconditional covenant, not based on feeling but on choice. We pledge to hang together in sickness and in health, until death separates us.

In my third pastorate I published **The Golden Stairway Discipleship Course**, and discipled 128 men at my house in ten years. These were **Covenant Groups,** where each man knew what was required. Perfect attendance was expected. Full circle prayer was required—with a pledge to confidentiality. Each wrote his life story, sharing one a week. Bible lessons were based on 2 Peter 1:1-11. Home assignment: read a book per week on marriage, parenting, spiritual-gifts, cults, evangelism, etc. We climaxed with a banquet, with wives as guests. No man ever dropped out!

An Ohio lady discipled women with this course. She wrote: "I have led many Bible study groups. It was refreshing to guide ladies in this way. I saw more growth, more closeness, more openness, more healing in thirteen weeks than I had in other groups that met for two years."

SOLOMON'S GLORIOUS REIGN June 9

"At Gibeon the Lord appeared to Solomon during the night in a dream, and God said, 'Ask for whatever you want me to give you?'... 'Your servant is here among the people you have chosen, a great people, too numerous to count or number. So give your servant a discerning heart to govern your people and to distinguish between right and wrong...' The Lord was pleased that Solomon had asked for this." (1 Kings 3:5, 8-10 NIV)

God was pleased that Solomon had not asked for long life, the death of his enemies, nor for wealth—so He promised him wisdom, honor and even wealth. The Bible tells us that Solomon, in his youth was humble, and sincerely loved God. He felt honored to be chosen to succeed his godly father David, and agreed to build a beautiful temple to worship Jehovah God.

If you and I would be asked to list our top craving, many of us would have to say wealth. We all have a natural yearning for more money. The person with $5,000 wants $10,000; the person with $50,000 wants $100,000; and the person with one million wants two million. Covetousness is a bottomless pit; it is never satisfied. Our hearts are vacuum-shaped and only God can fill them.

Even though King Solomon was promised wealth, he was not always a good steward of his estate. He saddled his people with an oppressive taxation. He built large pagan temples for his pagan wives. He amassed enormous wealth by controlling trade routes and using naval ships. Here is a strong lesson for us. The careful use of money is paramount—giving to God's Kingdom, to the church, to missions, and to benevolent causes. We need to use our wealth to evangelize the world!

WORLD'S WISEST MAN   June 10

"Let love and faithfulness never leave you; bind them around your neck, write them on the tablet of your heart. Then you will win favor and a good name in the sight of God and man." (Proverbs 3:3-4 NIV)

Here is one of Solomon's 3,000 proverbs. He also wrote 1,005 songs. He is the author of three Old Testament books: Proverbs, Ecclesiastes and Song of Solomon. It is stated in 1 Kings 10 that "King Solomon was greater in riches and wisdom than all the other kings of the earth." For this reason the whole world desired to visit him to hear his God-given wisdom. Each visitor gifted him with massive quantities of gold and other valuable treasures.

The Queen of Sheba got word of this famous God-fearing king. She came with a huge caravan, camels loaded with gold, spices and precious stones. She questioned Solomon on many subjects and marveled at his wisdom. When she saw Solomon's palace, with it's tables of food and it's attendants in uniform and the burnt offerings he made at the Temple of the Lord, she was overwhelmed. She said that she had heard much, but the half had not been told her! The Queen gave Solomon 120 talents of gold and the largest gift of spices he had ever received. In turn, Solomon gave the Queen of Sheba whatever she requested.

King Solomon ruled over Israel for forty years. His kingdom was the strongest and richest on earth. His wisdom gave him worldwide fame. A favorite Proverb of mine, one I have relied on many times is Proverbs 3:5-6: "Trust in the Lord with all your heart and lean not on your own understanding; in all your ways acknowledge him, and he will make your paths straight."

SOLOMON'S SAD APOSTASY   June 11

"If my people, who are called by my name, will humble themselves and pray and seek my face and turn from their wicked ways, then will I hear from heaven and I will forgive their sin and will heal their land. Now my eyes will be open and my ears attentive to the prayers offered in this place." (2 Chronicles 7:14-15 NIV)

When King Solomon was dedicating the finished Temple, God appeared to him at night and gave him a remarkable promise of forgiveness and healing if people did four things: 1) humble themselves, 2) pray, 3) seek God's face, and 4) turn from their wicked ways. This divine formula is always mentioned in our day, as well, when the need of revival is highlighted. What a comforting solution. What a grand promise. What a loving Heavenly Father!

Solomon had a grand beginning, with a humble godly attitude. He asked for wisdom and God honored that. Why then did he end so badly? Because he loved many pagan women—those God had forbidden Israelites to marry. "He had 700 wives of royal birth and 300 concubines...As Solomon grew old, his wives turned his heart after other gods, and his heart was not fully devoted to the Lord his God,...He followed Ashtoreth the goddess of the Sidonians and Molech the detestable god of the Ammonites, so Solomon did evil in the eyes of the Lord" (1Kings 11:3-6).

We today need to ask ourselves whether our present lifestyle is drawing us toward God, or driving us away. Annually, we need to test our priorities. We cannot rely on decisions made years ago. We need frequent recommitments. It is sad when Christians start with a glowing vibrant profession, and in old age live a compromised life that displeases God.

SOLOMON'S RISE & FALL   June 12

"Then Solomon stood before the altar of the Lord in front of the whole assembly of Israel and spread out his hands... 'Now Lord, God of Israel, keep for your servant David my father the promises you made to him when you said, You shall never fail to have a successor to sit before me on the throne of Israel if only your descendants are careful in all they do to walk before me according to my law, as you have done.'" (2 Chronicles 6:12, 16-17 NIV)

One of Solomon's great achievements was the building of a magnificent Temple, plus his own Palace. That took 20 years. He drafted 70,000 aliens to be carriers and 80,000 to be stonecutters in the hills, with 3,600 foremen over them to keep the people working. These aliens Solomon conscripted for his slave labor force. He did not make slaves of the Israelites; they were his fighting force, chariot commanders and supervising officials.

In his book, *Archeology of the Old Testament*, J. A. Thompson writes that Solomon made four grave mistakes, which sowed the seeds for revolt. (1) Solomon divided his kingdom into 12 zones, ignoring the old tribal boundaries. (2) He used forced labor and excessive taxation. (3) He had an extravagant building program. (4) He offended Israel's scruples by allowing his wives to erect pagan temples right beside the True Temple.

A fifth mistake that even trumps the others is Solomon's failure to train a godly successor from his own family—How Sad! Rehoboam succeeded his father and reigned wickedly. In five years the kingdom was divided and ungodly Jeroboam ruled over ten tribes. I am thankful that my three sons are Christians, raising their families in church. PRAISE THE LORD!

ENDING WELL FOR GOD   June 13

"The Lord became angry with Solomon because his heart had turned away from the Lord, the God of Israel, who had appeared to him twice. Although he had forbidden Solomon to follow other gods, Solomon did not keep the Lord's command. So the Lord said to Solomon, 'Since this is your attitude and you have not kept my covenant and my decrees, which I commanded you, I will most certainly tear the kingdom away from you and give it to one of your subordinates.'" (1 Kings 11:9-11 NIV)

I feel compelled to add another devotional on Solomon. After God awarded the king, wisdom, honor and wealth, and after Solomon's 40 year reign of amazing success, it is sad, so sad, that he turned his back on his Precious Lord, blatantly worshiping at the pagan altars of his ungodly wives.

It behooves all of us as Christians to determine to end well, to remain faithful to our Lord and Savior to our dying day! Unlike Solomon, we have the benefit of a caring church, the whole Bible, the teachings of Jesus and Christian support groups. In our homes, Bible reading and prayer need to be a priority. Our stewardship needs to be intentional, giving to worldwide missions, and locally helping Teen Challenge and Rescue Missions heal alcohol and drug addictions. Pro-Life groups need help in providing adoptions in place of abortions. We use our money to strengthen God's cause.

MY PRAYER: Dear God, Thank you for our salvation through faith in Jesus Christ. We are grateful for the forgiveness of sins, for peace of heart and for the hope of heaven. Thank you for the work of the Holy Spirit, enabling us to overcome sin, and empowering us to live Christlike. O Lord, we pledge our loyalty to you to our dying breath. In Jesus name, Amen.

COMPATIBILITY IN MARRIAGE   June 14

"You only have I chosen of all the families of the earth; therefore I will punish you for all your sins. Do two walk together unless they have agreed to do so?" *(Amos 3:2-3 NIV)*

The Prophet Amos refers to the special relationship God had with Israel. They are God's unique people, not because of their superiority, but because of the unusual covenant God made with their Father Abraham. With privilege came accountability, and hence the possibility of punishment. The Prophet Amos is basically asking the rhetorical question—Can God and Israel walk in agreement if they don't choose to? This same question is often applied to the marriage vow: "Do two walk together unless they have agreed to do so?"

I recall a news release, that for the first time in the history of America, one million divorces were recorded in a single year. In thousands of cases one reason was given: INCOMPATIBIL-ITY. This word is used, abused and misused. It is an umbrella to cover a whole family of ailments. It may refer to 1) adultery, 2) desertion, 3) anger, 4) immaturity, 5) alcoholism, 6) parental interference, 7) impatience, 8) laziness, 9) vice of gambling, 10) jealousy, 11) assault and battery, 12) diverse goals, 13) religious disagreements, 14) sickness, 15) incarceration, 16) sexual mal-adjustments, 17) professional differences—these are all listed under one common nomenclature: INCOMPATIBILITY.

In *The Birth Order Book*, Psychologist Kevin Lehman suggests that the ideal compatibility is the marriage of the oldest girl with three brothers to the youngest boy with three sisters—or—the youngest girl in a family of boys to the oldest boy with three brothers! Yet, most of us lack this ideal combination! Therefore, with deep love, prayerful effort and a gentle spirit we strive for a harmonious relationship with God's help!

ACHIEVING MARRIAGE HARMONY   June 15

"Submit to one another out of reverence for Christ. Wives, submit yourselves to your own husbands as you do to the Lord....Husbands, love your wives, just as Christ loved the church and gave himself up for her...." (Ephesians 5:21-22, 25 NIV)

Compatibility requires that two parties show willingness to adjust, to forgive, to support and to learn. Psychologists list five areas that need attention in marriage.

1. Economic Compatibility. The leading cause for divorce is finances. Everything we do relates to money. If one plans to use credit, and the other plans to use cash then this issue needs reconciliation. Dr. Kevin Lehman tells of a couple he helped, both were "last born," and neither was efficient with money. When they agreed to discard their credit cards for two years, harmony and happiness was restored.

2. Sexual Compatibility. Today, couples can easily talk to a medical doctor, pastor, or psychologist about sexual matters. Plenty excellent books are available as well.

3. Family Compatibility. Marriage counselors find that interference from parents can be a serious issue. If possible, they should not live too close together. The in-law problem is also large. I always tell couples, "Respect your own parents. They are your best friends. Try getting along with them in love and in harmony."

4. Crisis Compatibility. In the area of health, if a lady knows she will be childless, she should reveal this before marriage. Likewise, if the husband knows he might become incapable of working, he should reveal this key information to his spouse.

5. Spiritual Compatibility. Psychologists view the area of religion as supremely important. This needs open discussion. Ideally, husband and wife should settle on one church and model unity to their children. For Christians a mutual submission to one another is crucial. A common commitment to Jesus Christ will influence everything they encounter.

PLOWING STRAIGHT FURROWS   June 16

"Join with others in following my example, brothers and sisters, and just as you have us as a model, keep your eyes on those who live as we do. For, as I have often told you before and now tell you again even with tears, many live as enemies of the cross of Christ....But our citizenship is in heaven. And we eagerly await a Savior from there, the Lord Jesus Christ, who by the power that enables him to bring everything under his control, will transform our lowly bodies so that they will be like his glorious body." (Philippians 3:17-18, 20-21 NIV)

The Apostle Paul urges his hearers to observe the patterns lived out in the lives of those who are imitating Paul. They are all looking toward heaven, awaiting the coming again of Christ, their Lord.

As Paul pointed to patterns to follow, my dad taught me patterns for plowing a field. I first learned on a Model D John Deere tractor. Dad grabbed the flywheel and started the engine. Then I grabbed the steering wheel, and with my left hand pushed the throttle and with the right hand engaged the clutch. In the field dad stepped off 50 yards and hung a flag on the fence. Next he drove to the other end of the field (one quarter, or half mile) and placed a flag. So I dropped the plow and drove toward yonder flag. Looking back was forbidden—it made curves and crooks in the furrow. To make a straight furrow, I focused on the goal, but picked intermediate items to drive toward.

Paul warns us to avoid sidetracks—earthly attractions that take our eyes off of Jesus Christ and our heavenly goal. Friends, the lesson is clear. Our focus must be on Christ's work biblically assigned to us, and our heavenly hope promised to us!

MISSIONARY MIRACLE MEDICINE   June 17

"The Lord gives sight to the blind, the Lord lifts up those who are bowed down, the Lord loves the righteous. The Lord watches over the foreigner and sustains the fatherless and the widow, BUT HE FRUSTRATES THE WAYS OF THE WICKED. The Lord reigns forever, your God, O Zion, for all generations. Praise the Lord." (Psalm 146:8-10 NIV)

Here is a story of God's amazing protection. Levi Keidel Jr., author of *Footsteps to Freedom*, served as a Mennonite missionary in the Congo for 15 years. (He is a personal friend, having spoken in my recent church, and having written an endorsement for my discipleship book).

In one village, Levi and Eudene Keidel, taught a class of 40 boys and girls. Older men would squat at the edge, listening. They seemed hostile, but never harmed them. One after another the boys and girls opened their hearts to Christ and affirmed Christianity. This thrilled the missionaries, but it angered the village elders. One night an elder came and squatted by Keidel's fire. He wanted to talk. He said, "Your medicine is very strong?" Levi asked what evidence he had? "We tried to kill you, but your medicine is stronger than ours," replied the native!

The village elder explained that they resented the missionaries enticing the youth to leave the religion of their forefathers. So the elders decided to kill them. First, they cursed the coins collected for Jesus' birthday. Secondly, they poisoned Keidel's water. And thirdly, they gave the Keidels poisoned antelope meat. Yet, nothing killed them! Levi's heart jumped for joy at this news! The elder requested some of their protective medicine! So Levi handed him a Testament. "Read this Bible, God gave us this medicine. It tells us of our sin and how Jesus died to forgive us. You must invite Jesus into your heart also!"

PRAISE BROUGHT MIRACLES   June 18

"I will praise the Lord all my life; I will sing praise to my God as long as I live. Blessed are those whose help is the God of Jacob, whose hope is in the Lord their God. He is the Maker of heaven and earth, the sea, and everything in them—He remains faithful forever." (Psalm 146:2, 5-6 NIV)

Merlin Carothers, a convict, was marvelously converted in prison. In his book, *Praise Works*, he tells the story of the daughter of Frank Foglio, the International Director of the Full Gospel Business Men. Frank's daughter received severe brain damage in a car accident. Thousands of men around the world prayed, still her condition grew worse. Finally, she was placed in an Institution for the mentally ill.

When Frank's family stopped to visit her, they noticed the environment: some inmates, chained for 12 years, were strapped down for violence, others were like vegetables. Frank's own daughter had often clawed her way out of her straight jacket. It was now seven years since the accident, and her case looked hopeless. It took a toll on Frank's faith in God.

This staunch Christian, leader of many, wondered, "Can I really believe in God. He could have healed her!" Frank felt anger. Then a voice said, "Just praise me." I can't—he thought. The Holy Spirit persisted. His hard angry heart began to melt. His throat chocked: "Yes God, thanks that my daughter is here, and I know you love her." At that moment he heard, "I want my daddy." Frank rushed through the last gate to his daughter's room. Now clothed in her right mind for the first time in seven years, she embraced her dad! The nurses and guards all wept—her mind had come back. Praise God, today she is back home with her family!

THE THERAPY OF PRAISE   June 19

"Come, let us sing for joy to the Lord; let us shout aloud to the Rock of our salvation. Let us come before him with thanksgiving and extol him with music and song. For the Lord is the great God, the great King above all gods." (Psalm 95:1-3 NIV)

I remember teenagers used to sing the song, "Let's Just Praise the Lord." I like that song because it carries a great idea. There is something inspiring about praise. Praise is tonic to the soul, an antidote to discouragement. Praise is wholesome for your physical health, it is good for what ails you! For us as Christians, praise comes naturally. We owe God eternal praise for salvation, for forgiveness, for daily strength, for meaningful purpose in life and above all, the hope of heaven. Heaven will overflow with praise.

Keith Miller was a minister who traveled extensively holding seminars and workshops in the interest of church renewal. He once wrote about his six year old boy who prayed one night during family devotions, "Lord, forgive us for running all around the country telling people about Jesus, and then us being so grumpy when we are at home." We can all identify with that, can't we? A life of praise is the opposite of grumpiness, the opposite of discontentment.

Here is an A B C game for your family devotions. List opposites to praise. A=anxiety or anger; B=bickering or bad-mouthing; C=complaining or condemning, D=discouraging or demanding; E=egotistical or egghead; F=fighting or fussing; G=griping or gossiping and so forth (negating praise from A to Z). It is easy to take our children and youth to church, and easy to lecture them at home, but we as parents need to model joyful, praise-filled living each day.

170

COMPASSIONATE TO THE POOR   June 20

"Those who give to the poor will lack nothing, but those who close their eyes to them receive many curses." (Proverbs 28:27 NIV) *"Do not withhold good from those to whom it is due, when it is in your power to act. Do not say to your neighbor, 'Come back tomorrow; and I'll give it to you'—when you now have it with you."* (Proverbs 3:27-28 NIV)

The Bible urges people who experience prosperity to look with compassion on the poor. While Solomon, in his Proverbs, states that laziness and mismanagement can lead to poverty, he also urges our kindness to the poor, since many face uncontrollable circumstances, lacking a fair chance! We as Christians are obligated to exercise generosity.

In my Kansas pastorate, I counseled a poor couple living on welfare and food stamps. At times they attended my Couple's Bible Study. One day Bill (not his real name) told me that his $800 tool chest was in hock at the pawnshop and the deadline was near. The fee was $52. I went with Bill to the shop and offered the owner a check from our church for $52. He refused it and asked for cash. So I threatened to report him to the IRS! He jumped over the counter, shook his fist in my face, and ordered us out—never to come back! Three days later, I returned to his shop, accompanied by three men, and asked for the tool chest. He sheepishly apologized, gave us the chest and accepted the money in cash. As we walked out, Bill looked back, "What about the radio I left here?" "Oh, that's long gone," the owner said. Bill replied, "OK." There I saw the disadvantage of the poor: Bill lost his radio and paid 42% interest on a 60 day loan of $45. How unfair!

HONESTY IN BUSINESS   June 21

"The Lord abhors dishonest scales, but accurate weights find favor with him....The integrity of the upright guides them, but the unfaithful are destroyed by their duplicity." (Proverbs 11:1, 3 NIV)

In Bible times balancing scales were normally used. If you were selling a bushel of wheat, you would place a 60 pound weight on one side, and then pour grain into a container on the other side until it was evenly balanced. Cheating was possible but it was not God-honoring. Years ago, we were driving through New Mexico, and I stopped at a lonely service station. To my surprise I got 20 gallons of gas into my 18 gallon tank! Today, government inspectors periodically check the accuracy of gas pumps.

I remember as a lad I had a Sunday School teacher named Mr. Harder. I enjoyed him because he often told stories. One day he related this story: A farmer brought a truckload of wheat to our local elevator. The wheat looked beautiful and the man tested a sample and quoted a good price to the farmer. He agreed. As the front-end of the truck was hoisted, the wheat flowed out of the back. The elevator man noticed that the grain at the bottom looked dusty and shriveled, not the same quality as the top. The elevator man kept silent, but the farmer was proud of his clever deception. Sometime later the same farmer came to the elevator man and talked to him about Jesus Christ and left him a gospel tract. The man listened respectfully, but as soon as the farmer was out of sight, he crumpled up the tract, apparently thinking, if that's a Christian, I want no part of it! The farmer's testimony did not ring true. Friends, dishonesty never pleases God.

ENOCH WALKED WITH GOD   June 22

"When Enoch had lived 65 years, he became the father of Methuselah. And after he became the father of Methuselah, Enoch walked faithfully with God 300 years and had other sons and daughters. Altogether, Enoch lived a total of 365 years. Enoch walked faithfully with God; then he was no more, because God took him away." (Genesis 5:21-24 NIV)

When we approach the early chapters of the Bible, we need to take them at face value. In history, some have uncritically accepted the man-made theories of the Graf-Wellhausen Documentary Hypothesis and Darwinian Evolution, while subjecting the Bible to bitter scrutiny. We cannot accept the theory that the Bible is a patchwork of texts arranged by editorial redactors, nor that early man evolved from animism to polytheism and finally to theism in the days of Amos, the prophet. Nor can we espouse the view that man evolved from lower forms to apes and eventually to manhood millions of years ago. To college students I recommend a book of superb scholarship, *Introduction to the Old Testament*, by Dr. Roland K. Harrison of the University of Toronto.

I accept the Bible at face value: 1) the Bible shows an amazing unity, 2) mankind was created by God, and 3) man from the start believed in one God. In 1650 A.D., Archbishop Ussher dated Adam's creation as 4004 B.C. This many Evangelical scholars today don't accept, because there are gaps in the genealogies. In the Hebrew language, "John begot James" indicates lineage, but not whether James is son, grandson, or great-grandson.

Twice our text states, "Enoch walked with God." What a stunning biography. God transferred him to glory without death. As a child, I heard our pastor say, "I don't expect to die, I believe Christ will return soon!" Well, he died 50 years ago.

VICTORIES IN PRISON   June 23

"The seventy-two returned with joy and said, 'Lord, even the demons submit to us in your name.' He replied, 'I saw Satan fall like lightning from heaven. I have given you authority to trample on snakes and scorpions and to overcome all the power of the enemy; nothing will harm you. However, do not rejoice that the spirits submit to you, but rejoice that your names are written in heaven.'" (Luke 10:17-20 NIV)

In the years I pastored in Southern California, I remember a woman chaplain named, Mima Snodgrass, who worked at the county jail, the Terminal Island Woman's Facility and the Corona Institute for Women. I saw one of her reports.

Sixty-five percent of the women in Los Angeles County in jail are mothers. The faces of these mothers show dismal despair and remorse. Some are bitter and defiant, feeling that society has been unduly harsh. A helping hand goes a long way in gaining the confidence of distraught mothers. A frantic weeping mother, appealed to Chaplain Mima to visit her children, a girl age 13, and two preschool age boys. She also expressed anxiety about her husband—a good man when he leaves the bottle alone. In her visit, the chaplain led the girl to Christ. Then she visited a neighborhood pastor who enrolled the children in his Sunday School. Back at the prison, the Chaplain had the joy of leading the mother to Jesus Christ! After the mother was released from jail, her husband also accepted Christ and in a little neighborhood church, father, mother and daughter were baptized in the same service on the same day!

My friends, Jesus tells us that your greatest thrill in life should be that excitement you experience when you realize that your names are written in heaven. That's the grand miracle.

DINNER COST A FORTUNE   June 24

"When Jesus reached the spot, he looked up and said to him, 'Zacchaeus, come down immediately, I must stay at your house today.' So he came down at once and welcomed him gladly. All the people saw this and began to mutter, 'He has gone to be the guest of a sinner.' But Zacchaeus stood up and said to the Lord, 'Look, Lord! Here and now I give half of my possessions to the poor, and if I have cheated anybody out of anything, I will pay back four times the amount.'"
(Luke:19:5-8 NIV)

One day Jesus entered Jericho, the town where the wealthy tax collector Zacchaeus lived—a man, who was no doubt, dishonest, corrupt and guilty of extortion. Yet he was searching for truth. Being short of stature, he climbed a sycamore-fig tree, to get a good glimpse of Jesus. Jesus saw him and invited himself to his house for dinner. What a costly encounter for Zacchaeus. He promised Jesus half of his wealth for charity, and a fourfold restitution plan!

I remember attending a conference, where my roommate was Charles Farrah of the Navigators. They stress evangelism and man-to-man follow up. He said three factors keep Americans from Christianity: 1) Pride, fearing criticism, 2) Money, too busy for God, and 3) Sex, having freedom to live by feeling.

A Chinese man became a Christian. He was illiterate, had no Bible, and met no missionary. He explained that a no-good man in his village, an opium addict, who refused to work, went to another village for a few months. He came back changed. He uprooted his opium plants and assumed normal family responsibilities. He had become a Christian! The convert said, "for that reason I also became a Christian!" WOW, changed lives can win converts!

FROM SALVATION TO SERVICE   June 25

"For it is by grace you have been saved, through faith—and this is not from yourselves, it is the gift of God—not by works, so that no one can boast. For we are God's handiwork, created in Christ Jesus to do good works, which God prepared in advance for us to do." (Ephesians 2:8-10 NIV)

Here is the conversion story of my brother-in-law, David. He was a Canadian farm boy. He was a school dropout, and worked for four years on his brother's farm. As a teenager he lived in a state of rebellion toward parents and church. He took a job in the city working in a lumberyard. His friends arranged for him to work at Seagram's Distillery, so he could pitch on their city league ball team. For nine years his life was self-centered, with a feeling of emptiness and guilt.

As he was pondering life's meaning, Dave picked up a Bible. He read it with intense interest at work while whiskey was flowing from tank to tank. Then one evening in his dad's barn, surrounded by 30 munching cattle, he knelt down, "God, I need help. I've ignored you. I feel bad. I want to do what's right." As he prayed and wept, guilt vanished and a feeling of joy and peace welled up. When he shared this event with his parents, his mother played the piano and David sang, "Years I spent in vanity and pride, caring not my Lord was crucified, knowing not it was for me he died, on Calvary." At age 23, he entered college. There he met his future wife, and started training for the ministry. He has devoted many happy years to Christian service. As our text states, we're saved to serve.

AMAZING HUMAN BODY   June 26

"For you created my inmost being; you knit me together in my mother's womb, I praise you because I am fearfully and wonderfully made; your works are wonderful, I know that full well." (Psalm 139:13-15 NIV)

I often marvel at the amazing creation of God—the human body! We can prick a finger and test a drop of blood and discover the sugar content throughout the whole body. This week we picked up a newspaper with an article on health, written by Dr. Alan Frischer, former chief of medicine at Downey Regional Medical Center.

Here are some facts: 1) Your blood vessels, laid end-to-end, would stretch for about 60,000 miles. The heart pumps about 2,000 gallons of blood through those vessels daily. 2) Each day your brain uses 20 percent of your body's oxygen and calories, while it comprises only two percent of your body weight. 3) Each day, the average person will take about 23,000 breaths, and the heart will beat 100,000 times. 4) In any lifetime, a person might produce 25,000 quarts of saliva. That could fill two swimming pools. 5) A sneeze will expel air at a speed up to 100 miles per hour, and a cough expels air up to 60 miles per hour. 6) Humans shed about 600,000 tiny particles of skin every hour. That adds up to about a pound and a half per year, or over 100 pounds of skin by age 70.

Christian friend, your body is the temple of the Holy Spirit. Take good care of it by controlling blood pressure, managing cholesterol, ceasing smoking, and taking a baby aspirin—all under doctor's care. Moderate exercise is wholesome. Use prayer to control stress. A vital Christian faith will guarantee a happy fulfilled life.

EXPECTATIONS IN MARRIAGE June 27

"Marriage should be honored by all, and the marriage bed kept pure, for God will judge the adulterer and all the sexual immoral. Keep your lives free from the love of money and be content with what you have, because God has said 'Never will I leave you; never will I forsake you.'" (Hebrews 13:4-5 NIV)

Many couples enter marriage feeling that they can handle things with no outside help. And later they might enter the divorce court, still feeling they don't need counsel—If that is so, why do they want to quit?

In Los Angeles County, former Judge Louis H. Burke of the Superior Court, had an astounding technique in the realm of marriage counseling. He tried to get pro-divorce couples to reconsider. At one point, of 2074 divorcing couples that came before him, 887 decided to reconsider and signed his famous "Reconciliation Agreement." After one year, 75% of these were still holding together! Judge Burke, wrote a book, *With This Ring*, and in the Appendix you can find his 11-page "Reconciliation Agreement." He writes that every single area of concern that couples brought to him, is somewhere covered in the agreement. He deals with 40 distinct areas. The first is Marital Counseling, and the last one is Family Prayer. His book, *With This Ring*, was published by McGraw-Hill, and was very useful to me, in both premarriage and crisis marriage counseling. I highly recommend it!

Judge Burke was continually impressed with the number of people who did not know what was expected of them in marriage. Premarital counseling helps eliminate unexpected surprises. For example, if his family only bought with cash and her family only with credit card, then this needs to be processed. Friends, avoiding surprises will usually guarantee blissful harmony!

MARRIAGE & UNEQUAL YOKE   June 28

"Do not be yoked together with unbelievers. For what do righteousness and wickedness have in common? Or what fellowship can light have with darkness? What harmony is there between Christ and Belial? Or what does a believer have in common with an unbeliever?" (2 Corinthians 6:14-15 NIV)

The apostle Paul uses a metaphor of a double yoke under which two animals work side by side. He may have in mind the prohibition of Deuteronomy 22:10, "Thou shalt not plough with an ox and an ass together." Teaming up a horse and an ox would clearly be an unequal yoke. Paul does not specify exactly what he means—of course, he clarifies that believers and unbelievers don't have much in common—but he doesn't indicate whether he has the business world in mind. Already in first Corinthians, Paul alludes to believers and unbelievers in marriage (7:12-15, 10:27f., and 14:24). So probably this is his prime focus.

Over the years in my marriage counseling, I emphasized to our youth that a Christian should marry a believer. In one case, where a girl I had baptized on profession of faith, fell in love with an unbeliever, who had no interest in church attendance, I warned her of the danger of marrying a non-Christian. "Maybe I was not truly saved anyway," she glibly commented. HOW SAD! She proceeded with the wedding and thereby committed herself to years of living outside the Church.

My wife has a glorious ministry of praying for all her nephews and nieces each day, asking God that each will marry a Christian! What a delight to attend a wedding and find that our nephew or niece is marrying a believer. Young people, be careful whom you date and marry—sharing vows with another Christian can bring great joy, a blessing you'll never regret.

COMPASSION FOR CHILDREN   June 29

"He took a little child whom he placed among them. Taking the child in his arms, he said to them, 'Whoever welcomes one of these little children in my name welcomes me; and whoever welcomes me does not welcome me but the one who sent me.'" *(Mark 9:36-37 NIV)*

Growing up in the Midwest, I remember my Uncle and Aunt adopting twins. They were childless and opened their loving hearts to two boys needing a home. Both became responsible Christian men. Both married. One brother took over his dad's well kept dairy. Last year we attended my sister's memorial service at the church of my childhood. There I met my cousin, the dairyman, active in my home church. Being in charge of the control room, he requested my address, to send me a complimentary cassette of the service.

This morning, riding six miles on my Schwinn Airdyne, I was listening to Focus on the Family, interviewing a Canadian couple who had adopted numerous foster children. The wife told of turmoil at bedtime, so she decided to sing to the kids until they fell asleep. One night one of the boys said, "Sing the Jesus song," So she sang "Oh, how I love Jesus" and "Jesus loves Me" and others. Sleep came fast. The husband suggested that if every church in the USA and Canada would adopt one foster child, every child existing would have a loving Christian home! At the end, Jim Daly asked for 20,000 donors, each to send $45, to promote adoptions. I jumped off my bike and told my wife, "Let's do it!" My friend, what are you doing to spread the love of Jesus to these precious children?

PATTERN FOR EVANGELISM   June 30

"God is not unjust; he will not forget your work and the love you have shown him as you have helped his people and continue to help them." (Hebrews 6:10 NIV) "Whoever is kind to the poor lends to the Lord, and he will reward them for what they have done." (Proverbs 19:17 NIV)

I remember attending a seminar on "The Church and The Offender" featuring Dick Simmons as speaker. He shared a wealth of information about his prison ministry. He asserted that 80% of American prisoners come from broken homes. He outlined several patterns for evangelistic outreach in our present world.

EACH ONE, REACH ONE This was modeled by Christ. He promised to make his followers "fishers of men." Christ's work had a one-on-one pattern. He ministered individually to person after person. We too can witness to the wealthy and prominent, or to the poor and forgotten. All are candidates for the Kingdom of God.

GIVE THE MOST TO THE LEAST This was John Wesley's motto. Those having the least opportunity to hear the gospel, deserve to have the first chance. In world evangelism, Ralph Winter in Pasadena, has invited all mission agencies to help him divide up the unreached areas, so that all people can at least hear once.

GO TO THE WORST FIRST This was the motto of William Booth, Founder of the Salvation Army. Remember Christ paused at a well to win a Samaritan prostitute, a five-time-loser. She brought others to Christ. In Washington State, a black man sat in jail three years with no visitor or letter. Dick Simmons formed the M-2 program, sending 2000 Christians— each to visit a prisoner. This motivated the state to pass a law, giving each released prisoner six month unemployment pay, in a year when no other money bill was passed!

ANGELS OF PROTECTION   July 1

"Daniel answered, 'May the King live forever! My God sent his angel, and he shut the mouths of the lions. They have not hurt me, because I was found innocent in his sight. Nor have I ever done any wrong before you, Your Majesty.' The king was overjoyed and gave orders to lift Daniel out of the den. And when Daniel was lifted from the den, no wound was found on him, because he had trusted in his God." (Daniel 6:21-23 NIV)

The angel of God miraculously protected Daniel in the lion's den! While my father-in-law was still living, every time we left his South Dakota home, he took off his hat and said a prayer, "Dear God, place your guardian angel in front of their car, behind, and on both sides. Bring them safely home, in Jesus name, Amen!" Yes, friends, protecting God's children is one duty assigned to God's angels.

Each Saturday evening at 7:00 we listen to TBN where one of Billy Graham's Crusade Classics is aired. Yesterday, it was a 1975-program from western Texas. His sermon theme was angels. Dr. Graham told this story: A girl went to a medical doctor's home with an urgent request, "Please come to our house, my mother is critically ill and might die if you don't come!" The doctor explained that normally he did not make house calls, but due to her tender plea, he might consider. On further thought, he quickly went to the girl's house and told her mother that her daughter had requested help. "My daughter?" said the woman, "she died two months ago. Look at her closet—those are her clothes." Looking at the clothes, the doctor blurted out, "Why, those are the exact clothes the girl was wearing. She must have been an angel!"

ELIJAH'S CHARIOT OF FIRE   July 2

"As they were walking along and talking together, suddenly a chariot of fire and horses of fire appeared and separated the two of them, and Elijah went up to heaven in a whirlwind. Elisha saw this and cried out, 'My father! My father! The chariots and horsemen of Israel!' And Elisha saw him no more. Then he took hold of his garment and tore it in two." (2 Kings 2:11-12 NIV)

Elijah's dramatic exit from earth came as a chariot of fire swooped him up in a whirlwind and took him to heaven. A few chapters further (2 Kings 6:8-18) the Prophet Elisha was counseling the King of Israel how to fight off the King of Syria. One night the Syrians sent a host of men with chariots to surround Dothan to capture Elisha. Elisha's servant was scared stiff. But the prophet prayed that the servant's eyes would be opened and he saw the mountains full of horses and chariots of fire! God protected them. The Psalmist elsewhere speaks of 20,000 chariots and thousands of angels (68:17). One might assume that even Elijah's chariot ride to heaven was manned by angels!

Jesus told the parable of the rich man and Lazarus. When Lazarus died, he was carried by angels to Abraham (Luke 16:22). From my childhood, I remember a story of Pastor Ted Roth of the Swiss Mennonite Church of Whitewater. He went to the hospital to see a dying man, leaving his five year old boy in the car. The patient died. When Pastor Roth returned to the car, the boy said, "I saw an angel on the hospital." The father asked when? The boy told him. It appeared to be the very time the man died. Friends, be assured, that angels, usually invisible, are there to take Christians home!

HAPPINESS THROUGH HUMOR   July 3

"A happy heart makes the face cheerful, but heartache crushes the spirit." *(Proverbs 15:13 NIV)* *"Gracious words are a honeycomb, sweet to the soul and healing to the bones."* *(Proverbs 16:24 NIV)*

It is often stated that a cheerful disposition is healthy for both the body and the soul—for physical health and mental health. There is a fascinating connection between the two. In this whole area of "growing-old-gracefully," humor plays a crucial role. People enjoy keeping company with those of a smiling face and a jovial spirit.

In the senior group my wife and I attend, we jokingly ask, "Are you going to the next organ recital?" No, we aren't referring to music; we're talking about heart, liver, kidney, knees, gall bladder, lungs, or some other part of the body. Wife and I chuckle, when at prayer time, someone requests special prayer for his upcoming monumental colonoscopy!

In the aging process, all of us, to some degree, face the issue of forgetfulness. My wife brought home a napkin that said, "At my age I've seen it all, done it all; I just can't remember it all." A joke book on church humor spoke of the pastor who told a lady, "You need to think more about the hereafter." She replied, "I always do. I go to the basement, to the bedroom, to the garage, and to the kitchen, and ask myself—what am I here after." When we meet an old acquaintance, and they ask, "Remember me?" On the spur of the moment we have to say, "I never forget a face, but I have such a hard time remembering names!"

Humor is healthy for body and brain. I always say that health is a gift from God. We need to thank God while we have it!

LOVE YOUR MOTHER-IN-LAW   July 4

"But Ruth said, 'Entreat me not to leave you, or to turn back from following after you; For wherever you go, I will go; And wherever you lodge, I will lodge; Your people shall be my people, and your God, my God. Where you die, I will die, and there will I be buried. The Lord do so to me, and more also, if anything but death parts you and me.'"
(Ruth 1:16-17 NKJV)

In a time of famine, Naomi and her family left Bethlehem of Judah and migrated to Moab. There her husband died and her two sons married Moabite women. After ten years, the two sons also died, and Naomi urged her daughter-in-laws to return to their native families. Ruth insisted on following Naomi back to Judah. In a rare vow of devotion, Ruth pledged loyalty to her mother-in-law's country, people and even her God! What profound love.

In 1994 my in-laws moved into a nursing home in South Dakota. After two months Grandpa died, and at the funeral, I asked my mother-in-law whether she would like to move in with us in Nebraska. She took it as a voice from heaven! Promptly, she checked out of the nursing home: wheelchair, potty chair, Bible and all. For six years my wife cared for her saintly invalid mother! Her faith was great, disposition sweet, and mind clear. She loved the old hymns. After her 90th birthday she weakened. On a day in April, sitting at the supper table, she quietly slipped into eternity. The doctor said, "What a blessed way to go!"

Caring for my mother-in-law was no burden, it was a high privilege. My wife was very fond of her mother. To this day, my wife's sisters thank us every year—on anniversary dates—for our love and care of Grandma.

WHEN GOOD & READY   July 5

"But because of his great love for us, God, who is rich in mercy, made us alive with Christ even when we were dead in transgressions—it is by grace you have been saved. And God raised us up with Christ and seated us with him in the heavenly realms in Christ Jesus, in order that in the coming ages he might show the incomparable riches of his grace, expressed in his kindness to us in Christ Jesus." (Ephesians 2:4-7 NIV)

This passage tells us that when God offers salvation, to lost sinners like you and me, he does it because of his great love and his incomparable grace. And his kindness expressed to us through Jesus Christ is a guarantee of indescribable heavenly bliss in the ages to come. What a privilege to be a Child of God!

I was raised in a Christian home on the Kansas prairies. I came to assurance of salvation while attending a Christian High School. At the age of 20, while attending Bible College, I volunteered to go to Oklahoma, to teach Summer Bible School in the hills of the Ozarks. My partner was another farm fellow, who brought along his trombone. We stayed in school houses, where we conducted Bible School in the morning for children, and held evangelistic meetings in the evening. I was the preacher and my partner was the musician.

In the afternoon we did house visitation. We came to one house where their Grandma was visiting. She blurted out, "I'm not a Christian!" I sized her up for age and looked at the grandchildren. "Grandma," I said, "What are you waiting on?" "Mister, I won't do it until I'm good and ready." My dear friends, our death and Christ's coming are up ahead. We must have our suitcase packed to go!

INFLUENCING YOUR GRANDSON   July 6

"You then, my son, be strong in the grace that is in Christ Jesus. And the things you have heard me say in the presence of many witnesses entrust to reliable people who will also be qualified to teach others. Join with me in suffering like a good soldier of Christ Jesus." (2 Timothy 2:1-3 NIV)

This evening my grandson Jordan, a 20-year old college guy, in the San Francisco area phoned me to chat. His conversation warmed my heart—because I sensed advancement in his Christian commitment. I was reminded of the Apostle Paul, who mentored his spiritual son, Timothy, and gave him continual encouragement.

Jordan told me he had entertained a missionary from Indonesia last week. He even fed him breakfast (mandarin oranges, eggs, sausage, fried potatoes and deer meat). In their visit Jordan told the man that Grandpa had given him an idea about finding the will of God for one's life. As it is hard to steer a stalled car, so in life, it is easier for God to lead us when we continue moving in the direction he seems to be leading us.

My wife and I enjoy a close relationship with our grandchildren. Jordan has long hoped to become a forest ranger or park director. He loves fishing and hunting, and owns a hunting dog. He told me today that happiness comes from doing things you like to do, but real joy comes from doing things for Christ, like his recent missions trip to Chile and Peru! Then he added that if God called him into Christian service or mission work, there are certain plans and activities he would have to change! This thrilled my heart. We pray daily for our grandchildren, and at times participate in their activities, and always encourage them in their Christian commitment!

EXAMPLE: JOSHUA & CALLEB   July 7

"Then Caleb quieted the people before Moses and said, 'Let us go up at once and take possession, for we are well able to overcome it.' But the men who had gone up with him said, 'We are not able to go up against the people, for they are stronger than we…There we saw the giants (the descendants of Anak came from the giants); and we were like grasshoppers in our own sight, and so we were in their sight.'" (Numbers 13:30-31, 33 NKJV)

When the 12 spies returned from scouting out the "Promised Land," Caleb and Joshua remembered God's miraculous exodus from Egypt, and said "With God's help we can take the land." However, the ten gave a bad report, "We look like grasshoppers compared to those giants!" The children of Israel wept and murmured against Moses, "Why did we leave Egypt?" Caleb and Joshua pled with Israel to believe that God wants to give the Land—flowing with milk and honey—to them. But the people rebelled and threatened to stone Moses and Aaron (14:10). Moses prayed, and God promised pardon, but those over 20 (14:29) will wander 40 years in the wilderness and die, but Caleb and Joshua will enter.

What a lesson! We can look at the giants, our enormous problems, and give up in despair. Or we can open the Bible, claim God's promises, ask our churches to pray, and place it in God's hand. I have seen some marvelous answers to prayer. Yet ultimately, we will all sicken and die. Recently, I lost two sisters—one at age 70 of leukemia, the other at age 80 following heart surgery. I also think of two men, both died of cancer. One reached 70, the other 80. These Christians were all bathed in prayer. God's blessing was very evident!

FLORENCE NIGHTENGALE   July 8

"In Joppa there was a disciple named Tabitha (in Greek her name is Dorcas); she was always doing good and helping the poor. About that time she became sick and died, and her body was washed and placed in an upstairs room...Peter went with them, and when he arrived he was taken upstairs to the room. All the widows stood around him, crying and showing him the robes and other clothing that Dorcas had made...Peter sent them all out of the room; then he got down on his knees and prayed. Turning toward the dead woman, he said, 'Tabitha, get up.' She opened her eyes, and seeing Peter she sat up. He took her by the hand and helped her to her feet." (Acts 9:36-41 NIV)

The believer Dorcas was widely known in Joppa for her ministry to the poor and needy. When she died, two men hurried to Lydda to get Peter. He brought great excitement to the community when he raised Dorcas back to life! This woman reminds me of Florence Nightengale, the renowned nurse.

Florence lived from 1820 to 1910. In her 90 years she championed the profession of nursing, raising it to a respectable occupation. In England in the early 1800's, nurses were viewed as uneducated, often immoral and frequently alcoholics. Florence Nightengale came from a very wealthy family, but never pursued wealth. At age 31 she took nurses training in Germany and two years later became a hospital superintendent in London. She shied away from common allurements like art, literature and even marriage, and determined to garner respect and honor for the nursing profession. She deserves our deepest thanks.

One of my aunts and two of my sisters became nurses. What a noble profession for Christians—showing the love of Christ to people in their hour of pain.

ISAAC MARRIES REBEKAH   July 9

"And Abraham was now old...He said to the senior servant in his household, the one in charge of all that he had...'I want you to swear by the Lord...that you will not get a wife for my son from the daughters of the Canaanites, among whom I am living, but will go to my country and my own relatives and get a wife for my son Isaac...The Lord, the God of heaven...will send his angel before you so you can get a wife for my son from there.'" (Genesis 24:1-9 NIV)

In the book of Genesis (24:1-67) we find one of the most adorable wedding stories in history. Abraham sent his top servant to his hometown of Nahor, in the land of Mesopotamia, to secure a wife for Isaac, among his relatives. The servant took ten camels, loaded with wonderful gifts, and headed for the town of Nahor.

Outside the town's water wells, he had his camels kneel. There he prayed earnestly, asking the God of Abraham for success! He prayed for a sign. When he asks a young maiden for a drink—let the right one also offer to water the camels. A lady came and did that! He found out she was Rebekah, the granddaughter of Nahor, Abraham's brother! Excitedly he gave her a golden ring and arm bracelets. Rebekah ran to her mother, and the servant and his men were invited to stay for the night.

The servant refused to eat, until he explained his mission—finding a wife for Isaac. Rebekah and family consented. Gifts were distributed, and the next day Rebekah left home. She became Isaac's wife, and he loved her (24:67). What a lesson for our day. When courtship and marriage is bathed in prayer, God's blessing is always experienced!

AVOID SMUG CLANNISHNESS   July 10

"A women in that town who lived a sinful life learned that Jesus was eating at the Pharisee's house, so she came there with an alabaster jar of perfume. As she stood behind him at his feet weeping, she began to wet his feet with her tears. Then she wiped them with her hair, kissed them and poured perfume on them. When the Pharisee...saw this, he said to himself, 'If this man were a prophet, he would know...she is a sinner.'" (Luke 7:37-39 NIV)

When a church roots its identity in its common ethic names, recipes and birthplaces rather than in the gospel of Jesus Christ, newcomers will feel like outsiders. This could happen to Scottish Presbyterians, Swedish Baptists, or German Mennonites. Many smaller denominations face an overwhelming challenge—to move beyond the restricting limits of ethnicity while retaining the tenets of their biblical historical faith.

A Mennonite businessman from Los Angeles attended a Mennonite relief sale at Fresno. He gave the high bid on a 1923 Chevy roadster: $5700. He overheard two local men, "Who bought the car?" "Oh, some Mr. Johnston from Los Angeles. Isn't it a shame a Mennonite didn't buy it!" It is tragic when a man is valued by his name and not his character! The comment should have been, "Praise God, Mr. Johnston gave five thousand dollars to help us feed the hungry!"

This story hides a clue to a big obstacle in evangelism. Christians of a common ethnic group can display a snob-complacency and smug-clannishness. A basic prerequisite to sound mission work worldwide is identification with others who differ from us. To be Christlike is to feel with all people, and to include them in our circles of friendship. A true Christian spirit is ethnically inclusive.

LIKE LEACHED OUT SALT   July 11

"Salt is good, but if it loses its saltiness, how can it be made salty again? It is fit neither for the soil nor for the manure pile; it is thrown out." (Luke 14:34-35 NIV)

In the Sermon on the Mount, Jesus identified his followers as "Salt of the Earth." Here he clinches his discipleship lesson with another analogy from salt. In Kingdom-talk, in the cosmic struggle between good and evil, disciples not radically committed are like leached out salt—tasteless, useless and worthless.

If we could diagnose the heart condition of the typical USA churchgoer, would we find it healthy, vital and vigorous? What basic motivation drives us? David and Karen Mains on their radio program "Chapel of the Air" interviewed Leonard Ravenhill, an aging evangelist, a frequent speaker for The Full Gospel Businessmen's Association. In style, he resembled the Old Testament prophets. He recalls preaching at a church. The sanctuary was swank and three thousand had gathered for worship. At that sacred moment, when pastors and elders meet before they enter the worship service, one elder blurted out, "I wonder what score our football team will rack up today?" Ravenhill observed that America has one king—SPORTS and one queen—ENTERTAINMENT. Where is our devotion to Jesus Christ?

Our discipleship requires a full surrender to Jesus Christ—that's CONSECRATION. And it requires keeping our vows made to Christ and his church—that's INTEGRITY. And it requires all of our witness, service, and worship to surge forth from the overflow of a Spirit-filled life—that's PENTECOST. Discipleship is costly but so rewarding. It is time for every church and every believer to declare Jesus as LORD, and to bask in the joy and inspiration of his presence. We must be salt and light.

SHOWING LOVE TO ENEMIES July 12

"...Love your enemies, do good to those who hate you, bless those who curse you, pray for those who mistreat you....Then your reward will be great, and you will be children of the Most High, because he is kind to the ungrateful and the wicked. Be merciful, just as your Father is merciful." (Luke 6:27-28, 35-36 NIV)

The Bible accents forgiveness, yet Psychologist Archibald Hart found that a dozen of our current psychology textbooks don't mention forgiveness at all. That is surprising! Certainly, anxiety and guilt drives thousands to a therapist. A scholar of another age, Dr. Plummer said succinctly, "To return evil for good is devilish, to return good for good is human, to return good for evil is divine."

I knew a business man in California (we'll call him Joe) who joined two other lenders to give a man (we'll call him Bill) capital to start a new cement company. Unfortunately, Bill's enterprise eventually collapsed. He lost it all. The three lenders discussed their options. Two decided to take Bill to court to recover their investment; but Joe refused, "I will not sue another Christian brother." So the two took the beleaguered man to court. As Bill took legal action to protect himself, the prosecution lost the case and the two got nothing. Many years passed. One day Joe received a letter: "Dear Brother, I have never forgotten your kindness when I started my cement business. I have retired and sold my house. My wife joins me in sending you the money you loaned us. We wish you good health. Thanks again, Sincerely, Bill."

My friends, here is a lesson as we seek to demonstrate Christ-like love. Exercising patience and forgiveness, in our effort to leave all consequences in God's hand, pays rich dividends.

IMITATING JESUS CHRIST   July 13

"Therefore if you have any encouragement from being united with Christ, if any comfort from his love, if any common sharing with the Spirit, if any tenderness and compassion, then make my joy complete by being like-minded, having the same love, being one in spirit and of one mind...With one another, have the same mindset as Christ Jesus." (Philippians 2:1-2, 5 NIV)

In his book, *Strengthening Your Grip*, Charles Swindoll writes, "This may shock you, but I believe the single most significant decision I can make on a day-to-day basis is my choice of attitude. It is more important than my past, my education, my bankroll, my successes or failures, fame or pain, what other people think of me or say about me, my circumstances, or my position."

In context, the Apostle Paul urges Christians to "walk worthy of the gospel of Christ" (1:27). This requires them to live together in unity. This can be performed only with Christlike selfless humility. This prevents fragmentation in the church and like a magnet, draws unbelievers into the fellowship.

The fourfold "if" assumes each proposition to be true, so could be translated "since." The **first** is "Encouragement in Christ." Being new creations in Christ is an incentive to godly behavior. All hateful bickering must be replaced. The **second** is "Comfort of Love." When we contemplate God's amazing love to us undeserving sinners (Rom. 5:8), we shout with joy! The **third** is "Fellowship with the Holy Spirit." While Satan injects disharmony and strife, the indwelling Holy Spirit knits all believers beautifully together. The **fourth** is "tenderness and compassion." Paul himself models these traits (1:8-9) as he speaks of his affection for the Church at Philippi. Friends, if we adopt Christ's attitude of selfless humility, placing others ahead of ourselves, we bring great honor to Christ and his church.

THE PROSPECT OF HEAVEN   **July 14**

"But as it is written: 'Eye has not seen, nor ear heard, nor have entered into the heart of man the things which God has prepared for those who love Him.' But God has revealed them to us through His Spirit. For the Spirit searches all things, yes, the deep things of God." (1 Corinthians 2:9-10 NKJV)

One of the saints of old, a church apologist, argued that a commitment to Christianity was logically sound. If you are a believer and ultimately find out that heaven is not real, you have lost nothing. But if you reject the Gospel of Christ and later find out that heaven is real, you have lost everything!

The prospect of heaven is an incentive for evangelism—the hope of bringing others with us to glory. In one of my pastorates, a lady followed the Lord in baptism and joined our church. Her husband showed no interest. When he was hospitalized, I visited him. "Bill," I said, "Why don't you commit your life to Christ and join our church?" His response was: "Do you think I should if I don't feel like it?" Soon our church organized a concerted prayer effort for the unsaved in our community. One Easter Sunday at our worship, Bill came forward to accept Christ! Our whole church was ecstatic! Bill became active in the life of our church.

Friends, as you read this, please don't postpone a commitment. When you say, maybe someday, remember an indecision is really a "NO" decision. Good intentions don't cut it. God requires a "YES" or a "NO." You need to acknowledge your sinfulness, repent and accept Jesus Christ as your personal Savior. You need to find a Bible-Believing church and commit yourself for growth and service.

MY HEART CHRIST'S HOME   July 15

"Those whom I love I rebuke and discipline. So be earnest and repent. Here I am! I stand at the door and knock. If anyone hears my voice and opens the door, I will come in and eat with that person, and they with me." (Revelation 3:19-20 NIV)

The Presbyterian pastor and educator, Robert Munger, once preached a sermon, "My Heart-Christ's Home" based on Ephesians 3:17, sometimes translated: "That Christ may settle down and be at home in your hearts by faith." InterVarsity placed this in booklet form and distributed it widely. Few have so effectively dramatized the need to relinquish everything near and dear, to Jesus, as this sermon.

Bob gave Jesus a royal tour of the house: Library, Dining Room, Workshop and all. In each room Jesus made alterations. One day Jesus noticed a peculiar odor—something dead upstairs in the hall closet. Bob's self-talk was full of anger: "I gave him the run of the whole house and now he wants that tiny closet. True, those personal things are dead and rotten but I love them. I wanted no one to know about them." As the odor got worse, Jesus threatened to sleep on the back porch. Only then did Bob surrender the closet key. In a moment Jesus had the rotten putrefying filth cleared out. What victory!

Bob wearied of housecleaning. Rooms dirtied too fast. "Lord," Bob ventured, "is there any chance of you taking responsibility for the whole house?" "Certainly," said Jesus, "you can't be victorious on your own, but I'm only a guest, I have no authority to take over." Bob saw the light. He fell on his knees and declared Jesus, Lord of his house. He grabbed his deed of title and signed it over to Jesus. "All I am and have is yours forever!"

A CURE TO ANXIETY   July 16

"But blessed is the one who trusts in the Lord, whose confidence is in him. They will be like a tree planted by the water that sends out its roots by the stream. It does not fear when heat comes; its leaves are always green. It has no worries in a year of drought and never fails to bear fruit." *(Jeremiah 17:7-8 NIV)*

This text from Jeremiah blesses people who place their confidence in God. It promises victory (no fear, no worry, no failure). Here are several similar promises in the Psalms: "Commit your way to the Lord" (37:5), and "Cast your burden on the Lord" (55:22). The New Testament is full of such invitations to pray!

In a study, Dr Holmes at the University of Washington Medical School joined with others to publish a STRESS-RATING-SCALE. The top four items are: Death of a spouse—100 points, Divorce—73, Marital separation—65, and jail term—63. The experts say that when your stress level adds up to over 200, then you are in danger of exhaustion, poor decisions, and health risks: physically, mentally and spiritually.

Here are four common events: Fired at work—47, Retirement—45, Foreclosure of mortgage—30, and In-law trouble—29. Every things adds to stress. Being aware of this, encourages us to slow down and become more deliberate in decisions.

Even everyday occurrences are evaluated: Changing residence—20, Change in church activities—19, Taking vacation—13, and Experiencing Christmas—12. This teaches us to control our activities in life. Basically, we need to commit all our major concerns to God in prayer—daily! We need to calm down and size up what is happening in our lives. We need to reorder our priorities, and map out a schedule that gives comfort and peace.

COPING WITH YOUR STRESS   July 17

"Trust in him at all times, You people; pour out your hearts to him, for God is our refuge....One thing God has spoken, two things have I heard: that you, O God, are strong, and that you, O Lord, are loving. Surely you will reward each person according to what he has done."
(Psalm 62:8, 11-12 NIV)

The starting point might be to name your stress causes: irritating relationships, a nagging spouse, financial pressures, academic failures, family quarrels, business losses or some other? Use a stress-rating-scale to rate your stresses.

USE THE POWER OF PRAYER. The psalmist David invites us to pour out our hearts to God, thus unloading our burden on the Lord. This brings great relief. Before you run to a brother or sister, or even a therapist, try prayer!

SET PRIORITIES IN YOUR LIFE. Rise early, so you have time to organize the details of your day, before it becomes hectic. Take breaks; don't always live in the fast lane. At church, at home, or at school, accept only what you can handle well.

USE RELAXATION TECHNIQUES. Jesus gave his followers some good advice. "Come with me by yourselves to a quiet place and get some rest" (Mark 6:31).

ADOPT GOOD HEALTH PATTERNS. Exercise with regularity. I remember a medical doctor who had a nervous breakdown. After hospitalization, he returned to his practice. Every noon he would jog several miles—his daily therapy. Eat properly. Wholesome nourishing food is essential to good health. Sleep adequately. There is no pill that can replace lost sleep. To function well you need proper sleep.

PRACTICE THOUGHT-CONTROL OVER STRESS. Memorize consoling Bible verses like Romans 8:32 "He who did not spare his own Son, but gave him up for us all, how will he not also, along with him, graciously give us all things."

SAFEGUARDS FOR HEARTS   July 18

"My son, give attention to my words; Incline your ear to my sayings. Do not let them depart from your eyes; Keep them in the midst of your heart; For they are life to those who find them, and health to all their flesh. Keep your heart with all diligence, for out of it spring the issues of life." (Proverbs 4:20-23 NKJV)

The Bible is our key protection. We concentrate here on verse 23. In the paraphrased *LIVING BIBLE*, it reads, "Above all else, guard your affections, for they influence everything else in your life." Solomon here appeals to us to use our minds, our ears, our eyes and our hearts to appropriate the Word of God! Many of us have numerous Bibles, but when they sit on the shelf, or are hidden in a drawer, they may not be easily available. I like to see people carry their Bibles to church and always have them within reach at home or in the office. The Bible becomes part of our lives as we **HEAR** it taught at church, and as we **READ** it at home. A double blessing comes to those who teach Sunday School or lead a home Bible class because they are compelled to **STUDY** the scriptures to explain its meaning! We absorb the scripture by hearing, reading and studying. Two other verbs are crucial: **MEMORIZING AND MEDITATING.** In my childhood in rural Kansas, school ended on April 20. Then came six weeks, half day German school/ half day Bible school. One year I memorized 275 Bible verses. In one of my pastorates, an 80 year old saint taught a Bible memorizing class. He himself memorized each week! And as to meditating on God's word continually, that is the delight of the devoted man of God (Psalm 1:2).

BECOMING HEAVENLY MINDED   July 19

"Since then, you have been raised with Christ, set your hearts on things above, where Christ is seated at the right hand of God. Set your minds on things above, not on earthly things. For you died, and your life is now hidden with Christ in God. When Christ, who is your life, appears, then you also will appear with him in glory." (Colossians 3:1-4 NIV)

People at times joke about Christians who seem to be "too heavenly minded to be of any earthly good." This is especially said of people who judge others harshly, while judging themselves conveniently, neglecting the Christian virtues of love and compassion. The context here refers to people as "the old man" or "the new man" (3:9-10). The old self, with his earthly nature lives for sexual immorality, greed, evil desires, and even anger, rage, and filthy language. On the other hand, the new self with his heavenly nature lives clothed in kindness, humility, gentleness, forgiveness and love (3:12-14). The lesson for Christians is simple: put off the old, put on the new. If you are saved, or born-again, live like it!

We are admonished to set our hearts and minds on things above. A book on Christian humor tells of a family facing a crisis. Mother says to her husband, "Quick, Henry, call the doctor, Johnny just swallowed a nickel!" Father responded, "No, Mother, let's get the minister. He gets money out of anyone." Seriously, the heavenly minded start with prayer. They constantly feel their identity with Christ in his death and resurrection—"our life is hidden with Christ." We sense God's presence. Our hearts are filled with praise to God. Our prayer requests rise continually to God's throne. We have a gleam of heaven in our eye!

THE RICH FOOL CASE   July 20

"...Jesus replied....'Watch out! Be on your guard against all kinds of greed; life does not consist in the abundance of possessions.' And he told them this parable: 'The ground of a certain rich man produced a good crop. He thought to himself,...I will tear down my barns and build bigger ones...I will say to myself—You have plenty of grain laid up for many years. Take life easy....'" (Luke 12:13-18 NIV)

The "Rich Fool" was a symbol of success, the envy of the countryside. His office wall, no doubt, displayed a "Farmer of the Year" plaque. He was a whiz at farming, an expert at wheeling and dealing—and he turned a profit. But he ignored God. According to Jesus—he died just as he had lived—a fool!

What was his mistake? He stockpiled his wealth for personal security, high-style living, and a luxurious retirement. He flunked God's management test: (1) of allotting resources for God's kingdom, (2) of releasing funds for the needs of other people, and (3) of planning for dying. In short, he failed in estate planning.

How do we teach a biblical perspective of money? Tony Campolo tells of a Russian educator visiting Philadelphia—requesting to see social services enacted by religious groups. Tony showed him many projects including a school for disadvantaged children. At the debriefing, the Russian expressed surprise that the Christian children had more concern about making money, than about spiritual things.

Friends, this parable of Jesus cautions against greed. The joy and meaning of life is not wrapped up in accumulating wealth. The greedy poor are no better than the greedy rich. Nowhere does Jesus say that money, per se, is evil, but he hints that it is hazardous to handle. Caution—its allure can seduce us.

SEEKING A CHRISTIAN LIFESTYLE   July 21

"Do not labor for food that perishes, but for the food which endures to eternal life, which the Son of Man will give you, because God the father has set His seal on Him." (John 6:27 NKJV)

In this verse Jesus talks about priorities: setting our highest goal on eternal things, and after that, secondarily on temporal things. The American dream has been to own a three bedroom home with a double car garage. Few Christian writers have grappled as realistically with alternative lifestyles and the maximizing of money for God's kingdom as has Tom Sine. His book, *Wild Hope*, should be required reading for every Christian leader. He asserts, "We have programmed the Christian young to expect to have everything economically that their parents had and a little more. But while their parents could typically buy the split-level and everything that goes with it on a single income, that lifestyle today requires at least two incomes." Christians need to cope in new and creative ways.

In his book, *Master Your Money*, Ron Blue gives superb help for family money-management. The typical American family, he states is in a serious dilemma. Here is proof: "...only 2% of Americans reaching age 65 are financially independent; 30% are dependent on charity, 23% must continue to work; 45% are dependent on relatives. Additionally, 85 out of 100 Americans have less than $250 when they reach 65."

Jesus devoted one quarter of His teachings to the subject of possessions. In fact, He spoke more on wealth than on heaven and hell, or peace and forgiveness. Today, people need help in corralling the runaway horses of spending—it's out of control. The wise use of money, and estate planning, should be taught from every pulpit, class, and small group. Corporate prayer would help!

PURPOSE OF THE TITHE   July 22

*"Be sure to set aside a tenth of all that your fields produce each year. Eat the tithe of your grain, new wine and oil, and the firstborn of your herds and flocks in the presence of the Lord your God at the place he will choose as a dwelling for his Name, **so that you may learn to revere the Lord your God always.**"* *(Deuteronomy 14:22-23 NIV)*

From Genesis to Malachi, the Old Testament teaches that all blessings of life fall from heaven and that Jehovah God desires the first and the best portion of our earnings. In the New Testament Jesus our Lord never rescinded such spontaneous giving; it is our response to God's grace. Milo Kauffman in *Stewards of God*, suggests that the only argument against Old Testament tithing, in our day, is to go beyond the tithe. Should we do less than they?

My wife and I are tithers, as were my parents and my granddad. When my son Greg married, he and his wife also began with a covenant on tithing. After three years they came to a financial squeeze: They had a baby to feed, bills were coming due, Greg had taken his CPA exam but didn't know his score, he had no prospect of work. They had a mere $65 in the bank, and owed $45 tithe. At that moment they decided to give the tithe, and trust God (Malachi 3:10). Two days later the bank called, "An anonymous donor has placed $500 into your account!"

The purpose of tithing is to learn to put God first—to always revere Him. Walking with Jesus as Lord is more than claiming forgiveness; it mandates walking in newness of life. It behooves every Christian family to set monetary priorities, so our wealth benefits the Kingdom of God!

PRAYER BLESSINGS PROJECTED   July 23

"When famine or plague comes to the land, or blight or mildew, locusts or grasshoppers, or when enemies besiege them in any of their cities, whatever disaster or disease may come, and when a prayer or plea is made by anyone among your people Israel—each one aware of his afflictions and pains, and spreading out their hands toward this temple—then hear from heaven, your dwelling. Forgive, and deal with everyone according to all they do, since you know their hearts (for you alone know the human heart), so that they will fear you and walk in obedience to you all the time they live in the land you gave to our ancestors." (2 Chronicles 6:28-31 NIV)

Before he died, King David assembled all leaders of Israel at Jerusalem and told of his plans to build God's Temple. But God intervened, "You shall not build a house for my name, because you have been a man of war and have shed blood" (1 Chronicles 28:1-6 NKJV). God told David that Solomon would build the house.

King Solomon, for seven years, involved thousands of workers in the building of the beautiful magnificent Temple—one of the grandest structures in the world. At the Dedication, Solomon knelt on a bronze platform, three cubits high, in front of all the people and prayed fervently (see prayer above). He asked God to hear, forgive and enable men to faithfully walk—all lifelong—in God's ways.

The Greek philosopher, Socrates (469-399 B.C.) insisted that "Knowledge Is Virtue." To him all wickedness stemmed from ignorance, implying—if you know right, you will do right. But wait, look at Solomon, his life disproves this theory. He began knowing right, but sadly—"As Solomon grew old, his wives turned his heart after other gods" (1 Kings 11:4).

FORSAKE ALL FOR CHRIST   July 24

"Then he said to them all, 'Whoever wants to be my disciples must deny themselves and take up their cross daily and follow me. For whoever wants to save their life will lose it, but whoever loses their life for me, will save it. What good is it for someone to gain the whole world, and yet lose or forfeit their very self?'" (Luke 9:23-25 NIV)

These statements are often called *"the hard sayings of Jesus."* The multitude was shocked. They were looking for an easy Jesus Club—no cost, no sacrifice, no work, all play, all profit, all blessing. They wanted Christ to heal their sicknesses, feed them free meals, and tell them exciting parables. No way were they looking for a Lord to govern their lives. Even the disciples—the twelve—failed to grasp the meaning of discipleship until after the resurrection. Jesus made it clear that he required more than an emotional feel; he wanted a deliberate act of counting the cost.

When I was guest speaker at a rural church near Spokane, Washington, I stayed at the home of Pastor Unruh and he told me this story. Dr. David Lowry was a minister in London, England during World War II. He sought to win a couple to Christ, but they had no time for Christ or the church. They promised to consider it someday, when they were financially secure. One night Nazi planes bombed their area. It was the pastor's grim duty to identify bodies. They found an arm. The ring identified the woman he had witnessed to. They pried the fist open, it held a coin. She died, clutching the only thing she was living for—money. Jesus said, "Unless you are willing to forsake all, you cannot be my disciple!"

MEANING OF CROSS-BEARING   July 25

"But God forbid that I should glory except in the cross of our Lord Jesus Christ, by whom the world has been crucified to me, and I to the world." (Galatians 6:14 NKJV) "And whoever does not bear his cross and come after Me cannot be My disciple." (Luke 14:27 NKJV)

The general idea that these words of Jesus about bearing the cross refer to passive submission to all kinds of afflictions like disappointments, pain, grief, or sickness that come upon a person in life is not accurate. A further misuse of terms like self-denial and cross-bearing frequently comes at Lent, when people deny themselves of things like coffee, candy bars or cigarettes. Surrendering nonessentials might be a mild form of self-denial, but it is not Biblical Cross-bearing.

Back in Bible times, it was a common sight to see the Romans marching a robber or a rebel to an execution site. Every criminal carried his own cross of wood upon which he would be crucified. The modern parallel would be a man carrying his own rope to his own gallows, or a man carrying his own rifle to his own firing squad to face his own death. In each case it's an ugly symbol of death.

What did Jesus mean about cross-bearing? Norval Geldenhuys in the *New International Commentary* writes, "He who is not willing to die a most hideous death by crucifixion for the sake of his love and loyalty to Christ, cannot be my disciple." Yes, a willingness to die for Christ is key. But since Christ died for all, my sacrifices to share this news also counts. When I postpone buying a new car because I'm sending thousands of dollars overseas, to support missionaries who are spreading the Gospel—that's Cross-Bearing—in pure form as well!

THE VALUE OF GOALS July 26

"Do all things without murmuring and disputing, that you may become blameless and harmless, children of God without fault in the midst of a crooked and perverse generation, among whom you shine as lights in the world, holding fast the word of life, so that I may rejoice in the day of Christ that I have not run in vain or labored in vain." (Philippians 2:14-16 NKJV)

The apostle Paul was certainly one of the greatest missionaries of all time. He told his converts at Philippi to be blameless, harmless and faultless, shining as bright lights in a dark evil world. That way his goal of establishing a sound faithful church would be realized. He was truly goal-oriented!

I wrote a book entitled, *Discipleship Therapy: Healthy Christians, Healthy Churches.* I urged churches to disciple their converts, rather than letting them escape out of the back door as fast as they came in the front door. Just as child-care is hard work in parenting, so convert-care is time-consuming and strenuous in church evangelism. But it pays rich dividends. After writing eleven chapters on mentoring new believers, I wrote one on five-year goal-setting in: Following, Witnessing, Working, Praying, Forgiving, Giving, and Relating.

An acquaintance of ours, George Janzen, a missionary in Japan wrote that his small church had a new vision of what they could do for Christ. They set a goal to pray for 20 new converts who would follow through to baptism. That year they worked and prayed, reaching people one by one. At Christmas they baptized ten in one service! At year-end they counted 21! How remarkable. That was more than they had baptized in the previous five years. Friends, that was real cross-bearing, working wholeheartedly in the very enterprise for which Christ died.

HARD SAYINGS OF JESUS   July 27

"Large crowds were traveling with Jesus, and turning to them he said 'If anyone comes to me and does not hate father and mother, wife and children, brothers and sisters—yes, even their own life—such a person cannot be my disciple.'" (*Luke 14:25-26 NIV*)

We visualize Jesus as a kind, soft-spoken, gentle Lord. He was touched by the illness of people, he wept at funerals, he preached to the poor, he was kind and compassionate to Samaritans. Then on this occasion, surrounded by a great multitude, Jesus used shock-therapy and startled everyone: "If you don't hate your relatives, you cannot be my disciple." This is a figure of speech called an hyperbole. It is a teaching technique that exaggerates to make a point.

The scholar G.B. Caird writes, "The Semitic way of saying 'I prefer this to that' is 'I hate this, but I like that.'" Thus for the followers of Jesus to hate their families meant giving family second place in their affection. InterVarsity Press published a book by F. F. Bruce, *The Hard Sayings of Jesus.* He says it seems queer to hate our families, when we've been told to love our neighbors and even our enemies! He gives an easy explanation: The parallel passage, Matthew 10:37 states, "Anyone who loves his father or mother more than me, is not worthy of me."

Let me illustrate. Our missionaries in Japan held services, proclaiming Jesus Christ night after night. A college boy accepted Christ. At home he told his father, "I have become a Christian." "No, no," the fathers shouted, "Why do you hate us?" "I love you father, but I believe in Jesus Christ," the son responded. The father continued, "You're rejecting us, renouncing your Buddhist ancestors, you hate us, renounce Christ or leave!" The boy chose Jesus and moved out.

HUMILITY IN PRAYER   July 28

"To some who were confident of their own righteousness and looked down on everybody else, Jesus told this parable: 'Two men went up to the temple to pray, one a Pharisee and the other a tax collector. The Pharisee stood up and prayed about himself: God I thank you that I am not like other people—robbers, evildoers, adulterers—or even like this tax collector. I fast twice a week and give a tenth of all I get. But the tax collector stood at a distance. He would not even look up to heaven, but beat his breast and said, God, have mercy on me a sinner. I tell you that this man, rather than the other, went home justified before God. For all those who exalt themselves will be humbled, and those who humble themselves will be exalted.'" (Luke 18:9-14 NIV)

In my first pastorate I went with a Christian brother to his AA meeting. The Alcoholics Anonymous group met at the Women's Club. I was impressed. Each said, "My name is Joe, I'm an alcoholic, here is how my week went." One AA step reads, "We admit we were powerless over alcohol and our lives had become unmanageable." **What Humility!** Why can't we say in Church, "My name is Al, I'm a sinner. I was powerless over sin. I turned to Christ and he saved me. Please pray for me."

In my second parish, a distraught mother requested prayer. Her son had phoned, "My wife is leaving me next Friday." I called a prayer-circle for 10:00 p.m. We prayed fervently. We covenanted to fast the next evening—to pray over the dinner-hour. The anxious mother was so inspired, she skipped work, and prayed all afternoon. Late that evening the son phoned, "Praise God, my wife has decided to stay!" Humble prayers are powerful!

BANKING IN HEAVEN   July 29

"Do not store up for yourselves treasures on earth, where moth and vermin destroy, and where thieves break in and steal. But store up for yourselves treasures in heaven...For where your treasure is, there your heart will be also." (Matthew 6:19-21 NIV)

Some say it is better to have your bank in heaven, than to have heaven in your bank. That's worth a ponder. As a young pastor I read a book by Jack Haskell on taking $500 and building it into a fortune. His vision involved the Antelope Valley, north of Los Angeles. Since populations had increased from 26,000 to 82,000 in ten years, Haskell suggested buying 10-acre plots ahead of the expansion. I went to bed that night with dollar signs before my eyes. The very next morning my devotions were in Luke 12, "Beware of covetousness. A man's life does not consist in the abundance of his possessions!" This pulled me up short and forced me to re-examine my views on accumulating wealth.

Permit me to use an illustration that even a child can understand. A father and his son wanted to capture a monkey. They fastened down a jar and placed some peanuts inside. They came back an hour later and a monkey was there with his hand in the jar, clutching peanuts. The monkey could have opened his fist and pulled his hand out and escaped. But because of greed he refused to release the peanuts and the father and son walked right up and caught him!

When we use all our time and wealth to accumulate more, we are prisoners of our own greed. God owns all, and loans some to us—to help his kingdom—thus laying up treasures in Heaven. When we die, we leave all, and our works follow us (Revelation 14:13).

MIGHTY POWER OF PRAYER   July 30

"The effective, fervent prayer of a righteous man avails much. Elijah was a man with a nature like ours, and he prayed earnestly that it would not rain; and it did not rain on the land for three years and six months. And he prayed again, and the heaven gave rain, and the earth produced its fruit." (James 5:16b-18 NKJV)

The Bible gives us much encouragement to pray. As humans we have a Heavenly Father who loves to hear His children pray. In our spiritual growth as Christians we learn the art of prayer, and gradually gain discernment on how to pray in God's will. At times we will see marvelous answers to our petitions!

Here is an inspiring prayer-story. One of my seminary professors, Dr. F. Carlton Booth, when he taught at a Bible college in Philadelphia, witnessed a miracle. The school was in cramped quarters, and heard of a beautiful spacious campus for sale. The value of the property was about $325,000. The entire student body devoted a day to prayer and fasting, as the Board calculated their bid. Knowing that another party was also bidding, the Board settled on $330,000. One person suggested $331,000, but another one liked $331,001. That was the final decision submitted at the Court House. The lawyers opened the school's bid of $331,001. Then they opened the second bid, and the lawyers were stunned—the bid was $331,000 even. When the students heard that the Board had outbid the opposition by one dollar, they jumped for joy with Hallelujahs and praise to God!

Such amazing prayer victories, build faith in all people involved. They never forget that experience. So as they go through life, they know that prayer is always a potential answer to their problems. God is our solution. God answers prayer!

HEAVENLY TICKET SECURED   July 31

"The Son is the radiance of God's glory, and the exact representation of his being, sustaining all things by his powerful word. After he had provided purification for sins, he sat down at the right hand of the Majesty in heaven." (Hebrews 1:3 NIV)

In Kansas where I grew up, it was customary to hire a lawyer, when we purchased real estate. His duty was to study the abstract, to check on prior debts, liens and restrictions, as well as mineral rights. Later in Los Angeles County where we bought some apartments, the escrow officer requested a title search to see if the title was clear. Then the title company guaranteed that no encumbrance existed.

Our ticket to heaven, our trust-deed of ownership, is guaranteed and secured by the true eternal Word of God. Titus 1:2 states, *"a faith and knowledge resting on the hope of eternal life, which God, who does not lie, promised before the beginning of time."* Our basic sinfulness, which we must acknowledge, would keep us out of heaven, were it not for the amazing redemption plan of God. The Bible repeatedly says, "and the blood of Jesus, his Son, purifies us from all sin" (1 John 1:6-10). What a comfort to everyone who has accepted Jesus Christ as Lord and Savior!

At the moment of belief we are declared righteous, through the merits of Christ. From that point we begin a struggle against sin in our lives—ever hoping to become more Christlike. This morning at our church's MAN-UP breakfast, our director, Fred, challenged us to live pure lives for Christ, protected by the armor of God (Eph. 6). At the end of his 30 minute speech, he invited us to come and accept a wrist band, with the words: **Man of God 24/7.**

CATTLE ON THE HILLS   August 1

"Listen my people, and I will speak; I will testify against you Israel: I am God, your God....for every animal of the forest is mine, and the cattle on a thousand hills....Sacrifice thank offerings to God, fulfill your vows to the Most High, and call upon me in the day of trouble; I will deliver you and you will honor me." (Psalm 50:7, 10, 14-15 NIV)

I was raised on a Midwest farm. Annually, we bought 100 calves, from the Texas SMS Ranch. Each spring we drove them 20 miles to pasture. At age six, I rode a horse in the chase. When I turned 16, Dad's herd brought $100 net profit per head, in the very year our new 1947 Chevrolet Fleetline cost $1700. Yes, the cattle on a thousand hills belong to God.

Each morning we hear radio teacher David Jeremiah. As an alumnus of Dallas Theological Seminary, he told a story from the school's early history. Once the school was in debt and creditors threatened foreclosure. As the Board prayed, Harry Ironsides said, "God, you own the cattle on a thousand hills; please sell some and help us." Later that day, a man wearing cowboy boots entered the seminary, "I have sold two loads of cattle at Fort Worth, and decided to donate this to you." President Lewis Sperry Chafer looked at the check—the exact amount of the debt, signed by a local cattleman! He shouted, "Mr. Ironsides, your cattle are sold!"

Psalm 50 teaches that all animals and birds belong to God. Bringing a sacrifice has meaning **ONLY** if hearts are filled with love to God, with obedience and submission to his will. When we fulfill our vows to God, we can call on God in our troubles and he will deliver.

COMPEL THEM TO COME   August 2

"And the servant said, 'Master, it is done as you commanded, and still there is room.' Then the master said to the servant, 'Go out into the highways and hedges, and compel them to come in, that my house may be filled. For I say to you that none of those men who were invited shall taste my supper.'" (Luke14:22-24 NKJV)

Jesus told a parable of a man who invited people to a Great Banquet. Invitations were met with wild excuses. Finally, the man invited the poor, the lame and the blind. Still there was room, so he instructed his servants to go to the highways and compel them to come in!

I cringe when pastors use trickery to bring people to the altar. I shudder when soul-winners forcefully demand a decision, when no friendly relationship has been established. There is a saying, "A man convinced against his will, is of the same opinion still." Yet the parable of Christ seems to indicate that evangelism cannot use a casual take-it-or-leave-it approach. In our witness for Jesus, we need to be so sincere and persuasive, that when people reject our Christ, they will sense our disappointment that they have refused Christ's wonderful offer!

In my college days I taught DVBS in Ozark schools, helping workers of The Go Ye Mission at Alderson, Oklahoma. They told me this story. A man at their church, attended regularly, always friendly, but refusing to become a Christian. A visiting missionary asked him, "Do you want to accept Christ today?" He replied, "I don't know if I'm ready?" The missionary grabbed him by the hand and forced him down. On their knees, the man was led in a prayer of acceptance. The conversion was genuine—he was eternally grateful that someone had compelled him to come in!

CHEERFULNESS IN GIVING   August 3

"Each of you should give what you have decided in your heart to give, not reluctantly or under compulsion, for God loves a cheerful giver. And God is able to bless you abundantly, so that in all things at all times, having all that you need, you will abound in every good work."
(2 Corinthians 9:7-8 NIV)

Somewhere around 1940, Solomon Mouttet had a vision to evangelize Eastern Oklahoma, in the beautiful hills of the Ozarks. He established the Go Ye Mission with offices in the town of Tahlequah. His mission workers went to public grade schools and taught weekly Bible lessons. In the summertime, they conducted camps for young people. As they were leading many children to Christ, some from non-Christian homes, it occurred to Mr. Mouttet that public high schools did not provide a good atmosphere for these young Christians.

He had a vision to start a Christian High School called Markoma Academy—where students would be encouraged in their Christian faith. He visited churches like ours in Kansas, to raise money. He hoped to buy a farm, so the Academy would be self-supporting, and where students could work to help pay their tuition. Homer, Solomon's son, was one of the Academy instructors who told me this story.

A nearby farm became available for about $60,000. One day a Kansas farmer showed up. He examined every inch of that farm. "I will buy it," he said, "but the school will own it." As they were signing the papers, the lawyer said, "It must feel great to give like this to God's work!" The farmer, a man of few words responded, "Lawyer, God spoke to me very strongly before I did this!" For the Go Ye Mission this was a marvelous answer to prayer.

FIGHT THE GOOD FIGHT OF FAITH   August 4

"But you, man of God, flee from all this, and pursue righteousness,
godliness, faith, love, endurance and gentleness. Fight the good fight
of faith. Take hold of the eternal life to which you were called when
you made your good confession in the presence of many witnesses."
(1 Timothy 6:11-12 NIV)

Few professors in recent times have so eloquently written
about the defense of the faith as did the President of Fuller
Theological Seminary, the late Edward J. Carnell. In the 50's
I sat in his classes, and bought his brilliant books, *An Introduc-*
tion to Christian Apologetics (1956) and *Christian Commitment-An*
Apologetic (1957). Our duty to defend the faith is clearly outlined in scripture. *"But In your hearts set apart Christ as Lord.*
Always be prepared to give an answer to everyone who asks you to
give the reason for the hope that you have. But do this with gentleness
and respect" (1 Peter 3:15).

Dr. Carnell asserted that in sales work, we are taught to
start with the most attractive positive aspects, and after that
bring up price and sales-commitment. But Christianity starts
with the negative—our sin and our need of redemption. While
lecturing at the University of California at Berkeley, a student
asked, "How do you know Christianity is the right religion if
you haven't spent your whole life studying world religions?"
Dr. Carnell replied, "Why, that's simple. I check the basic pre-
suppositions. Only Christianity teaches that humans are lost,
straying and falling short of God's glory. They must humbly,
on their knees, open their hearts to Jesus Christ and accept
salvation. All other religions, to achieve favor with God, teach
that men by self-improvement, self-punishment, self-restric-
tion or self-suppression can gain favor in God's sight." So it's
divine atonement, not human attainment that really counts.

THE HALL OF FAITH   August 5

"And without faith it is impossible to please God, because anyone who comes to him must believe that he exists and that he rewards those who earnestly seek him." (Hebrews 11:6 NIV)

In 1974 we as a family vacationed on the Atlantic Seaboard. We arrived in Washington D.C., on the very day President Richard Nixon left the White House. En route home we visited the Baseball Hall of Fame at Cooperstown, New York, the place where baseball was born. We saw the historical exhibits of the "baseball greats" like Babe Ruth and Sandy Colfax. We saw the uniforms, the bats, the hats, and the photos. My three sons posed for a picture beside the bust of Mickey Mantle.

In Hebrews 11 we have the Christian's Hall of faith. Out of thousands and thousands, only nine are given full length feature and nine are given honorable mention. You may remember these Bible stories at your mother's knee. By faith Abel offered a better sacrifice. By faith Enoch walked with God. By faith Noah heard God's warning and built an ark. By faith Abraham obeyed God and went to a strange country. By faith Sarah gave birth in old age. By faith Isaac blessed Jacob and Esau. By faith Jacob blessed the sons of Joseph and worshiped. By faith Joseph gave instructions regarding his burial. By faith Moses, when he came to years, refused to be called the son of Pharaoh's daughter, esteeming the reproach of Christ greater riches than the treasures of Egypt.

The honorable mentions are: Joshua, Rahab, Gideon, Barack, Samson, Jephtha, David, Samuel and the prophets. "All these people were still living by faith when they died. They did not receive the things promised; they only saw them…from a distance. And they admitted they were aliens and strangers on earth" (11:13).

THE POWER OF FORGIVENESS   August 6

"Therefore, as God's chosen people, holy and dearly loved, clothe your-self with compassion, kindness, humility, gentleness and patience. Bear with each other and forgive one another if any of you has a grievance against someone. Forgive as the Lord forgave you." (Colossians 3:12-13 NIV)

The Bible is clear and emphatic that Christians, who have experienced the loving forgiveness of their Heavenly Father, are obligated to forgive others—with the same measure of love! Harboring anger, grudges and unforgiveness is displeasing to God, and is even harmful to physical health and psychological well-being. It is sad when people refuse to forgive others. They only hurt themselves.

The Bible has a practical solution—practice forgiveness each day before you go to bed. "In your anger do not sin. Do not let the sun go down while you are still angry, and do not give the devil a foothold" (Ephesians 4:26-27 NIV).

Our Lord Jesus often said, "your sins are forgiven." At times we need to do the same. When Bruce Larson was Senior Pastor at the University Presbyterian Church of Seattle, he wrote the commentary on Luke in the *Communicator's Commentary*. He wrote about Dr. Bill Wilson, a psychiatrist at Duke University. In their hospital they had a patient, nonfunctioning for years. In Vietnam he was responsible for many deaths and the staff felt that he was unable to forgive himself. One day this Christian physician, Dr. Wilson, sat on the patient's bed and said, "Your sins are forgiveness. I have authority to tell you, through Jesus Christ, that your sins are forgiven." That marked the beginning of healing in that man's life! Today he is back in society, functioning normally. Dr Wilson says that many people seeking therapy groups are actually struggling with guilt and we Christians have the solution.

AMAZING PARENTAL INFLUENCE   August 7

"Then the Lord said, 'Shall I hide from Abraham what I am about to do? Abraham will surely become a great and powerful nation, and all nations on earth will be blessed through him. For I have chosen him, so that he will direct his children and his household after him to keep the way of the Lord by doing what is right and just, so that the Lord will bring about for Abraham what he has promised him.'" (Genesis 18:17-19 NIV)

When God was contemplating the future of Sodom and Gomorrah, he gave high praise to Abraham who was chosen to lead his children in the ways of God, to do what is just and right. God foretold the blessings that would accrue to all nations of the world through the faithfulness of Abraham. We know the fulfillment of this came through the life, teachings and death of Christ!

The influence of parents is amazing. When their speech does not line up with their daily shouting and yelling, the children have no helpful pattern to imitate. Clean gentle godly speaking is such a blessing. It is soothing, it is quieting, it is comforting and brings godly security to the children!

To prepare our children for leadership in the church, it is helpful when Dad and Mom set a good example. If parents come home from church overly critical, criticizing the sermon, pastor or teacher, will their children learn to love the church? Will the children ever volunteer to be a Sunday School teacher, church officer, or pastor? A positive praying attitude in the home is essential if we want our children to become supporting, praying, tithing, serving, enthusiastic church members! (It may be wise for parents to discuss and pray about critical church matters in private).

GOD'S SPECIAL GUIDANCE   August 8

"You are my hiding place; you will protect me from trouble and surround me with songs of deliverance. I will instruct you and teach you in the way you should go; I will counsel you with my loving eye on you. Do not be like the horse or the mule, which have no understanding but must be controlled by bit and bridle or they will not come to you." (Psalm 32:7-9 NIV)

This psalm of David promises that God will watch over us, he will protect us from trouble, and he will guide us where to go. When my in-laws, Joe and Susie Walter, were still living, we at times drove to South Dakota for a visit. They welcomed us with open arms, and when we left they always blessed us with a unique prayer: "God, put your Guardian Angel in front of the car, behind, and on both sides, AMEN" To this day we use that prayer when we travel.

In the 15 years we lived in Nebraska, one Saturday night at 9:00 p.m., we were coming home from Kansas, and our car stalled on Interstate I-35 near Salina. We prayed. I walked a quarter mile to a housing area, and saw two ladies, one was pushing a baby carriage. She said I could use her phone. I called Sam Entz at Newton, a retired missionary who was an auto mechanic, "Can you come 60 miles and help us?" He came, checked things out and concluded, "I can't help you, it's the fuel pump." I told him that the home where I phoned, has a new Chevy fuel pump. He drove and picked it up. It fit perfectly! By midnight the car was running like new. What a miracle! God had led me to the exact home that had a spare fuel pump! Praise God.

AUTHENTIC COMMUNITY   August 9

"You were taught...to be made new in the attitude of your minds; and to put on the new self, created to be like God in true righteousness and holiness....Follow God's example, therefore, as dearly loved children and walk in the way of love, just as Christ loved us and gave himself up for us as a fragrant offering and sacrifice to God." (Ephesians 4:22-24, 5:1-2 NIV)

Recently our church has highlighted "Authentic Community" and today's sermon centered on that theme. The subjects covered were authenticity, transparency, and accountability. This issue has interested me, ever since my doctoral studies on Convert-Care. At that time the Southern Baptists outshone most church groups in their successful evangelism; however, my research found, they had no more success with discipleship than the rest of us! One leader lamented that only half of their 15,000,000, showed up on a given Sunday.

Ephesians 4 states pointedly that Authenticity is experienced when we put off the old self with all of its lust and impurity, and put on the new self, created to be like God. Transparency is realized when we reject falsehood, and speak truthfully with others, even controlling our anger—denying the devil a foothold. Such a life of love mirrors the very character of God, whom we are to imitate. Accountability is demonstrated when we utilize wholesome talk to build others up, when we strive to meet their various needs. Small classes or discipleship groups are helpful for holding each other accountable and ministering to each other.

Praying for each other is a grand way to guarantee spiritual growth in our own lives, and it helps us bless our community, our church and our country. In our attempt to win people to Christ, when they shut out our witness, we still have the powerful avenue of prayer.

REVIVED IN REVIVAL   August 10

"Will you not revive us again, that your people may rejoice in you? Show us your unfailing love, Lord, and grant us your salvation. I will listen to what God the Lord says; he promises peace to his people, his faithful servants—but let them not return to folly." (Psalm 85:6-8 NIV)

Past generations often gave glowing testimonies of how Revival Meetings had blessed their lives. How they had been motivated to become a Christian, or how as a backslider, they had been revived dramatically.

In my first pastorate in southern California, we had a godly member, Grandma Preheim, in her 80's. She rode 12 miles on the city bus twice a week—to Sunday morning worship and to the midweek Woman's Mission Society. She always brought a whole bushel basket full of clothing for the needy. Her late husband was a minister, and she had a large family.

On New Year's Eve at our Watch Night service, Grandma Preheim stood to share a testimony, "Years ago I grew spiritually cold. I felt my husband's prayers were too long. I quit my devotional life. Then Revival Meetings came to our community. For a week and a half there was no response to the altar call. Then the evangelist asked parents to come forward if they were willing to pray for their children. Again, no response— even I resisted. At home I tried to pray, and couldn't. It dawned on me, I had forfeited my right to pray for myself. I humbly asked God for forgiveness. The next evening I went forward to pray for my children." The joy of the Lord was restored to her! Old-timers often sang, "Revive us again, Fill each heart with thy love, May each soul be rekindled with fire from above."

OUR MEASURE IS USED   **August 11**

"He said to them, 'Do you bring in a lamp to put it under a bowl or a bed? Instead don't you put it on its stand?...If anyone has ears to hear, let him hear. Consider carefully what you hear,' he continued. 'With the measure you use, it will be measured to you—and even more. Whoever has will be given more; whoever does not have, even what he has will be taken from him.'" (Mark 4:21, 23-25 NIV)

Just as lamps are designed to illuminate things, not to hide them, so Christ's parables were to reveal truth, even though some listeners had no discernment, and considered them mere stories. As listeners assume responsibility, the measure of attention given to Jesus, is the same measure of understanding and blessing that listeners will receive. The more receptive we are to Jesus' teaching, the more discernment will be granted to us.

In the game of football, the more a receiver excels, the more opportunities he will get to catch passes, gain yards or achieve touchdowns. Recently, Mike Greenberg and Mike Golic, ESPN talk show hosts campaigned to get Cris Carter inducted into the Pro Football Hall of Fame. Cris Carter had a stellar pro-career as a receiver. He caught 1,101 passes, gaining 13,899 yards, and made 130 touchdowns. He was asked about his potential for the Hall of Fame? He replied, "I see it this way—the Hall of Fame is writing a story, and is the Hall of Fame complete without you?" Humbly, he was leaving it to the experts, to evaluate his importance.

In the game of life, God will be our judge. While heaven is free to all believers through the merits of Christ, our work for Christ will be richly rewarded as we enter the Heavenly Hall Of Faith!

HELPING SELF AND OTHERS   August 12

"If you have any encouragement from being united with Christ, if any comfort from his love, if any common sharing in the Spirit, if any tenderness and compassion, then make my joy complete by being likeminded, having the same love, being one in spirit and of one mind. Do nothing out of selfish ambition or vain conceit. Rather, in humility value others above yourselves, not looking to your own interests, but each of you to the interests of others." (Philippians 2:1-4 NIV)

Here is a marvelous passage. Paul is saying that if you have enjoyed the gracious benefits of the Christian faith: the encouragement, the comfort, the fellowship, and the compassion, then shape your life according to that. In that way you imitate Jesus Christ, your Lord—who humbled himself to become a human, a servant, and died for us all (2:5-11). The big lesson: be as much concerned about others as you are concerned about yourself!

In my third pastorate my goal was to disciple 12 men annually. One father, hearing about my work of mentoring men, brought me a cake: "Pastor, I have several sons. Won't you take one of them in your next group?" That was a parental concern I adored! One day a wife phoned me, "Pastor, you will remember inviting my husband to one of your groups and he turned you down. Well, time has passed and I believe he might be ready now." I explained that I don't wish to be a nuisance, so I don't normally ask the same person twice. But she persisted, "I think he is ready!" Since I appreciated her vision for her husband, I invited him and he accepted!

How heartwarming when people have a spiritual concern for another! That's being Christlike. How about you?

AFFIRMING OUR YOUTH   **August 13**

"My son, do not forget my teaching, but keep my commands in your heart, for they will prolong your life many years and bring you peace and prosperity. Let love and faithfulness never leave you; bind them around your neck, write them on the tablet of your heart. Then you will win favor and a good name in the sight of God and man. Trust in the Lord with all your heart and lean not on your own understanding; in all your ways submit to him, and he will make your paths straight." (Proverbs 3:1-6 NIV)

Here are some sound principles for our youth. Lay ahold of love and faithfulness and never let them go. As a reminder, hang them around your neck and inscribe them on your heart. Trust the Lord for guidance. Lean wholeheartedly on God and he will direct your paths. Already as a teenager, I clung to these verses; and they are still my favorites.

In one of the churches I pastored, we had a need for more teachers. In my background I was used to Adult Teacher Training courses. However, this church historically and periodically gave training to teenagers. Two ladies in the Board of Education, Marlene and Amy, conducted a class for seniors in High School. They taught Biblical principles, sound educational methods and hands-on training right in classes alongside experienced teachers. As the years passed some teachers testified that their love for teaching stemmed from their teenage training.

Affirming young people is so crucial. Since we retired to Bakersfield, California, our current church annually sends 100 youth to Mexico to build three houses, to teach a week of Vacation Bible School, and to offer recreational fun to children. Of course, 30 adult sponsors go along. These missionary activities are very wholesome for our youth.

A HEARTFELT RECEPTION   August 14

"As Jesus and his disciples were on their way, he came to a village where a woman named Martha opened her home to him. She had a sister called Mary, who sat at the Lord's feet listening to what he said." (Luke 10:38-39 NIV)

This was about six months before Christ's betrayal and crucifixion. The Jewish leaders were mounting a strong opposition. Finding a secure haven at Martha's home was such a comfort. This was at Bethany, two miles from Jerusalem. Scholars place this event before Christ raised Lazarus (John 11) and Mary's anointing (John 12). Luke alone records this story. In a day when Jewish culture downgraded women's standing, Luke alone named three prominent women who financially supported Christ and his ministry: Mary Magdalene, Joanna, wife of Herod's steward, and Susanna (Luke 8:1-3). John's Gospel tells us that Jesus loved Martha, sister Mary and brother Lazarus (11:5). This was truly a warm personal relationship.

My first 13-year pastorate was in Downey, California. We operated a church bus where Levi, the driver, and Hilda, the Church Visitor, worked as a team, building a warm rapport with the neighborhood. The bus brought youth to Sunday School, Summer Bible School, and occasionally took kids to summer camp. We had a great time, reaching and teaching children for Christ. The parent's were so appreciative of our ministry to children, that when I advertised a three month class for neighborhood parents—teaching the Life of Christ—sixteen enrolled!

Take a girl named Marilyn. She rode our bus to church and embraced Christ. After college she took a teaching job at a church school. Decades passed; we lost touch. Praise God, last year we met her again. Now living in Texas, she and husband, both employed, both active in church, have raised their children to be church-attending Christians!

226

MARY AND MARTHA   August 15

"As Jesus and his disciples were on their way, he came to a village where a woman named Martha opened her home to him....But Martha was distracted by all the preparations that had to be made. She came to him and asked, 'Lord, don't you care that my sister has left me to do the work by myself? Tell her to help me!' 'Martha, Martha,' the Lord answered, 'you are worried and upset about many things, but few things are needed—or indeed only one. Mary has chosen what is better, and it will not be taken away from her.'" (Luke 10:38, 40-42 NIV)

Jesus stopped at Martha's house at Bethany, on the eastern slope of the Mount of Olives. Apparently, Mary lived with her sister. But clearly Martha was the predominant person. It was her house. She is the hostess. She welcomes Christ. The welcome mat was always out for Jesus and his disciples.

Martha was busy in the kitchen, Mary chose to sit at Jesus' feet. The Canadian scholar, E. Earl Ellis, writes, "...the story reflects a dinner scene, as was the custom. Jesus reclined on his side at the table. Mary...sat at the Lord's feet. The picture is that of a Rabbi instructing his pupil...Judaism did not forbid women to be instructed in the Torah, but it was very unusual for a Rabbi to lower himself to this."

Martha, working alone in the kitchen became upset. She obviously had the spiritual gifts of Hospitality and Service. Jesus gently rebuked her. Mary's gifts are harder to discern. Some suggest Teaching and Exhortation. At any rate, Jesus praised Mary for her wise choice! We all need to guard against allowing our busyness to crowd out our quality time with Christ. And further, we should refrain from criticizing people with gifts different from ours!

THREEFOLD BEHAVIOR LESSON   August 16

"Jesus asked the Pharisees and experts in the law, 'Is it lawful to heal on the Sabbath or not?' But they remained silent. So taking hold of the man, he healed him and sent him away. Then he asked them, 'If one of you has a child, or an ox that falls into a well on the Sabbath day, will you not immediately pull it out?' And they had nothing to say." (Luke 14:3-6 NIV)

One Sabbath day when Jesus went to eat at the house of a prominent Pharisee, he was carefully watched. There Jesus taught them three behavioral lessons. **Lesson No. 1, True Lesson on Helpfulness.** The Gospels record seven cases of healings on the Sabbath and Luke records five of these miracles. At that house, Jesus saw a man suffering from dropsy, so he healed him. Sensing the Pharisees were shocked, Jesus defended his action by asking whether they wouldn't pull a son or an ox out of the well, if they fell in on a Sabbath day? That was legal!

Lesson No. 2, True Lesson on Humility. Jesus noticed that dinner guests were choosing seats of honor. He suggested that guests could start with lower seats, and let the host usher them to a higher room. It's embarrassing to be demoted! Jesus knew that pride kept many from accepting his message of sin and salvation.

Lesson No. 3, True Lesson on Hospitality. Next Jesus spoke of a godly host who didn't just invite relatives and rich friends—they will invite you back. The ideal guest list includes the poor, the crippled, the lame and the blind. They can't invite you back. You will be repaid at the resurrection of the righteous! What a lesson for our day. Whom could you invite? Heaven has some great rewards!

AMAZING HUMAN EXCUSES   **August 17**

"Jesus replied: 'A certain man was preparing a great banquet and invited many guests. At the time of the banquet he sent his servant to tell those who had been invited, Come for everything is now ready.' But they all alike began to make excuses. The first said, 'I have just bought a field, and I must go and see it. Please excuse me.' Another said, 'I have just bought five yoke of oxen, and I'm on my way to try them out. Please excuse me.' Still another said, 'I just got married, so I can't come.'" (Luke 14:16-20 NIV)

As Christ is dining with the Pharisees, he told a parable of a man who prepared a great banquet. Many folks refused his invitation. Remember the Old Testament had announced the coming Messianic Kingdom, and Jesus was now making his rounds saying, "Come join, the Kingdom has come!" But many refused.

Excuse No. 1. Pressing Circumstances. One man wants to visit his land-purchase. I once urged a man to accept Christ and the church. His reply was, "I would if I was younger, but at age 53, I don't have time. Having had a heart attack, I have to work hard to provide for my family while I can!"

Excuse No. 2. Personal Convenience. One man wants to try out his new yoke of oxen. In our day it may be a tractor, golf clubs, motor boat or a hopped-up sports car. Little time or money is left for Christ's Church.

Excuse No. 3. Private Consideration. Another man said, "I just got married!" Wow! The banquet invitation was a "No Brainer." Most newlyweds want to economize. Men could take their brides to this complimentary banquet! So in life, people can accept God's marvelous forgiveness and salvation, but sadly reject it to their own peril.

EXPERIENCING AN EARTHQUAKE   August 18

"God is our refuge and strength, a very present help in trouble. Therefore we will not fear, though the earth be removed, and the mountains be carried into the midst of the sea; though its waters roar and be troubled, though the mountains shake with its swelling....God is in the midst of her, she shall not be moved; God shall help her, just at the break of dawn." (Psalm 46:1-3, 5 NKJV)

After my 13-year pastorate in Southern California at Downey, we moved to Glendora, while I worked on a doctorate at Fuller Seminary in Pasadena. On the morning of February 9, 1971 a severe earthquake, registering 6.5 on the Richter Scale, struck Los Angeles. The center of devastation was in San Fernando and Sylmar. Tremors were felt for 300 miles. Sixty-five persons were killed and 1,000 injured. Loss of life was heavy in Sylmar where a four-story Veterans Hospital collapsed.

I was home with my three sons. I awakened as my bed started jerking around. Some items fell from shelves. Thank God for protection—we were unhurt, and the house was undamaged. My wife was working that night at a newborn nursery in a local hospital. They were all safe.

Our text affirms that we need not fear, God is "a very present help in trouble." In the megalopolis of Los Angeles, out of seven million people only 65 were killed! Here is an amazing observation: electricity, gas, water and telephones cut out simultaneously. Why is that important? When the gas lines ruptured, the electric lines were already dead. A big fire, an horrendous fire, was averted. There was no water pressure to fight fires! Despite heavy suffering, God be praised for such miraculous loving protection! The devastation could have been exceedingly worse!

RECOVERING FROM EARTHQUAKE   August 19

"May the glory of the Lord endure forever; May the Lord rejoice in His works. He looks on the earth, and it trembles; He touches the hills and they smoke. I will sing to the Lord as long as I live; I will sing praise to my God while I have my being." (Psalm 104:31-33 NKJV)

In the 1971 Los Angeles earthquake, in the town of San Fernando 258 homes were destroyed and 1520 badly damaged. Yet, less than one per cent of the populace moved away. In 1975 the City Administrator, Robert James was interviewed. He was pleased how merchants and home owners had repaired and rebuilt their properties. He saw no reason for persons to flee—every area has some potential problem—floods, fires, hurricanes, twisters or some freak of nature. One family did move to Louisiana, only to be wiped out by Hurricane Camille.

The LA earthquake struck on a Tuesday morning, and 80,000 evacuees were forbidden to return to their homes until 4:00 p.m. on Friday, when LA Mayor Yorty allowed it. The Van Norman Dam was badly cracked, and 14 feet of water—half of the lake's water—was released before residents below the dam were permitted to return.

Fire Chief Edmund Friand said, "You know people have taken more interest in their town, in their government, and in each other, as a result of this experience. San Fernando is a better place than it ever was." The Fire Chief was most impressed with how kindly people helped one another.

We know that normal life will have lots of trials. As Christians we seek to praise God no matter how severe the trials are. We trust God—He alone knows the reason behind certain events. Christians commit themselves into God's care.

LAUNCHING INTO EVANGELISM   August 20

"When they had done so, they caught such a large number of fish that their nets began to break...When Simon saw this he fell at Jesus' knees...For he and all his companions were astonished at the catch of fish they had taken, and so were James and John, the sons of Zebedee, Simon's partners. Then Jesus said to Simon, 'Don't be afraid; from now on you will fish for people.'" *(Luke 5:6, 8-10 NIV)*

That day on the shores of the Sea of Galilee, Jesus told Simon Peter to launch into the deep and they caught such a huge amount of fish, they filled two boats. Peter and his comrades were amazed. This miraculous catch convinced Peter that Jesus was more than a mere human. At this point Peter left his fishing nets and began following Christ. From the teachings of Christ, Peter soon learned that this man claimed to be the Messiah, the Son of God!

In his book, *Mere Christianity*, C.S. Lewis, who became a Christian late in life, made this observation that when we read the gospels, we can only come to one of three conclusions. Either Christ was a crook, deceiving people, or a loony, eligible for an asylum, or he really was the Son of God and we need to kneel and worship him!

Jesus told Simon Peter that he would start "fishing for men." What a challenge for every Christian. When Bruce Larson pastored in Seattle, one parishioner, a tiny lady, would go out at night on dangerous streets to witness for Christ. In her purse she carried a note, "My dear friend, so you're in trouble and stole my purse. I love you and God loves you. Here is my address and phone number. Contact me and I will help you." What a courageous fisher-woman!

BEING HIS WITNESSES   August 21

*"Then he opened their minds so they could understand the Scriptures.
He told them, 'This is what is written: The Messiah will suffer and
rise from the dead on the third day, and repentance for the forgiveness of sins will be preached in his name to all nations, beginning at
Jerusalem. You are witnesses of these things. I am going to send you
what my father has promised; but stay in the city until you have been
clothed with power from on high.'"* (Luke 24:45-49 NIV)

Before Christ returned to heaven, he foretold that his death
and resurrection would be preached in all nations. He reminded
them that they were witnesses, and after being empowered by
the Holy Spirit, they were to share this witness everywhere. In
my Kansas pastorate I challenged people to evangelism. Fifty
persons signed a statement, including an 80-year-old deaconess
at the Bethel Deaconess Hospital. Sister Anna Marie wrote, "I
would like to love someone to Jesus this year." Setting goals is
extremely beneficial! It is very motivating.

Matthew's Gospel contains what we call "The Great Commission" (28:16-20). It contains one imperative, "MAKE
DISCIPLES" and three qualifying participles: going, baptizing,
and teaching. In his opposition to the Anabaptist Movement,
Martin Luther insisted that the Commission was exhausted, and
did not apply to us. The Anabaptists disagreed. They attempted
to restore New Testament Christianity. The Methodist scholar,
Franklin H. Littell, in *The Anabaptist View of the Church*, writes,
"The Anabaptists were among the first to make the Commission binding on all members. In the organization, the promise
to go where sent, was part of the ceremony of admission to the
true church." Church historians suggest that these Christians
were the forerunners of the modern missionary movement of
the 18th and 19th centuries. What a grand complement.

FINDING YOUR NICHE   **August 22**

"Better is one day in your courts than a thousand elsewhere; I would rather be a doorkeeper in the house of my God than dwell in the tents of the wicked. For the Lord God is a sun and shield; the Lord bestows favor and honor; no good thing does he withhold from those whose walk is blameless." (Psalm 84:10-11 NIV)

Here is a beautiful text of God's protection, and his favor, honor and goodness bestowed on his devoted followers. What a heartwarming testimony of a man who would rather be a humble doorkeeper in the house of his God, than dwell in the tents of the wicked! What niche would you prefer in the Church of Jesus Christ today? Where would you feel most fulfilled?

In the churches of America, in recent decades, there has been a heavy emphasis on volunteerism. Placing people carefully in certain positions is extremely important. When people are placed in jobs that don't fit with their abilities, experience or their gifting, they will soon burn out, or get bored. Spiritual Gift Discernment is needed. Yet one lady recently wrote in a magazine that her background makes it difficult to say, "My gift is teaching, or mercy, or service etc., it sounds boastful, and contradicts humility!" It sorta sounds like bragging. Frankly, I have led many groups in gift discernment, and have always found them beneficial. If individuals are required to say what they think their gifts are, then the group can evaluate. If all agree, this gives him or her the desired affirmation. This is very encouraging.

My friend, what about you? Are you regular in your church attendance? Are you an active participating member? Have you found your niche in the church? Are you praying, tithing and helping? Your Spiritual Gifts are needed!

TRUST NOT IN WEALTH   August 23

"Command those who are rich in this present world not to be arrogant nor to put their hope in wealth, which is so uncertain, but to put their hope in God, who richly provides us with everything for our enjoyment. Command them to do good, to be rich in good deeds, and to be generous and willing to share." (1 Timothy 6:17-18 NIV)

My sister Frieda, school teacher in Leavenworth, Kansas, gave a gift to our son, Steven, when he graduated from high school. It was William DeWitt's book, published in 1970, *HISTORY'S 100 GREATEST EVENTS.* Event #1 is "Israelites flee; Receive Commandments." Event #100 is "America First on the Moon." Event #91 caught my interest, "Stocks Crash in Wall Street's Worst Day." To many investors, this was the end of the world!

The fateful day was October 29, 1929. An unbelievable 16,000,000 shares of stock changed hands that day, with prices plummeting. By year-end, in terms of security values, the trading had wiped out fifteen billion dollars of Investments. As rumors spread, there was a "run" on the bank in many towns. In 1930 there were 1,352 bank failures and in 1931, another 2,294. Business failures reached a peak in 1932, when 31,822 firms closed down. This brought economic shock worldwide. In America, an ever expanding prosperity was ingrained in every mind; political leaders had spoken of two cars in every garage. Now it all collapsed. Men, young and old alike, jumped out of windows to their death.

My parents were married in 1927. On a Kansas farm, between 1928 and 1942 they had eight offspring. We children experienced the depression days, yet we never went hungry. We milked our own cows, planted a big garden, fed a flock of chickens. My Christian parents trusted God—He never failed us!

REACHING YOUR NEIGHBORHOOD   August 24

"My brothers and sisters, believers in our glorious Lord Jesus Christ, don't show favoritism. Suppose a man comes into your meeting wearing a gold ring and fine clothes, and a poor man in filthy old clothes also comes in. If you show special attention to the man wearing fine clothes and say, 'Here is a good seat for you' but say to the poor man, 'You stand there,' or 'Sit on the floor by my feet.' Have you not discriminated among yourselves and become judges with evil thoughts?"
(James 2:1-4 NIV)

The ministry of Jesus was exemplary—devoid of any discrimination. Rich or poor: Jesus ate dinner with wealthy Zachaeus, and he praised the destitute widow who gave her last coin. Jew, Gentile or Samaritan: Jesus healed the servant of a Gentile centurion and praised the Samaritan who rescued the injured man. Men or Women: Jesus chose 12 men as disciples, but allowed a group of women to offer financial support (Luke 8:2-3).

Recently our Sunday School teacher contrasted two churches. The one noticed the changing neighborhood and built a high wall around its premise—with barbed wire on top, to protect itself. The other church, with a declining membership, decided to reach the newcomers around them. They organized a strong Awana program. They removed the pews in the sanctuary, so the space was usable for children and youth activities. Worshipers sat on folding chairs. The church grew nicely as people felt the welcome of a loving church!

Loving acceptance is the hallmark of every successful missionary enterprise. Any healthy church should be able to assimilate folks from any race—yet the late Donald McGavran, church growth expert insisted that people prefer to worship with their kind: Chinese with Chinese, Blacks with Blacks, Hispanics with Hispanics. No doubt, that's often true.

THE PRODIGAL SON   **August 25**

"Jesus continued, 'There was a man who had two sons. The younger one said to his father, Father, give me my share of the estate. So he divided his property between them. Not long after that, the younger son got together all he had, set off for a distant country and there squandered his wealth in wild living.'" (Luke 15:11-13 NIV)

One son, too impatient to wait for his father's death, demanded his inheritance now. Father obliged. The younger son apparently got one-third. He may have been revolting against rules and regulations at home. Discontent, he chose to run from reality. Imagine his last night at home, "Father, I want my freedom!" Father's response, "Son, freedom is doing what you should do; living by lusts and desires leads to awful slavery!"

The son left. In a far country he squandered his wealth in reckless riotous activity. You name it—carousing, drinking, gambling and partying all night—he did it all. His living "high-off-the-hog" did him in. Impoverished and hungry, he found a job of feeding pigs for a Gentile! THERE HE CAME TO HIS SENSES. Repenting at heart, he began yearning for his father's love—feeling unworthy, willing to be a servant.

What a homecoming! The father ran to meet him and embraced him. The son confessed his sin against both God and family. Father called for the best robe, ring and shoes. He asked servants to kill the fattened calf for a feast and celebration. Jesus told this story to show the Pharisees that when publicans and sinners repent, God is thrilled! My friend, as you read this, be assured that God is waiting for you with open arms. He will forgive your wicked past and accept you. Opening your heart to Jesus will ring the bells of heaven!

THE PHARISAICAL SON   August 26

"Meanwhile the older son was in the field. When he came near the house, he heard music and dancing. So he called one of the servants and asked him what was going on. 'Your brother has come,' he replied, 'And your father has killed the fattened calf because he has him back safe and sound.' The older brother became angry and refused to go in. So his father went out and pleaded with him." (Luke 15:25-28 NIV)

On this day Jesus was teaching. His audience contained Pharisees, publicans and sinners. The parable of the prodigal son coming home to a forgiving father, showed how Matthew, a tax collector, could be a disciple, and how Mary Magdalene, rescued from evil spirits, could be a follower (Lk. 8:2). However, the older son was a perfect portrayal of a Pharisee—always criticizing and condemning Jesus—with a holier-than-thou attitude.

The older son, coming home from work and hearing the music inquired, "What is the meaning of this celebration?" He was told, and became angry with a furious rage and refused to join in! Father came out to tenderly plead with him. "This son of yours squandered his health and wealth on prostitutes, then traipses home as a ragged vagabond seeking help from his father and you reward such irresponsible behavior?" "Yes," said Father, "He was dead, now he's alive, we had to throw a party!" But the son retorted, "Why should I have served you all these years, totally unrewarded?" "You didn't," said Father, "You inherited all I owned."

When we waste money or ruin our bodies; or when we drag our childhood faith through the gutter of an adult world—Surprise, Surprise—God never gives up! Here is a big lesson—God yearns for every straying son, waiting for his return.

BOASTING ABOUT TOMORROW   August 27

"Now listen, you who say, 'Today or tomorrow we will go to this or that city, spend a year there, carry on business and make money.' Why, you do not even know what will happen tomorrow....Instead, you ought to say, 'If it is the Lord's will, we will live and do this or that.'" (James 4:13-15 NIV)

In daily conversation, the phrase "Lord Willing" is not heard as often as it used to be. In fact, in my younger years on a Kansas farm, I recall people jokingly say, "Lord willing and the creeks don't rise." But seriously, in our Christian viewpoint, we know, our Sovereign Lord knows every cloudburst, thunder clap or lightning strike. He allowed the tornado that struck our farm near midnight while I was a lad of nine. It is comforting to know that God Almighty, our Sovereign Lord is our Loving Heavenly Father who watches over us night and day!

James reminds us that life is fragile, like a mist that soon vanishes. Our boasting about our "living and doing" tomorrow is futile. We don't even know if we'll be alive. Take my sister Martha, she was a missionary nurse in Africa's Sudan and Ethiopia, for 30 years. In retirement, she conducted Bible classes in Wichita for women from Iran and surrounding countries. At age 80, doctors sent her to the K.U. Medical Center at Kansas City for heart valve replacement. Because she had a cold, the surgery was postponed one week. So she went on a shopping spree and bought a beautiful red dress. She expected a fast recovery. On surgery day, she had two valves installed, but that evening a severe stroke took her. At the funeral she wore that dress!

Friends, let's keep the words "Lord Willing" in all of our future plans!

GOD'S ALL-SEEING EYE   August 28

"For the eyes of the Lord run to and fro throughout the whole earth, to show Himself strong on behalf of those whose heart is loyal to Him."
(2 Chronicles 16:9a NKJV)

This verse is a gem! It was spoken by Hanani, the seer, in the days of Asa, King of Judah. The seer reminded King Asa that when he relied on Almighty God, in the battle against the huge army of the Ethopians and the Lubim, with their countless chariots and horses, God had given Asa an overwhelming victory. But in the current battle, with Baasha, King of Israel, Asa had not sought God's counsel, but rather took gold and silver out of God's temple, and bribed Ben-Hadad, King of Syria to help him. This displeased God and God sent Hanani to tell Asa that his move was very foolish, and as a result, his future would be filled with wars. This made Asa furiously angry, and he sent Hanani to prison.

A few years later, Asa died, and Jehoshaphat, his son ruled. This was good news, because he was a godly man. Our text was a powerful promise to him—he was a "King whose heart was loyal to God!" And God blessed him abundantly.

My friends, this verse is a heartwarming message to you and me. If we love God with our whole heart and remain loyal to Him, He will keep His eye on us, and He will show Himself strong on our behalf. What a promise! Here is a verse to memorize. It belongs in your heart, and on your desk or refrigerator. God's strength is available for your every test, every trial, and every temptation. God loves to hear His children cry to Him for help. He waits for their phone call.

WISDOM CAREFULLY APPLIED   August 29

"Who is wise and understanding among you? Let them show it by their good life, by deeds done in the humility that comes from wisdom....But the wisdom that comes from heaven is first of all pure; then peace-loving, considerate, submissive, full of mercy and good fruit, impartial and sincere. Peacemakers who sow in peace raise a harvest of righteousness." (James 3:13, 17-18 NIV)

What a beautiful scripture! The context in James contrasts God's wisdom and the devil's wisdom. The former is pure and lovely, the latter is unspiritual, feeding on bitter envy and selfish ambition, leading to disorder and every evil practice (v.16). However, God's wisdom is shucked full of qualities that bring peaceful tranquility!

Life requires lots of practical wisdom. Let me illustrate: When wife and I got married some 50 years ago, she said, "I'll gladly wash the dishes, and I'll leave the preaching to you." (Actually she feared public speaking). In a seminary homiletics class, Dr. Clarence Roddy told us young upstarts, "When you're ill-prepared to preach on a given Sunday—then preach a little louder and a little longer!"

At each church I pastored, I as senior pastor, led an old-fashioned Wednesday night prayer meeting. I led it myself, to demonstrate the importance of corporate prayer in the life of a congregation. Our attendance ranged from 50 to 100. We met for one hour, dividing it into three equal parts: sharing, Bible teaching and praying. My wife always attended. Even though she never accepted a speaking assignment at a Mother-Daughter Banquet, at the prayer hour, she regularly stood and prayed—with joy, vigor and confidence. How could she do it? The answer is simple. She had the spiritual gifts of Helps and Service. She was so eager to make the prayer meeting a dynamic success!

A MILLIONAIRE'S JOY   **August 30**

"The law of the Lord is perfect, reviving the soul. The statutes of the Lord are trustworthy, making wise the simple. The precepts of the Lord are right, giving joy to the heart. The commands of the Lord are radiant, giving light to the eyes." (Psalm 19:7-8 NIV)

Millions of Americans envy the millionaire. You and I may not have the erroneous concept that he is free from all worry and heartache, but to many Americans he is the symbol of the highest good, a comfortable living, and a portrait of well-being. You may have worked hard from sunrise to sunset, earning a living by the sweat of your brow—yet over a span of years you may have accumulated little. **Yet my friend, when you take inventory of your wealth, above all, use God's standard. If you have Christ in your heart, you are a SPIRITUAL MILLIONAIRE!**

Wealth No. 1 PARDON: Missionaries tell us that people worldwide suffer from guilt. Primitive tribes fear an angry God. Yet our Gospel floods joy into our hearts—in Christ Jesus we are accepted and pardoned. Jesus died for our sins and set us free. Our sins are removed as far as East is from the West (Psalm 103:12).

Wealth No. 2 PROVISION: God will supply all our needs (Phil. 4:19). A man in the Hills of Kentucky, managed a Christian orphanage. Once he took boys along to a store. Promptly, they ordered ice cream. But he was short of money: "Lord, what do I do?" Suddenly someone shouted, "the treats are on me." God provided!

Wealth No. 3 PRESENCE: God has promised his abiding presence (Hebrews 13:5). A surgeon at the City of Hope told me "Now that I accepted Christ, I feel God's presence during every difficult surgery!" God's presence is a great comfort!

WORKS VALIDATE FAITH   August 31

"What good is it, my brothers and sisters, if someone claims to have faith but has no deeds? Can such faith save them?...Was not our father Abraham considered righteous for what he did when he offered his son Isaac on the altar?... And the scripture was fulfilled which says, 'Abraham believed God, and it was credited to him as righteousness,' and he was called God's friend. You see that persons are considered righteous by what they do, and not by faith alone." (James 2:14, 21, 23-24 NIV)

It is well known that Martin Luther, the great promoter of "Justification by faith" felt that the book of James did not belong in the Canon of Holy Scripture. Our Sunday School class recently studied James. Our teacher gave us: SIX PHASES OF JUSTIFICATION, gleaned from *Believer's Bible Commentary* by Wm. McDonald.

1. It's by **GRACE** (the principle—Rom. 3:24) declared by God—unmerited favor.
2. It's by **FAITH** (the means—Rom. 5:1) justified by faith, we experience peace.
3. It's by **BLOOD** (the price—Rom. 5:9) Christ's death appeases God's wrath.
4. It's by **GOD** (the agent—Rom. 8:33) the ultimate Judge declares us forgiven.
5. It's by **POWER** (the dynamic—Rom. 4:25) the resurrection guarantees it.
6. It's by **WORKS** (the results—James 2:24) our faith demands deeds of proof.

My forebearers, the Anabaptists of the Reformation, often challenged Lutherans about church standards. With compulsory infant baptism, everyone was on the church roll. Many church members were living ungodly lives. The Anabaptists sought to restore New Testament Christianity with Biblical standards and church discipline. They espoused freedom of religion, separation of church and state, believer's baptism, and total discipleship. To their credit, the Lutherans of Europe, in 2011, contacted Mennonite leaders to apologize for persecuting Anabaptists in the Reformation. We gladly forgive!

CONSEQUENCE OF COMPLAINING   September 1

"The Lord said to Moses and Aaron: 'How long will this wicked community grumble against me? I have heard the complaints of these grumbling Israelites. So tell them, As surely as I live, declares the Lord, I will do to you the very things I heard you say: In this wilderness your bodies will fall—everyone of you twenty years old or more who was counted in the census and who has grumbled against me. Not one of you will enter the land I swore with uplifted hand to make your home, except Caleb...and Joshua...'" (Numbers 14:26-30 NIV)

When the Israelites reached Kadesh Barnea, God asked Moses (13:1) to send 12 spies on a 40 day study-trip to spy out the land of Canaan. Upon their return all people assembled eagerly. All 12 agreed the land "flowed with milk and honey" and the fruit was gorgeous. They brought a huge cluster of grapes, hanging on a pole between two men. But ten spies told of huge men and fortified cities. Caleb silenced the crowd, "We can possess the land, we can do it" (13:30). The ten said, "We can't attack those people, they are stronger than we are...We felt like grasshoppers in the presence of those giants" (13:31-33)!

That night people wept and grumbled, wishing they had died in Egypt or in the desert. Caleb and Joshua intervened, promising that God would help them take the Promised Land. But the assembly talked about stoning Moses and Aaron! Then the glory of Lord appeared (14:10). God threatened to destroy them all, due to their unbelief—after all His miracles. But Moses interceded and God relented. Ultimately, the consequence was severe: The ten died of a plague (14:36-37), and all Israel was sentenced to forty years of wandering in the desert (14:26-35).

ERADICATE YOUR GRUMBLING   September 2

"Offer hospitality to one another without grumbling" (1 Peter 4:9 NIV). *"Do everything without grumbling or arguing, so that you may become blameless and pure, children of God without fault in a warped and crooked generation. Then you will shine among them like stars in the sky as you hold firmly to the word of life..."* (Philippians 2:14-16a NIV)

Both Peter and Paul urge us to eliminate all grumbling and complaining, all murmuring and arguing, as we shine as stars in our depraved generation. What a heartwarming challenge. In the Old Testament, the grumbling of Israel destined them to 40 years of sheepherding in the wilderness. Only Caleb and Joshua wholeheartedly followed the Lord. In the New Testament Church, followers of Christ are asked to cut out all griping and grumbling, so that people will listen as they share the word of life. A negative disposition tends to repel people; but a loving compassionate spirit attracts. Our goal is to "become blameless and pure, without fault" in any hostile environment.

Whether at home, at church, or at work, a grouchy grumpy behavior blesses no one. Our continual griping is annoying, but a warm smile and a kind word will lift the spirit of others. It promotes peace! My friend, if this subject touches your heart, and you long for victory in gaining a Christ-centered disposition, then be sure to include this in your daily prayers.

Dear Heavenly Father, I'm a believer in Jesus Christ, your son. I have opened my heart to him for salvation. But Lord, I struggle with a grumbling spirit. I nag, I shout, I criticize and say words I regret later. Purify my thoughts today. Purify my words. Grant me a loving gentle disposition. Enable me to be a shining star for Jesus. In his name I pray, Amen.

BLENDING SOVEREIGNTY & HUMANITY September 3

"Therefore, my dear friends, as you have always obeyed—not only in my presence, but now much more in my absence—continue to work out your salvation with fear and trembling, for it is God who works in you to will and to act in order to fulfil his good purpose." (Philippians 2:12-13 NIV)

The relationship between the free will of man and the sovereignty of God is a fascinating subject. When people isolate verse twelve, and ignore the context, they conclude that salvation is primarily self-achieved. This contradicts what Paul wrote to the Ephesians, that salvation is a gift, not a work of our doing (2:8-9). However, verse thirteen clarifies the issue—in salvation, God has worked his purpose within us , and we are to work out the ramifications!

In the philosophy of salvation, there is an obvious tension between man's freewill and God's sovereign will. Which should we emphasize? When we compare frail finite humans with Almighty God, Creator and Sustainer of the Universe—to me—the issue is resolved. The gospels insist that no one comes to God, unless he is divinely drawn. It's not us, searching out God; it's God drawing us in.

The God-Man relationship can be likened to a bicycle ride. The right pedal is God, the left pedal is us. First God instructs and pushes his pedal forward, next we agree and push our pedal, and we continue to work in harmony. In the book of Ezra we read: "Everyone whose heart God had moved—prepared to go up and build the house of the Lord in Jerusalem" (1:5). In the book of Galatians we read, "For God, who was at work in the ministry of Peter as an apostle to the Jews, was also at work in my ministry as an apostle to the Gentiles" (2:8).

OUR EXALTED LORD   September 4

"And when I saw Him, I fell at His feet as dead. But He laid His right hand on me, saying to me, 'Do not be afraid; I am the First and the Last. I am He who lives, and was dead, and behold, I am alive forevermore. Amen. And I have the keys of Hades and of Death. Write the things you have seen, and the things which are, and the things which will take place after this.'" (Revelation 1: 17-19 NKJV)

After one year at Hesston College, I transferred to Grace College of the Bible in Omaha and there I met my future wife, Susan Joann Walter, a farm gal from the vicinity of Huron, South Dakota. In our courtship, we enjoyed Sunday evening church attendance at Omaha Gospel Tabernacle, where noted pastor, R.R. Brown often spoke on the Second Coming of Christ—with great enthusiasm! Fifteen years later, during my first pastorate in California, I attended the Annual Revival Prayer Fellowship, under the leadership of Armin Gesswein, where 100 ministers met for three days. To my surprise, one year R.R. Brown was the guest speaker. White haired, now walking with a cane, he gave a memorable sermon.

He spoke of John's vision of the Risen Christ (Rev. 1:1-20). John, on the Island of Patmos, was in the Spirit on the Lord's day. Christ's appearance was stunning. His voice, like a trumpet v.10, and many waters v.15, His hair white as snow, His eyes like a flame of fire, His feet like brass, His mouth had a sword, His face shone in sunlight brilliance. John saw Christ and fell as dead. But Christ said, "Do not be afraid...I'm alive forevermore...I have the keys of Hades and of Death." **MY FRIENDS, NEVER FEAR THE FUTURE. CHRIST HAS CONTROL OF EVERYTHING!**

THE GOOD SHEPHERD CARES   September 5

"My sheep listen to my voice; I know them, and they follow me. I give them eternal life, and they shall never perish; no one can snatch them out of my hand." (John 10:27-28 NIV)

The portrait of Jesus being a gentle caring shepherd breeds confidence in the hearts of his sheep. However, the security factor does not apply to those who merely mouth allegiance to Jesus, it covers those who truly "Follow" him. A personal commitment is mandatory.

Today I heard the Focus On The Family radio program interviewing Sheila Walsh, author of *The Shelter of God's Promises (Nelson)*. She spoke with such humility and tenderness, as she recounted her experience in a psychiatric ward. During a period of severe depression, one night she was under a suicide-watch. In the middle of the night a man entered and gave her a small gift. As he started to leave, he turned and said, "The Shepherd always knows where you are." As she contemplated the meaning of this encounter, she concluded that God had sent an angel to encourage her!

One day Sheila Walsh was invited to speak at a woman's club. The clothing and jewelry of the audience depicted wealth. She wondered whether her speech would interest these ladies. But she spoke frankly about her depression and her psychiatric experiences. At the end, a leader of that meeting came to Sheila, took off her diamond-studded golden bracelet, and showed her the scar where she once slit her wrist! My reader friends, if you struggle with depression and wonder whether life is worth living—by all means—secure Sheila Walsh's book. Her sympathetic suggestions will be very therapeutic. And above all, turn your life over to Jesus Christ, He helped Sheila, and He certainly will help you.

SMALL CHILD'S SENSITIVITY   September 6

"Then people brought little children to Jesus for him to place his hands on them and pray for them. But the disciples rebuked them. Jesus said 'Let the little children come to me, and do not hinder them, for the kingdom of heaven belongs to such as these.' When he had placed his hands on them, he went on from there." (Matthew 19:13-15 NIV)

Jesus had such a "tender touch" when dealing with children. As the disciples wanted to chase them off, Jesus welcomed them! Dr. Paul Welter, University Professor at Kearney, Nebraska, teaching Educational Psychology, asked a class of 42 students to assist him in analyzing children. The outcome was Welter's good and delightful book, *Learning From Children*. He advocates that we view children as Master Teachers—our Spiritual Mentors! In my own words, I'll relate two of his powerful illustrations.

Childlike—Healing Brokenness. Grandmother died, being a young 56. Her daughter was utterly devastated, feeling tremendous grief. The three year old granddaughter noticed her mother's sorrow. One day, a gospel song on radio triggered an outburst of crying. The child grabbed her toy telephone, and handed it to her mother, "Here, someone wants to talk to you, it's Jesus, he wants to tell you he is taking good care of Grandma." Those words started the healing process!

Childlike—Empathetic Sensitivity. On Jeremy's first day at preschool, he was scared and tongue-tied when asked to stand for show-and-tell. He stood silent, under the gaze of 20 pairs of eyes. Another three year old got up and stood beside him. "Teacher, leave him alone, he needs more time to be shy." So the teacher went on, having learned a key lesson on sensitivity!

My friends, if you have the gift of "Showing Mercy" you can bless your church with words of encouragement, comfort and healing!

CHILD & COURAGEOUS FRIENDLINESS September 7

"O Lord, our Lord, how majestic is your name in all the earth! You have set your glory in the heavens. Through the praise of children and infants you have established a stronghold against your enemies, to silence the foe and the avenger." (Psalm 8:1-2 NIV)

Our text affirms that, "From the lips of children…you (God) have ordained praise." John Haggai of Atlanta, Georgia is one of the world's most successful mission executives, having trained thousands of nationals (doctors, pastors, bankers, mayors, lawyers, Company presidents, and other leaders) in Singapore and Hawaii and sending them back home to win millions. No other mission organization comes close in the volume of converts! In Haggai's book, *"Be Careful What You Call Impossible" (Harvest, 1989)*, he included a story of a 10 year old girl in Singapore named Lori and her mother named Linda.

Lori befriended a girl named Tracey, who regularly used bad language. During evening devotions, Linda shared a story about Corrie ten Boom and the Jews. (Tracey's family was Jewish); so Lori and Linda began praying for them. One day Tracey read Lori's Christian comic book from cover to cover. She told Lori that she wanted to become a Christian, so Lori led her in a prayer of accepting Christ. Next Lori got Tracey a Bible. Tracey ran home to see if she could accept this Bible? Her mother said, "Yes, but you can't go to church with Lori." The next day Tracey came to study the Bible. Later Lori told her mother—Tracey hardly said a bad word today, and she has started to pray!

Amazing, adults are fearful about witnessing to their own kind, much less to a Hindu, Jew or Moslem. But children readily witness across cultural lines. Jesus likes that—each human is a candidate for the kingdom!

OUR TRIALS & TRIBULATIONS   September 8

"They preached the gospel in that city and won a large number of disciples. Then they returned to Lystra, Iconium and Antioch, strengthening the disciples and encouraging them to remain true to the faith. 'We must go through many hardships to enter the kingdom of God,' they said." (Acts 14:21-22 NIV)

A foreign missionary spotted a witch doctor performing a miracle in public: he levitated a man horizontally three feet above the ground. The mission worker ridiculed the whole matter: "Sir, this must be a trick of some kind!" Suddenly, an invisible power grabbed the missionary by the throat; He gasped for air. Then he understood! He went home to pray. Returning, he witnessed the same feat. "In the name of Jesus," he commanded, "let this power be broken." The man dropped to the ground. Of course, the witch doctor was furious that this "Jesus-Power" had broken his spell. The general public took notice that the Christians were not intimidated by the witch doctor's magic (see Revelation 12:11).

The book of Revelation depicts the unrelenting enmity of Satan against the people of God which often finds historical expression. George Ladd, in his monumental work, *A Theology of the New Testament*, writes, "The modern evangelical fear of suffering in the great tribulation has forgotten the biblical teaching that the church in her fundamental character is always a martyr church (Acts 14:22). The true victory consists in conquering the Beast by loyalty to Christ to death" (Rev. 15:2).

Despite worldwide advances in tolerance and human rights, even today, somewhere in the world the Church of Jesus Christ faces severe opposition. Thousands die for Christ annually. The Upper Room Discourse of Jesus gives perspective: "...No servant is greater than his master. If they persecuted me, they will persecute you also" (John 15:20).

SEVEN MIRACULOUS SIGNS   September 9

"Jesus performed many other signs in the presence of his disciples, which are not recorded in this book. But these are written that you may believe that Jesus is the Messiah, the Son of God, and that by believing you may have life in his name." (John 20:30-31 NIV)

While a senior student at Wheaton College, I took a class on the Gospel of John under Dr. Merrill C. Tenney. He had published a book, *JOHN: The Gospel of Belief (Eerdmans, 1951)*. This gospel lists seven miracles (or Signs) revealing the supernatural power of Christ (exclusive of the Resurrection and fish-catch in the Epilogue). John insists that these were performed "in the presence of his disciples." The recording of the miracles was to elicit "belief"—the underlying Greek word, pisteuo, is used 98 times in this gospel.

Sign 1—Changing water into wine (2:1-11). Here Christ revealed himself as the master of quality—what the vine grew in months, he did in a moment of time. Sign 2—Healing the son of a Nobleman (4:46-54). Jesus showed himself as the master of distance. The boy he healed was about twenty miles distance away. Sign 3—Healing of the Impotent Man (5:1-9). Jesus is the master of time. This diseased man had been afflicted for thirty-eight years. He was healed instantly. Sign 4—Feeding of the 5000 (6:1-14). Jesus took 5 loaves and 2 fishes and fed 5000 men, besides women and children. Jesus was indeed a master of quantity. Sign 5—Walking on water (6:16-21). He again showed his mastery over nature. Sign 6—Healing a man born blind (9:1-12). Christ was a master over misfortune. Sign 7—Raising up Lazarus (11:1-46). Yes, this proved Christ's mastery over death. **JOHN'S GOAL IS TO GIVE YOU ETERNAL LIFE—VIA BELIEF IN JESUS, GOD'S SON!**

OUR GREATEST MIRACLE September 10

"What Jesus did here in Cana of Galilee was the first of the signs, through which he revealed his glory, and his disciples believed in him...After he was raised from the dead, his disciples recalled what he had said. Then they believed the Scripture and the words that Jesus had spoken." (John 2:11, 22 NIV)

Jesus Christ, our precious Lord and Savior, made his entrance into our world through the Miracle of the Virgin Birth, with no human father involved. And he made his departure from this life through the Miracle of the Resurrection with no human agent assisting. The birth of Jesus was spectacular, but philosophically, the Resurrection of our Lord was the MIRACLE-OF-ALL-MIRACLES!

Often today, the Virgin Birth is too lightly dismissed. That it appears in only two gospels is no argument. On that ground the Sermon on the Mount could be nullified. The view that Christians copied pagan-hero ideas is also untenable. Central to pagan thought is the idea that mythical gods cohabited with mortal women. The Bible text has a rare dignity, devoid of any immoral lust. The writer of the birth account, Luke the physician, may well have consulted Mary, to validate his story.

The bodily Resurrection of Jesus is the world's greatest miracle. No one—not Mohammed, nor Confucius, nor Joseph Smith, nor Pope John, nor Martin Luther, nor John Calvin, nor Menno Simons died for our sins and arose from the dead! Jesus alone merits this honor. "Salvation is found in no one else, for there is no other name under heaven given to men by which we must be saved" (Acts 4:12). Christ, the Risen Lord, walked and talked with his followers for forty days, prior to his Ascension. Christians today are also assured of a heavenly body, not subject to time and space!

LIVING THE GOLDEN RULE   September 11

"Give to everyone who asks you, and if anyone takes what belongs to you, do not demand it back. Do to others as you would have them do to you." (Luke 6:30-31 NIV)

When human relationships become irritating, strained or even broken, who is responsible to mend them? Who should initiate healing? The answer of Jesus may surprise you. First of all, if you have wronged someone, it is your duty to right it—to seek forgiveness and to make amends. Secondly, if someone else wrongs you, it is again your duty to take the initiative to bring about reconciliation, to demonstrate a spirit of forgiveness, and to harmonize your differences. Under all circumstances, the followers of Jesus are required to claim ownership to their own rapport with others.

Guideposts told a story of Norman Vincent Peale driving a rented car. He was lost and running late; he risked missing his plane. While speeding down a freshly oiled road he sprayed another car with tar. The offended driver roared past him, moved to the center of the road, slowing to a crawl. As Peale felt the awful urge to blast his horn, a verse flashed into memory: "A soft answer turns away wrath, but grievous words stir up anger" (Prov. 15:1 KJV). So he prayed for patience and turned the controls over to God.

The car ahead stopped, blocking the road. The irate driver asked him where he was going? Peale apologized for spraying his car. He explained that he couldn't find the airport entrance. The man relaxed, and offered to lead him to the airport. My friends, in all our relationships, the blessing of love goes miles further than the blasting of hate. Living out the Golden Rule offers a remedy to many strained relationships!

PERIL OF PROCRASTINATION   September 12

"Settle matters quickly with your adversary who is taking you to court. Do it while you are still together on the way, or your adversary may hand you over to the judge, and the judge may hand you over to the officer, and you may be thrown into prison. I tell you the truth, you will not get out until you have paid the last penny." (Matthew 5:25-26 NIV)

Jesus urges a prompt and expeditious handling of all reconciliation matters. Procrastination can be costly! In the ancient world debtors were jailed till the debts were paid. Jesus insisted on immediate action since malicious anger is so evil—and God's judgment is so certain (5:22). Therefore, we need to do all in our power to resolve conflict and settle disagreements with dispatch.

Churches need to provide fence-mending, bridge-building, injury-bandaging events to restore damaged relationships. Unresolved problems can fester for years. As a physician lances a boil to guarantee healing, so a Christian therapist can facilitate a reconciliation encounter to repair broken relationships. The therapist can even be a brother or sister in the church who possesses skills of counseling and has the "spiritual gift of mercy." Thus everyone benefits!

Estrangement, bickering or even avoidance between members can damage the witness of any church. The unchurched public is never attracted to a feuding fellowship. **Always remember: as a car runs on gasoline, the Church of Jesus Christ runs on love.** It was Jesus who declared **LOVE** to be his chosen insignia. And it was Jesus who urged followers to settle disputes quickly. With proper healthy confession and restitution, no lingering hate should remain. Pastors and Elders have a unique duty, admittedly difficult, to alleviate the friction areas of the church. A Spirit-led harmony is a great blessing to any church.

FAMILY DEVOTIONS PRACTICED   September 13

"But the fruit of the Spirit is love, joy, peace, forbearance, kindness, goodness, faithfulness, gentleness and self-control. Against such things there is no law. Those who belong to Christ Jesus have crucified the flesh with its passions and desires. Since we live by the Spirit, let us keep in step with the Spirit." (Galatians 5:22-25 NIV)

One summer, while we were living in Nebraska, we took a trip to California to visit our children in San Jose. We had the joy of joining them for their daily family worship. They used, *The ONE YEAR Book of Family Devotions*, from the Children's Bible Hour of Grand Rapids. Each page had a Bible passage on the right side and a contemporary story on the left. The April 16 page was designed for ages (8-13), just right for our oldest grandson, Josh.

Here is the story in capsule form: Helen's father was taking her to church choir practice, when they saw a bumper sticker: "Have you hugged your kid today?" "Hmmmph," Dad snorted, "That stupid bumper sticker makes me mad. I wonder how many kids have hugged their parents today?" Helen had been praying for her Dad's salvation. Later that day she cleaned her room and washed the dishes. Dad said, "What's gotten into that kid?" Before going to bed Helen hugged both of her parents. As she went to her room she overheard Dad say, "You know Helen is a nice girl. I think I'll go to church tomorrow to hear her choir sing." Helen's hope was that love in action might someday win her Dad to Christ!

Dear friends, I encourage you to practice family devotions. If your children are young, read Bible stories daily. A good Bible Story Book with ample pictures is a valuable tool in learning and teaching Bible knowledge.

PARENT'S SPIRITUAL ROLE   September 14

"My son keep your father's command and do not forsake your mother's teaching; Bind them always on your heart; fasten them around your neck. When you walk, they will guide you; when you sleep they will watch over you; when you awake they will speak to you. For this command is a lamp, this teaching is a light, and the correction and instruction are the way to life." (Proverbs 6:20-23 NIV)

In context, this passage says that obedience to parents will keep us on the "straight and narrow," on the path of truth and moral chastity. My forebearers did set a shining example. Take my Grandpa, John Epp Sr., who migrated from Europe in 1881 and settled on a farm in Kansas. I was born 50 years later and sometimes, as a lad, stayed at his farm overnight. For breakfast he ate steaming hot oatmeal, covered with a good dose of cream and sugar. He poured his hot coffee into a saucer, to cool it off, and drank out of the saucer. And always he read his German Bible at the breakfast table. He was a respected elder at our church. His nine children and a host of grandchildren always gathered at his farm on holidays for singing, scripture and prayer. He was a generous giver, helping many needy folks.

I was raised on a farm, one mile from Grandpa. My parents, John and Marie Epp, were devout Christians. They took us regularly to church, as well as to every Community Revival Meeting, and the Newton Annual Bible Conferences. At home they taught us Bible stories, and each evening gathered us together to hear Father read a Bible portion. Normally, we would kneel by our chairs, as several prayers were offered. We memorized both English and German prayers, which we said before going to bed.

EXALTING GOD TOGETHER　　　September 15

"I will extol the Lord at all times; his praise will always be on my lips. I will glory in the Lord; let the afflicted hear and rejoice. Glorify the Lord with me; let us exalt his name together." (Psalm 34:1-3 NIV)

The Psalmist David invites all to join him in exalting the Lord. In a Christian home husband and wife need to model togetherness from day one. As children are added, they need to be included in the daily worship of praise.

As children were born into our home, they were rocked to sleep with songs like "Jesus Loves Me" and "Jesus Loves the Little Children." We laid them into bed with a prayer. As they grew, we gave them pictorial Bible Story books. As they viewed the pictures, we read the stories. We taught them to fold their hands for a meal prayer. We took them to church—entrusting them to loving Nursery Care Workers.

As the youngsters grew we adjusted family worship to relate to them on their level. When our three sons were teenagers, the best togetherness-time was at dinner. After eating, we had Scripture reading and prayer, with all participating. Eventually, the boys left home for college, and we experienced the Empty Nest Syndrome.

Now that we're retired, we have an hour, every morning for worship and prayer. We seek to glorify the Lord and exalt his name. High on our prayer list, are our three sons, their spouses and children, and our wider family. We pray for our church, our Country and missionaries we support, and Christian workers from churches we pastored. This is not bragging—we're simply seeking to be faithful. Our goal is to inspire you to enlarge your prayer life. It will bring blessings of enormous proportions!

ANGEL OF THE LORD   September 16

"This poor man called, and the Lord heard him; he saved him out of all his troubles. The angel of the Lord encamps around those who fear him, and he delivers them. Taste and see that the Lord is good; blessed is the one who takes refuge in him." (Psalm 34:6-8 NIV)

In an earlier devotional, I have alluded to my late father-in-law's famous prayer: "Dear God, as this car is leaving, place your Guardian Angel in front of the car, behind the car, and on both sides. Bring them safely home. Amen." As a rule, wife and I pray daily for the car-driving safety of our children and grandchildren. So let me tell you what happened yesterday to our grandson, Jordan, living in the greater San Francisco area.

He was driving his gray 1996 Saturn to a class assignment. He is a student at West Valley College, learning to become a Park Ranger. He was turning off of Highway 101, at Morgan Hill, going 60 miles per hour, when apparently he fell asleep. His car drifted off the pavement. He grabbed the steering wheel and over-corrected. The car rolled over onto its top, and Jordan was upside down, hanging in his seat belt. He could not unlatch the belt. Two off-duty firemen saw the accident and rushed to get him out. He was alive, with only minor bruises. His professor happened to come by, picked him up, and took him to his class assignment. Later the professor even took him home.

Jordan is a sincere Christian. Praise God, "The angel of the Lord encamped around him and delivered him!" What a miracle—a marvelous answer to prayer! Our sovereign Lord does watch over his own.

TRUE LOVE TESTED   September 17

"On one occasion an expert in the law stood up to test Jesus. 'Teacher,' he asked, 'what must I do to inherit eternal life?' 'What is written in the Law?' he replied. 'How do you read it?' He answered, 'Love the Lord your God with all your heart and with all your soul and with all your strength and with all your mind; and love your neighbor as yourself.' 'You have answered correctly,' Jesus replied. 'Do this and you will live.'" (Luke 10:25-28 NIV)

Already, in the Old Testament Israel was told, "Love the Lord your God with all your heart and with all your soul and with all your strength" (Deuteronomy 6:5), as was also the command to love one's neighbor (Leviticus 19:18). But notice the wording: loving with the totality of our being is reserved for God. We are not instructed to worship our neighbor with our whole heart. Love neighbor "as yourself" is the instruction. It is assumed that everyone will have a fair degree of self-worth, self-esteem and wholesome pride. The therapist Dr. Sullivan, writing in *The Readers Digest* (January, 1974) said that genuine love exists only if the well-being and satisfaction of others is as important to you as your own well-being.

The Great Commandment, as we call it, is practical and relevant—it's where "the rubber hits the road." Christianity, beyond accepting forgiveness, denotes living in newness of life. C.S. Lewis, in *Mere Christianity*, writes, "If conversion to Christianity makes no improvement in a man's outward actions—if he continues to be just as snobbish or spiteful or envious or ambitious as he was before—then I think that we must suspect that his conversion was largely imaginary...Fine feelings...in religion mean nothing unless they make our actual behavior better." So our love for God is tested.

TURNING THE OTHER CHEEK September 18

"...If anyone slaps you on the right cheek turn to him the other also. And if anyone wants to sue you and take your shirt, hand over your coat as well. If anyone forces you to go one mile, go with them two miles. Give to the one who asks you and do not turn away from the one who wants to borrow from you." (Matthew 5:38-42 NIV)

If struck on the cheek, a disciple absorbs the insult and pain. Turning the other cheek will startle the enemy. It is not an act of cowardice; it is a symbol of courage and love. It is a clever strategy to break the cycle of revenge—a true protection for the forgiver.

Myron Augsburger in *The Christ-Shaped Conscience* (Victor, 1990) tells this story about his father. In 1941, due to ill health, Clarence Augsburger moved his family for the winter to Newport News, Virginia. He worked as a foreman on a house construction job. Bearing a German name, and being a Mennonite opposed to the war, he became the object of considerable criticism. One day, Bob, one of his severest critics, was laid off by another foreman. Days later, when Mr. Augsburger needed two more workers, he intentionally chose Bob, knowing he needed food for his family. Fifteen years later, Myron was invited to conduct an evangelistic crusade at Newport News. On the first Sunday evening, at the invitation to surrender to Jesus Christ, an older man came down the aisle. He said to Myron, "Do you know Clarence Augsburger?" "Why, yes, he's my dad." Tearfully the inquirer continued, "That man is why I am here today!"

When we respond lovingly, we leave outcomes to God. Turning the other cheek—more often than we dream—wins people to Jesus Christ.

BLESS AND FORGIVE   September 19

"Bless those who persecute you; bless and do not curse." (*Romans 12:14 NIV)*

Every Christian needs a big heart of appreciation for the saints who sacrificed their lives to bring us the Gospel! My heritage stems from the Anabaptist movement of the Reformation. In a home Bible study, in Zurich, Switzerland, on January 21, 1525 the Swiss Brethren under George Blaurock and Conrad Grebel lead participants in baptism and ordination. This was the start of a rapidly growing movement. About that time in Europe, it became illegal to be an Anabaptist, whether in the Catholic, Lutheran or Reformed provinces. Persecution grew intense. Some 5,000 Anabaptists were martyred in the next several decades. They died heroically singing praise to God!

Here is what they believed: (1) Separation of church and state, (2) Believer's Baptism replacing Infant Baptism, (3) Freedom of religion with no coercion, (4) the Great Commission is the duty of every believer (Matt. 28:16-20), and (5) Total Discipleship is part of the Churches' message. Praise God—in America today, these truths are held by many churches!

Here is a neat story from Holland. In 1551 Menno Simons ordained Leenaert Bouwens, a dynamic speaker, as Bishop. Leenaert's wife objected, the risk looked too big. In a letter of loving tenderness, Menno recited the urgency of the work, pleading with her to trust God. Leenaert kept a list of all he baptized—all 10,252. He died in Hoorn, Holland in 1582—amazingly—of natural causes! Finally, my friends, who are the heroes in your Heritage? Never forget their sacrifices.

You and I need to thank God repeatedly for the saints that have gone on before. At times we extend love and forgiveness. Remember Christ's example: "Father, forgive them for they know not what they do."

CONVERSION BRINGS CHANGE   September 20

"Yet to all who did receive him, to those who believed in his name, he gave the right to become children of God—children born not of natural descent, nor of human decision or a husband's will, but born of God." (John 1:12-13 NIV)

Bent toward sin—selfish to the core—we're called to a major transition from death to life (John 5:24). Rather than aiding Satan's kingdom, disciples of Jesus, by means of repentance and childlike faith, deliberately cross over to the Kingdom of God. Basic orientations change. Life that once revolved around the big "I" now revolves around Jesus Christ (2 Corinthians 5:17). Christ becomes central.

In his excellent book, *The Upside-Down Kingdom*, Donald Kraybill warns of the danger of cheapening and sugarcoating a costly gospel. "We slice off the call to discipleship and focus on spiritual fluff, froth, and fizz....Just follow Jesus we are told, and we'll be successful....Be born-again and we'll win more beauty contests, hit more home runs, make more sales, and receive more rewards." His underlying assertion is that conversion leads to a serious following of Jesus, a path that is likely to be difficult and counter-cultural, rather than easy and popular. Obedience to Jesus will likely encroach upon one's behavior.

Discipleship is actually costly. Welcoming new members to any church is far easier than retaining members. Many converts drop out, when a church fails to disciple the new members. Churches need personal mentorships and intentional organized discipleship training groups. Convert-care requires work, much work! Just as raising children demands years of care and nurture, so also developing converts demands years of intentional organized training. Churches need to be willing to pay the price. The rewards are great. The Great Commission does not ask us to win members, but to make disciples.

PARABLE OF THE SOWER   September 21

"...A farmer went out to sow his seed. As he was scattering the seed, some fell along the path, and the birds came and ate it up. Some fell on rocky places, where it did not have much soil. It sprang up quickly, because the soil was shallow. But when the sun came up, the plants were scorched, and they withered because they had no root. Other seed fell among thorns, which grew up and choked the plants. Still other seed fell on good soil, where it produced a crop—a hundred, sixty or thirty times what was sown. Whoever has ears, let them hear."
(Matthew 13:3-9 NIV)

The meaning of this parable is explained by Jesus (Matthew 13:18-23). How people respond to the message of the Kingdom, is compared to a farmer sowing his seed. The first three are negative. The seed that falls on the roadside, speaks of a person that does not understand the message, and the "evil one," clearly the devil, snatches the thoughts from his memory. The second case is the seed falling on rocky soil. The person gladly receives the word, but since he has no root, he is short-lived. When trouble or persecution comes, he quickly falls away. The third case is the seed falling on thorny ground—meaning that the worries of life and the deceitfulness of riches choke out the message, and it is unfruitful.

In the fourth case, seed falls on good soil, meaning that the hearer is responsive and bears fruit, a hundredfold, sixtyfold or thirtyfold. On our farm in Kansas my Dad once planted a bushel of a new wheat variety on a two and a half acre plot. He harvested 99 bushels. The lesson: responsive Christians will produce bountiful fruit for the Kingdom of God!

CHRISTIAN'S WORK TESTED   September 22

"For no one can lay any foundation other than the one already laid, which is Jesus Christ. If anyone builds on this foundation using gold, silver, costly stones, wood, hay or straw....fire will test the quality of each person's work. If what has been built survives, the builder will receive a reward. If it is burned up, the builder will suffer loss; but yet will be saved..." (1 Corinthians 3:11-15 NIV)

This speaks of Christians who build life on Jesus Christ. When Christ returns, some believers will be rewarded, some will suffer loss. Obviously, gold, silver and precious stones will withstand fire; wood, hay and straw will be consumed.

In *The Communicator's Commentary*, Vol. 07 (Word, 1985) Kenneth Chafin writes of Karen, who was commissioned by his Baptist church for missionary work in Mexico. The service was very inspirational. Later, one by one, people told Pastor Chafin how they were involved in Karen's life. One had cared for her during preschool, another had helped during teen-days, one led a choir she was in, and another had introduced Karen to the idea of mission work in a group study. Each had the self-satisfaction of bringing Karen to this point of commitment to Jesus Christ. Karen was their "gold, silver and precious stones."

How will things be rewarded. God alone knows, but here is my personal opinion. All works done unselfishly, in obedience to God and his word, all for the glory of God, will be rewarded. Deeds done for selfish reasons, or with impure motives, will probably be the "wood, hay, and stubble." All sacrificial effort to bring people to Christ and his church pleases God. All work of comforting, teaching and nurturing the saints pleases God. Jesus said that a cup of cold water given in his name would not go unrewarded (Matthew 10:42).

EXPERIENCES SHAPE US   September 23

"Honor your father and your mother, so that you may live long in the land the Lord your God is giving you." (Exodus 20:12 NIV)

The missionary anthropologist, I. M. Friedmann, in his book entitled: *Helping Resolve Conflict* (Herald) tells a fascinating story. He noticed his own violent behavior whenever he was falsely accused. Perplexed about this knee-jerk reaction to certain events, he sought counsel. The therapist thought that, perchance, some childhood event could still be affecting him.

One day he quizzed his mother. Tearfully, she recalled an experience back in Russia when he was a mere lad of three. She was baking those double-decker zwieback buns and left them on a baking sheet to rise. Returning, she found them all pressed flat. She inquired who had done this. The children accused him, but he vehemently denied it. Mother spanked him until he admitted to it, only to learn later that another child had actually done it. This whole event was still fresh in Mother's memory after all these years.

The chat between Mr. Friedmann and his elderly mother had a twofold benefit. It gave her another opportunity to make peace with her son. And, he was delighted to assure her of forgiveness. At the same time, he gained new insight to help him cope more effectively with certain stressful experiences.

Since parents are fallible and prone to mistakes, even the best of them need to be forgiven. Truthfully, children need to learn to forgive their parents, whether they are alive anymore or not. Carrying grievances forward from year to year violates the command of Jesus to forgive. On top of that, a bitter unforgiving spirit is hazardous to your health. Practicing Christlike forgiveness, in a psychological sense, brings a wonderful gift of release for all concerned.

VISION TO EDUCATE   September 24

"Let the morning bring me word of your unfailing love, for I have put my trust in you. Show *me the way I should go, for to you I entrust my life....Teach me to do your will, for you are my God; may your good spirit lead me on level ground." (Psalm 143:8, 10 NIV)*

The vision to open a school in northern Iraq, according to educator George Grant was born in a Nashville bagel shop. The goal was to build a school that used a mainly Christian curriculum in a largely Muslim Kurd environment. In the 1990's Saddam Hussein had ravaged the Kurdish population of northern Iraq with mass slaughters and chemical weapons. The hard-working self-sufficient Kurds found themselves victims in an international aid bureaucracy that rationed food and medical care.

An Arab Christian pastor named Yousif Matty chose to help the Kurds. He linked up with George Grant of Nashville to accept a foundational curriculum, which Grant had pioneered in 1992—a trailblazer in the Classical Christian education movement. Grant observed that a school where their children could earn an American high school diploma would be like gold for them. Matty agreed to manage the first school.

In 2001 The Classical School of the Medes was established in Sulaymaniyah, next one was started in Dohuk, and a third school was started in 2003 in the regional capital, Erbil. These three schools have grown faster than any of Grant's similar schools in America. These three Iraqi schools in 2012 had 2000 students, nearly all Muslim, with 27 American teachers assisted by the Iraqi faculty. Yousif Matty serves as senior director of all three schools. What a marvelous Christian visionary ministry in an area that needs to feel the love of Christ! What an opportunity.

GEM OF A FELLOW   September 25

"What is more, I consider everything a loss because of the surpassing greatness of knowing Christ Jesus my Lord, for whose sake I have lost all things. I consider them garbage, that I may gain Christ and be found in him, not having a righteousness of my own that comes from the law, but that which is through faith in Christ—the righteousness that comes from God on the basis of faith." (Philippians 3:8-9 NIV)

Jeremiah Small, born to Alaskan missionaries, Dan and Rebecca Small, who moved to southwest Washington to run a Bible Camp, was the oldest of seven children. He was a committed Christian, who graduated from Central Washington University. He learned about the "Classical School of the Medes" in the city of Sulaymaniyah, a city of one million people in northern Iraq.

There he taught for six years. As Paul gave up all to follow Christ, so did Small. He had an ideal mission-trait, **identifying with his people!** One student wrote: "He was very Kurdish, very hospitable, very connected to all of our lives." Another student said, "He became the ablest and favorite teacher of the school, and had the friendliest face."

The magazine, *World* (Mar.24, 2012) where this story is featured, told of his open love for Jesus, frequently mentioned in his classes. His lessons were steeped in Shakespeare, John Bunyan, C.S. Lewis and American-made movies. In class he taught History and English; out of class, he taught students rock-climbing, and organized trips to Europe over summer break. He helped launch a student-run newspaper called "Median Ink." He taught classes how to compare the Quran with Bible texts, including the book of Romans. It was said that Jesus was always ubiquitous everywhere in his life. He was truly a remarkable witness for Jesus!

MARTYR FOR JESUS CHRIST   September 26

"Blessed are you when people insult you, persecute you and falsely say all kinds of evil against you because of me. Rejoice and be glad, because great is your reward in heaven, for in the same way they persecuted the prophets who were before you." (Matthew 5:11-12 NIV)

Jeremiah Small was a superb teacher in The Classical School of the Medes in Iraq. He was a radiant Christian, the favorite teacher of many. But there was one eighteen year old Muslim student, a professed atheist, who liked to argue with his professor. The 11th grade student, Bayar Sarwar, even threatened to kill teacher Small. Jeremiah was asked about this danger and assured friends that he thought the issue was resolved. Then to everyone's dismay, and utter shock, on March 1, 2012, as Jeremiah Small bowed his head to open his class with prayer, Bayar shot and killed his teacher with bullets to the head and chest. Then he turned the gun on himself.

According to the article by Mindy Belz, in the *World* (March 24, 2012), at the Muslim funeral the next day at a downtown mosque, Bayar was remembered. Even Jeremiah Small, the 33 year old Christian teacher from the state of Washington, was honored. The Small family chose to bury their son in Iraq, where he had taught for six years. That funeral was held at the Art Hall in Sulaymaniyah on March 6. Attenders included students and faculty from various schools, the Kurdish regional minister of education, as well as members of both the Sarwar family and the Small family. The scene was one of remarkable reconciliation. The murderer's father Rashid Sarwar openly apologized for the murder event. The teacher's father, Dan Small assured everyone that they held no hatred in their hearts for the Sarwar family. Both men embraced!

STARS, MOON & UNIVERSE   September 27

"When I consider Your heavens, the works of Your fingers, The moon and the stars, which You have ordained, What is man that You are mindful of him, and the son of man that You visit him? For You have made him a little lower than the angels, and You have crowned him with glory and honor." (Psalm 8:3-5 NKJV)

This is called a Messianic Psalm. Here Christ is referred to as the Son of man, made a little lower than the angels, while in Psalm 2 He is called God's son and king. In the New Testament Ps.2 and Ps.8 are tied together, showing that Christ would "taste death for every man," thus "bringing many sons into glory" and as a result He would be crowned with glory and honor (Hebrews 2:5-11)! The Psalmist was overwhelmed by the massive universe which God had created. How could this majestic Creator have a loving compassion for sinful humanity?

We have a grandson, Adrian, who has an intense interest in astronomy. When he was about seven years old, he requested a telescope for Christmas from his grandparents. This didn't surprise us, since he often chose to differ with his siblings. They each took piano lessons and violin lessons; but Adrian chose to play a saxophone. After Christmas, he enjoyed scanning the skies, trying to identify certain stars and galaxies. Of course, he didn't resist the temptation of using his telescope to watch cars a mile away on Interstate-80.

When Adrian was about ten, his family visited California. We toured the Griffith Park Observatory in Los Angeles. The impressive auditorium presentation showed a ceiling-replica of the vast starry sky. Finally, one by one, we viewed the heavens through the huge telescope. Adrian was first! God's creation is truly marvelous.

GOD'S MIGHTY ACTS   September 28

"Praise the Lord. Give thanks to the Lord, for he is good; his love endures forever. Who can proclaim the mighty acts of the Lord or fully declare his praise? Blessed are they who act justly, who always do what is right." (Psalm 106:1-3 NIV)

This psalm commands us to praise God, to thank God, and the reason is—because God is good and God is everlastingly loving. The only logical attitude for any of us is to be abundantly thankful, and constantly live with a heart full of praise. Being grateful, any therapist will tell you, is far more healthy and wholesome, than being grumpy!

The Psalmist asks a pertinent question: "Who can proclaim the mighty acts of the Lord, or fully declare his praise?" We can't even comprehend the extent of God's protection, provision and overall providence in the affairs of our daily lives. And if we could, our praise would still fall short.

If my wife and I would start naming "God's Mighty Acts" we would start with God's redemptive works in our immediate family. We both were raised in Christian homes, I in Kansas, and she in South Dakota. Parental influence was powerful. We each accepted Jesus Christ as Lord and Savior, due to the enthusiastic example of our parents and eagerly joined the church. Each of our three sons are also raising their families in the church. God's provision of salvation stands at the top of our "PRAISE LIST!" In addition, we praise God for his provision of health, and breathe. We praise God for his provision of food, work and income. We praise God for his protection on busy highways, on icy roads and hazardous streets. Yes, we owe God our praise; we are still alive due to God's marvelous care!

FOOTPRINTS TO FOLLOW   September 29

"By faith Abraham obeyed when he was called to go out to the place which he would afterward receive as an inheritance. And he went out, not knowing where he was going. By faith he sojourned in the land of promise as in a foreign country, dwelling in tents with Isaac and Jacob, the heirs with him of the same promise; for he waited for the city which has foundations, whose builder and maker is God." *(Hebrews 11:8-10 NKJV)*

In the Bible's famous "FAITH" chapter, Abraham is featured as the notable patriarch who followed God's instructions to leave his home, not knowing where he was going, totally relying on God to show him where to settle. He left his relatives behind at Paddan Aram, leaving Haran and settling in Canaan as a tent dweller, herding vast flocks, in the very land where Joshua would one day lead Israel into the promised land. Abraham lived to be 175, yet in his lifetime he never owned one acre in Canaan, except for the plot he bought to bury Sarah.

My third pastorate was Bethesda Mennonite at Henderson, Nebraska. The church was founded by 35 families who migrated from Molotschna, South Russia in 1874. Mrs. Peter Friesen loaned me the diary written by her grandfather, Gerhard Dyck, who came in 1877 from Russia. He was baptized on Pentecost Sunday in 1872, at age 20. In 1877, Dyck came on the ship, Faterland, with 1,000 passengers. The trip from Ukraine to Sutton, NE cost $64.00 per person when a day's wage was $1.00. In reflecting later, Dyck remembers friends in Russia ridiculing him for going to "Crazy America." (But the wealthy Johann Abrams, who bought the Dyck farm, later died of starvation)! Dyck felt his coming to America was providential, in obedience to God.

RETIRED & SERVING GOD   September 30

"...The harvest is plentiful but workers are few. Ask the Lord of the harvest, therefore, to send out workers into his harvest field." *(Matthew 9:37-38 NIV)*

Our church in Bakersfield has a healthy view toward world missions. The annual programs, the short term service trips and the "Market of Hope" project that recently raised $52,000 for overseas mission needs, all stoked mission interest. My wife and I supported two projects in Kenya, providing a milk cow for a pastor, and providing a sheep for a widow.

We were recently delighted when Doug and Myra Gentry reported to our Prime-Timers Sunday School Class regarding their two-year stint of mission service in Lisbon, Portugal. They had assisted Otto and Marjie Ekk, Mennonite Brethren church planters who supervised several Portuguese churches and two Russian churches. Doug and Myra came along side the Ekks and relieved them of many mundane jobs, so these veteran missionaries could devote more time to the major concerns.

Here are tasks they assumed: When important people flew in, the Gentrys picked them up at the airport. When Bible classes ended with a meal, or when the worship group ended with a meal, the Gentrys cooked the meal, fed the group and cleaned the kitchen. They hosted Bible Studies at their apartment, and so encouraged local believers in spiritual growth. They were always available to assist the Ekks in any special needs. The Ekks enjoyed their loving friendship and eager assistance in everything.

Doug and Myra are longtime members of our church. When Doug retired from his career as a Fireman, he and Myra accepted a two year assignment to assist our missionaries in Portugal. What a thrill to see our own members serve the Lord in such a significant way in retirement!

RETIRED AND REASSIGNED   October 1

"Stand up in the presence of the aged, show respect for the elderly and revere your God. I am the Lord. When a foreigner resides among you in your land, do not mistreat them. The foreigners residing among you must be treated as one of your native-born. Love him as yourself, for you were foreigners in Egypt. I am the Lord your God." (Leviticus 19:32-34 NIV)

When Doug and Myra Gentry finished reporting to the Prime-timers about their two years in Portugal, they turned next to their future plans. Their next goal was to assist Tim and Rachel Uthmann, serving refugees in Rome, Italy. This young couple, also from our church in Bakersfield, had served one term in Rome in a very needy ministry. The Gentrys had visited Rome to familiarize themselves with the challenge, and then flew to Chicago to attend orientation sessions sponsored by "International Teams." Doug and Myra committed themselves to two years of service in Rome.

The refugee problem is enormous worldwide. They number about 44 million and are people who are forcefully displaced due to war, famine or persecution. Rome, Italy has some 8,000,000 refugees. Some have traveled on foot a thousand miles to reach Rome! Fortunately, there are churches in Rome who have periodic feeding days where refugees can come for a free meal. Tim and Rachel Uthmann have opened a Reading Room where refugees can enter to read, to rest and find fellowship in a warm room—escaping inclement weather. It becomes an ideal setting for listening to people's story, for winning friendships, and for sharing the hope found in the Christian Gospel. Caring in Christ's name is so meaningful when working with people who have nearly lost hope in humanity. Sharing God's love and salvation with these refugees is a rare privilege.

HAVING SUITCASE PACKED   October 2

"Let not your heart be troubled; you believe in God, believe also in Me. In My Father's house are many mansions; if it were not so, I would have told you. I go to prepare a place for you." (John 14:1-2 NKJV)

It has often been said that none are prepared to live, if they have not made preparations to die. Since life is uncertain, and precarious at best, we need to have our suitcases packed and ready to go any moment. No matter whether we are thinking of the Lord's return or our personal death, we must be ready!

This was abruptly brought to our attention last week. My wife's brother, Johnnie, age 88, living in Roseburg, Oregon, died suddenly. He had enjoyed a men's meeting in the morning. His son later took him to a chiropractor. After the treatment, Johnnie got off the table and immediately collapsed. All resuscitation attempts failed. Since Johnnie's wife had died 15 months earlier, we knew the trip to his funeral was a 705-mile-run up Interstate I-5.

When a person dies, a lot dies with him. This was true of Johnnie. His siblings relied on him to accurately recall details of family history. He was a retired pastor, having served smaller churches in the Dakotas and Nebraska. His hobby was restoring Model-T Fords. He had an amazing ability at this craft. Each child was offered a fully operational Model-T. In his retirement, he set tombstones in many rural cemeteries, while living in Nebraska.

John 14 is one of the most comforting funeral texts. Jesus is preparing a place in heaven for every Christian. My friend, do you have the assurance of salvation? If not, please seek counsel! Prepare your heart and Jesus will prepare a place for you.

GOD'S BEAUTIFUL WORKMANSHIP   October 3

"For we are God's handiwork, created in Christ Jesus to do good works, which God prepared in advance for us to do." (Ephesians 2:10 NIV)

In this text the Apostle Paul portrays the transformed life—the honorable Christian life—as God initiated. It is not man-made nor self-induced. We dare not brag because it is not earned, it is received by faith as God's undeserved gift! It is God's design of taking sinful humanity and creating a transformed life!

I grew up on a farm in Kansas. When I was a teenager, my father bought a 1947 Fleetline Chevrolet for $1,700. He drove it 162,000 miles and sold it to me. I kept it operational for decades. In 1996 when we moved from Nebraska to Bakersfield, I drove the car into the moving van. Ten years later (2006) I took the car to the Farrar Rod shop, Lancaster, CA for a three year restoration job. What a radical transformation! I picked it up in September of 2009. With a new 350 Chevy engine, Ford Mustang suspension, and Camaro rear end, the car was roadworthy. The glass, upholstery, and paint (Indigo blue) were all new—with CD radio, seat belts, air-conditioner, Centerline Rims and Cooper Tires .

My wife and I, attended the annual National Street Rod event in Bakersfield. There were 1,896 cars registered (04-28-12) and ours was one of them. It was fun seeing all those cars on display, and interacting with folks displaying their cars!

As Christians we are God's workmanship. Is God really pleased with the good works we are displaying in our daily lives? God has planned our lives in advance. And we need to fit into that plan. Through Bible reading, daily prayer, and church fellowship we can discern God's will. We need to shine for Jesus!

MOTHER GREATLY HONORED   October 4

"A wife of noble character who can find? She is worth far more than rubies. Her husband has full confidence in her....She watches over the affairs of her household and does not eat the bread of idleness. Her children arise and call her blessed; her husband also, and he praises her." (Proverbs 31:10-11, 27-28 NIV)

My wife loves work and busyness. She is my partner of 59 years, and I have jokingly said that I would imprint on her tombstone, "Not a lazy bone in her!" From house-keeping, to meal-preparation, to record-keeping, to yard-work, she excels. She is a rare woman indeed!

Some months ago my sons began making secret phone calls to me, their dad, regarding plans to surprise Mother on her 80th birthday. I kept this super idea under wraps for weeks. On second thought, it occurred to me that I needed to divulge the good news. Certainly, mom would feel better if the yard was trimmed, and the house was immaculately clean, and the boy's favorite pastries were all baked, soups all cooked and salads all prepared! Yes—we got ready indeed.

Friday was BIRTHDAY. On Thursday two sons flew into LAX. Greg, a CPA , Division Manager for an oil company, flew in from Nebraska, and Nathan, a Hospital Surgeon, flew in from Indiana. Our son Steven, a Computer Programmer from San Jose, CA drove in by car, with wife and son. What a weekend! We visited, played games, saw slides from early days, prayed together, and did extensive reminiscing. Of course, we all went to church together on Sunday.

Mother was "tickled-pink." She felt highly honored. All three sons love their mother, and hold her Christian character in high esteem. The sons truly fulfilled the scripture, they "rose up and called her blessed!"

SERVING JESUS CHRIST   October 5

"Whoever is kind to the poor, lends to the Lord, and he will reward them for what they have done." (Proverbs 19:17 NIV)

The Bible lays a strong emphasis on helping poor and needy people. Each day we see someone with a sign, "Help, I'm homeless. I am hungry—can you help?" Today I met with a friend who had made a public profession of faith in Christ, a few months ago as he visited a church in Camarillo. I meet with him for mutual encouragement—to pray, to discuss events, to explain the Bible, and to foster spiritual growth. On Mother's Day his family had revisited that church and the pastor had challenged the congregation to help people in need. He invited 25 persons to come and accept a $100 check each—with the understanding that they would report back to the church on how they had used the money—to buy food for someone, to buy glasses, to pay for a doctor's visit, to buy shoes or clothes, or to pay for some other needed item. My friend did not respond, but the concept was vividly impressed on his memory.

A few days later, while on his evening job, working for a utility company, he saw a homeless fellow begging for food. He offered to buy him some, but the nearby fast-food places were already closed. So he took him to a service station that sold food. The man quickly grabbed potato chips and a can of pop. "No," responded my friend, "I will buy you food." So he settled on some sandwiches and a banana. The African-American clerk asked, "Are you paying for him?" "Yes." Her response was, "Then you must be a Christian!" What a thrilling affirmation to this new believer!

CHRIST'S DELIVERANCE METHOD   October 6

[Christ said] This, then, is how you should pray: "Our Father in heaven, hallowed be your name, your kingdom come, your will be done on earth as it is in heaven. Give us today our daily bread. Forgive us our debts, as we also have forgiven our debtors. And lead us not into temptation, but deliver us from the evil one." (Matthew 6:9-13 NIV)

Here is the prayer commonly called The Lord's Prayer. It is a sketch of a model prayer Christ gave to his disciples. It begins with giving honor to God's name and acknowledging his sovereign control over both heaven and earth. In the center are several requests: one for daily food and the other for forgiveness, providing we have a forgiving heart ourselves. The prayer ends with a plea for deliverance from evil. While the Greek language may be somewhat ambiguous here, numerous translations and commentaries prefer—-"deliver us from the evil one." (That's how it's rendered in Phillips, RSV, NEB, NIV, NKJV and The Living Bible).

Since every human is confronted by evil, and specifically by Satan, the evil one, it is only natural that Jesus would include this request in the Lord's Prayer. We trust God for deliverance. We need not fear. In Christ's name we can overcome. The scriptures urge us to resist evil: "Submit yourselves, then, to God. Resist the devil, and he will flee from you. Come near to God and he will come near to you. Wash your hands, you sinners, and purify your hearts, you double-minded" (James 4:7-8). We as Christians need to live close to the Lord, and in that way we will be assured of an overcoming victorious life. My friend, have you humbled yourself before God? Have you relied on God for his deliverance power?

SHOUTING FOR JOY   October 7

"With praise and thanksgiving they sang to the Lord: 'He is good; His love toward Israel endures forever.' And all the people gave a great shout of praise to the Lord, because the foundation of the house of the Lord was laid." (Ezra 3:11 NIV)

In the days of Ezra, the Persian king, Cyrus was led by God to encourage the Israel people to return to Jerusalem to build the temple. In the first year, those returning from captivity, built the altar and began offering sacrifices to God. In the second year they laid the foundation for the temple. When this was finished, the priests and Levites, with trumpets and symbals made great noise in celebration. And all the people gave a great shout of joy. The newcomers all joined in with shouts of praise, while the old-timers, remembering the former temple, wept for joy—but both groups made so much noise, you could not tell which group was the loudest! This was a great day!

In the decade of the 70's, I was pastoring a church in Kansas. One weekend, my home church, Emmaus of Whitewater, celebrated their 125th anniversary, and I was invited to be the guest speaker. What an honor! I used a text from Deuteronomy that said—when you come to a new land, and enjoy prosperity, by all means, don't forget your God!

Some years later the church building burned down. The congregation bought 20 acres, two miles south of the old site, at the edge of Brainerd. They built a six million dollar edifice (Sanctuary, Office, Social hall and Classrooms). This rural 400-member church is vigorous! They are big Mission-givers. Last year I saw the beautiful new church and my heart sang praises to our God!

SHOWERS OF BLESSING October 8

"Do any of the worthless idols of the nations bring rain? Do the skies themselves send down showers? No, it is you, O Lord our God. Therefore our hope is in you, for you are the one who does all this." (Jeremiah 14:22 NIV)

The Old Testament affirms that showers of rain are clearly blessings from God, especially when people honor God. Rain made crops grow; this fed people. But adversely, disobedience to God often brought drought. In this way, God caught their attention—it drove them to prayer.

In recent centuries the Christian communities in various countries, have experienced great revival movements. The Holy Spirit moved so mightily upon people that their behavior was radically altered. These waves of renewal were often called "showers of blessing." We used to sing words written by Major D. W. Whittle: "There shall be showers of blessing. This is the promise of love. There shall be seasons refreshing, sent from the Savior above."

In the 1800's, revival meetings made a profound impact in America in the spread of Christianity. First of all, Christians were revived, and secondly, unbelievers were brought to salvation. Some of the revival movements brought over a million converts into the churches! On the western frontier, some of the methods of winning converts seemed a little crass and manipulating. However, one scholar of American religion made an astute observation—the voluntary freedom of religion in revivalism was far superior to the method used in some other countries, where converts were forced to adopt religion by the threat of a sword!

America today needs revival in the churches. I have prayed for this for years. The book of Acts tells of the Holy Spirit falling on the Early Church in mighty power, and such an outpouring is needed today.

GLORY BE TO GOD   October 9

"Not to us, O Lord, not to us but to your name be the glory, because of your love and faithfulness." (Psalm 115:1 NIV)

This verse is straight forward; we need to raise high the name of God. Jesus reinforced the idea in the Lord's prayer: "Our Heavenly Father, may your name be honored" (Matthew 6:9 Phillips). In my own experience, when I was an 8th grader, we boys walking home from school, down the Missouri-Pacific railroad track, would use filthy language. We swore a blue-streak. Each tried to outdo the other. In the middle of high school, when I surrendered my life to Jesus Christ, it dawned on me, it makes no logical sense to profane God's name—if I expect God to save me for all eternity. Praise God, I have not sworn for years, God is my best friend!

This verse urges us to glorify God, because of his love. Already in the Old Testament, saints were commanded to love God with their whole heart. And God showed us how: *"For God so loved the world that he gave his one and only son, that whoever believes in him shall not perish, but have eternal life" (John 3:16).*

The second reason we give God glory is due to his faithfulness. My wife and I are alive because he has granted us health. God has also provided food for our table. We have assurance of salvation because God's promises are true. Our daily prayer for God's protection has been answered—our grandson rolled his car—he was hanging upside down in his seatbelt, but was unharmed! Our church group has provided wonderful prayer and fellowship. Because of our attempt to honor God with our finances, God has "opened the windows of heaven and poured out a blessing." God is faithful.

CALEB'S WHOLEHEARTED ATTITUDE   October 10

"So on that day Moses swore to me, 'The land on which your feet have walked will be your inheritance and that of your children forever, because you have followed the Lord my God wholeheartedly.'" (*Joshua 14:9 NIV*)

Joshua and Caleb were the two spies who urged the people to wholeheartedly obey God and take Canaan, while the other ten discouraged Israel from trying. As a result, Moses sadly told them they were destined for forty years in the wilderness, as punishment. After Moses died, Caleb, now 85, still strong and vigorous, agreed to go possess Hebron, the city and area promised him by Moses. Caleb acknowledged that his health was a gift from God, since he had followed his God—wholeheartedly! What an inspirational picture.

Each of us, as we transition through life, need to work wholehearted while God gives breath. My parents each reached 94, but that does not guarantee that each of their eight children will reach 94. Already two of my sisters have passed on. Frieda, a retired school teacher, died at age 70 of acute leukemia. She had a mere 60 days to make arrangements. Martha at age 81 was sent to the KU Medical Center to replace two heart valves. Following surgery she died of a massive stroke. So life is very fragile.

My wife, Susan Joann, and I are both 80. We are in fair health, and are currently grabbling with plans—plans on what we can do for God in the years ahead. We take courage from Bible heroes like Caleb. As long as God affords us breath we want to live wholeheartedly for God. People who advice others on how to prepare for passing on into eternity, suggest we should be so busy, that when God calls, we still have some things unfinished!

REDEEMED AND OWNED   October 11

"But now, thus says the Lord, who created you, O Jacob, and He who formed you, O Israel: 'Fear not, for I have redeemed you; I have called you by your name; You are Mine.'" (Isaiah 43:1 NKJV)

Through the prophet Isaiah, God gives to His special people a very intimate and personal word. God claims ownership to them because He (1) created them, (2) redeemed them, and (3) called them by name. God says, "You are Mine."

The historical origin of Israel stemmed from the miraculous birth of Isaac, when Abraham was 100 and Sarah 90. All Israel descended from Isaac. The redemption statement may refer to the miraculous rescue of the Israelites from Egypt, when the Sea parted and they crossed on dry land. And God sustained them for 40 years in the wilderness, before they entered the Promised Land.

The phrase, "Fear not, for I have redeemed you," also applies to Christians today. We are saved through the death and resurrection of Christ Jesus! Paul wrote, "In Him we have redemption through His blood, the forgiveness of sins, in accordance with the riches of God's grace" (Eph. 1:7). This salvation is undeserved, but given freely as a gift, through the mercy of God!

The idea of God calling us by name and claiming us as His own possession, is also appropriate. The Gospel of John has a beautiful statement spoken by our Lord Jesus, "My sheep listen to My voice; I know them, and they follow Me. I give to them eternal life, and they shall never perish; no one can snatch them out of My hand" (John 10:27-28). The saving and keeping power of God gives us great assurance, providing we are obeying Christ and following Him in complete surrender.

FUTURE IN YOUR HANDS   October 12

"On that night God appeared to Solomon, and said to him, 'Ask! What shall I give you.' And Solomon said to God: 'You have shown great mercy to David my father, and have made me king in his place....Now give me wisdom and knowledge, that I may go out and come in before this people; for who can judge this great people of Yours?'" (2 Chronicles 1:7-8, 10 NKJV)

As a Kansas teenager, I remember Dwight Wiebe, a Tabor College student coming to our church and giving his National Peace Oration—which won him 1st place. He told a story from ancient Greece. A man had a bird in his hand and asked "dead or alive?" If the listener guessed dead, he opened his hand and let it fly. If he said "alive," he squeezed the bird and showed it dead. The fate of the bird was in his hand. Then Dwight said, "The future of planet-earth is in our hands, we can preserve a clean earth, or destroy it with our armaments and the pollution of our inventions."

Our generation is obsessed with self-gratification. I read of a girl who went to a psychiatrist. Her lifestyle was an endless round of pot, booze and sex. "Have you ever thought of dropping these activities?" he asked. Her reply, "You mean I really don't need to do the things I want to do?"

God asked Solomon what he wanted. In the 1940's three UCLA students met for prayer. They prayed for extraordinary accomplishments in their future lives. One was Bill Bright, founder of Campus Crusade, hoping to train 10,000 university leaders. One was Dawson Troutman, founder of Navigator Discipleship work. One was Dan Fuller, professor at Fuller Seminary, where 1,000 students train annually. Friends, your future is in your hands.

AGING IN GOD'S WAY   October 13

"Satisfy us in the morning with your unfailing love, that we may sing for joy and be glad all our days." (Psalm 90:14 NIV)

In recent generations, according to our US Bureau of Census, the population of persons over 65 has doubled. Retired folks are a tremendous reservoir of wisdom and experience and knowledge. The church needs the seniors, and the seniors need the church. Dr Paul Johnson, a Professor of Psychology of Religion, has shown the importance of the church in the lives of the elderly. When the morale of a person weakens, then health, happiness and social usefulness decline in rapid succession. The church is in a position to retrieve them from isolated senility, and draw them into a dynamic church fellowship!

First of all, the Elderly need Belongingness and Acceptance. The Psalmist prayed, "Do not cast me away when I am old; do not forsake me when my strength is gone" (71:9). I recall visiting a hospital patient. He said, "I was laying in my bed and I heard a voice 'you're not a Christian.' I had not had doubts for years. I got out of my bed, got on my knees and prayed to make sure Christ was in my life!" I reassured him with scripture: "This is the record that God has given to us eternal life and this life is in his Son. He who has the Son of God has life" (1 John 5:11).

Secondly, the Elderly need Self-Esteem and Self-Worth. We naturally dread growing old. Often retirement parties accent our successes. But it is an empty honor to be placed on the shelf with the inactive list! Marks of aging can shake self-esteem. But it is imperative to remain active in the church "all our days!" Instead of dwelling on our sins and failures, we need to rejoice in God's mercy!

AGING IN GOD'S PLAN   October 14

"The righteous will flourish like a palm tree....They will still bear fruit in old age." (Psalm 92:12a and 14a NIV)

The elderly need (1) Belongingness and (2) Self-Esteem.
Thirdly, The Elderly need Purpose and Direction. Dr. Seward Hiltner of the University of Chicago once lectured at the School of Psychiatry at Topeka, KS. He asserted that he and his colleagues came finally to the same conclusion: **Older people are today what they were before and only more so.** Being resourceful or being despondent is not caused by aging, it reflects their earlier traits. A woman, who in the middle years took care of six children, various dogs and cats, and a lazy husband and always looked busy, now in later years shows a great capacity for human relatedness and sensitivity for appreciation of aesthetic realities. While another woman, busy with her family for years, but never taking initiatives, never learning new activities, now sits despondent blaming old age. Both women are what they always were, but only more so.

Fourthly, The Elderly need Companionship and Love. Dr. Paul Johnson insists that it's not wholesome for older people to live with "older people." They miss the exuberance of youth. My wife and I agree. We visited retirement centers in Phoenix, San Diego and Los Angeles. We bought a house in Bakersfield in a community of all ages. We chose a church of all ages, and enjoy it greatly!

Recently our church had their annual Picnic. We invited David and Beth Ann to eat with us. We provided the food. They had moved in from North Dakota 14 years ago. Beth Ann graduated from NDU and Bakersfield educators recruited her to teach. Her husband David works for a rental store. Their children, Ben, six, and Sarah, three, ate with us. What a joyful encounter.

SAM'S UNIQUE WITNESS   October 15

"Those who sow in tears shall reap in joy. He who continually goes forth weeping, bearing seed for sowing, shall doubtless come again with rejoicing, bringing his sheaves with him." (Psalm 126:5-6 NKJV)

It is interesting to ask people how they came to Christ. Who sowed the seed and reaped the harvest? So often when a person responds to a church altar call, the convert will feel that altar calls are the key method in evangelism. When a person is won to Christ by a friend in one-to-one evangelism, he might see that as the preferred witnessing technique. When, on the other hand, a person is converted reading a Gospel Tract, he will feel that that is the most effective outreach—and that was the case of my parishioner named Sam.

After seminary, my first pastoral charge was in Southern California. Sam was an enthusiastic member living in the suburb of South Gate. One day he told me his story. He had been a custodian and while emptying wasted paper baskets, his eye caught sight of a leaflet, a Gospel Tract. He read it repeatedly, and there at age 50, he accepted Christ. Next he affiliated with our church. To be a witness, to reach others, he started a tract ministry. He rolled several tracts in cellophane and with a kind of paper-gun, shot the tracts 30-40 feet onto people's lawns and porches. He rode a little red electric car, down the sidewalk, dispensing the Gospel throughout his neighborhood! One day he had another novel idea. He bought a tape-recorder and asked me, as pastor, to read a tract onto his tape, so he could play the gospel message to neighbors!

My friend, what evangelistic method are you using? Bringing others to heaven will give you joy, greatly pleasing Christ.

GIVING WITH WILLLINGNESS   October 16

"Remember this: Whoever sows sparingly will also reap sparingly, and whoever sows generously will also reap generously. Each of you should give, what you have decided in your heart to give, not reluctantly or under compulsion, for God loves a cheerful giver. And God is able to bless you abundantly, so that in all things at all times, having all that you need, you will abound in every good work."
(2 Corinthians 9:6-8 NIV)

This is one of the key biblical passages that encourages financial giving with a wholesome, grateful and generous attitude. This passage is so motivating since it promises abundant blessing for bountiful giving. It uses agriculture for its vivid illustration. Abundant harvests require abundant seeding.

My grandson, Jordan, at age 21, is finishing his second year at a local Junior College. At church he heard lectures from Dave Ramsey, a financial counselor, on how to adopt sound money patterns. So, he gives God his first tithe and sets aside a second tithe as an emergency fund. He earns his money as a security guard—he has a good job. This month he was tempted to omit his tithe. He is applying to a Christian University in the Chicago area, where the cost nears $35,000.

He phones us several times every week. Last week an academic scholarship of $7,000 was offered him, plus a $2,000 football scholarship. And he can apply for a Christian Service Merit Scholarship—for his South American Mission trip, for leading a weekly Bible Study, and for helping coach a freshman football team. Last week a man came 400 miles to buy his motorcycle for $1,400. Recently his landlord lowered his rent to $200, to help him. He said, "I felt guilty, I saw God's blessings, and cheerfully gave my tithe!" Our Grandson makes us proud.

THE SOLID TRUTH   October 17

"The Lord executes righteousness and justice for all who are oppressed. He made known His ways to Moses, His acts to the children of Israel." (Psalm 103:6-7 NKJV) "Jesus said to him, 'I am the way, the truth, and the life. No one comes to the Father except through Me.'" (John 14:6 NKJV)

The Bible is God's self-revelation. Starting with the first five books of the Old Testament—often known as the Books of Moses. The psalmist affirms that God made his ways known to Moses. God's fullest revelation came in the person of Jesus Christ. Jesus is the only way, "No one comes to the Father except through Me." This rules out the popular concept that any belief is valid, as long as people are sincere. There are not many ways to heaven!

At church our Youth Pastor related an experience with an eleven year old boy. "Would you like to accept Jesus as your Savior?" He answered, "Why should I, there are many religions, and all are good." The pastor insisted, "The Bible teaches there is one way, that is absolute truth." The boy retorted, "No, there are many ways, I don't believe in absolutes!" "Okay, then," the pastor continued, "From now on, I will call you a girl." "No, No I'm a boy," he shouted. The pastor replied, "If opposites can be true, then you are a girl!"

The Early Church taught that Christ is the key: "there is no other name under heaven given among men whereby we must be saved" (Acts 4:12). The Apostle John wrote: "These things I have written to you who believe in the name of the Son of God, that you may know that you have eternal life" (1 John 5:13). What wonderful words of assurance! Praise God.

AVOIDING PRESUMPTUOUS SINS   October 18

"Keep back Your servant also from presumptuous sins; Let them not have dominion over me. Then I shall be blameless, and I shall be innocent of great transgression." (Psalm 19:13 NKJV)

In Psalm 19 King David speaks of the value of God's law, statutes, and judgments which are more valuable then gold. They serve as a warning, and our obedience to them holds great reward (19:7-11). David's prayer is that God would deliver him from presumptuous sins (or willful sins NIV, or deliberate wrongs LB). This refers to "an overstepping of proper boundaries" (Webster).

David had a good upbringing. He learned the regulations, including the fabulous Ten Commandments. These rules are excellent for any age. So he clearly knew that adultery was forbidden, yet in the hour of temptation he saw a beautiful woman bathing, and ignoring his brilliant prayer, he invited her for a sexual encounter. How tragic! He hid this for a whole year—until God sent Nathan the prophet to confront King David. Nathan told David of a rich man who had robbed from a poor man. David became angry, but Nathan pointed his finger, "You are the man" (2 Samuel 12:1-14)!

David's prayer request for deliverance from deliberate wrongs is so apropos for our era as well. Every person who counsels others, whether a teacher, policeman, lawyer, pastor, or professional counselor, knows certain confidential details about the people they serve. This is a sacred trust that dare not be violated. It becomes a huge temptation, but with God's help victory is ours!

Our day needs men and women who keep themselves morally pure. This requires dedication to principle, determination of the will and an utter dependence on God. Such exemplary living inspires others, and will be richly rewarded in time and eternity.

PRAYER REQUIRES PATIENCE   October 19

"In a certain town there was a judge who neither feared God nor cared what people thought. And there was a widow in that town who kept coming to him with the plea, 'Grant me justice against my adversary.' For some time he refused. But finally, he said to himself, 'even though I don't fear God...yet because this widow keeps bothering me, I will see that she gets justice, so that she won't eventually come and attack me!'" (Luke 18:2-5 NIV)

Jesus told his disciples this parable to show them that they should continually pray and not get discouraged. You and I wonder why we pray for the salvation of persons and see no answer, or pray for healing and see no change, or pray for reconciliation between two parties and see no miracle. Jesus' lesson is "DON'T GIVE UP!" Yes, my friend, don't give up.

Let me share our experience. We retired to Bakersfield 16 years ago. For most of these years we had a concern for the spiritual welfare of one of our neighbor families. We prayed for them and maintained a friendly relationship. One day they attended a baby christening at their church. Later at the home-celebration, after some drinking, a fight developed over the use of chairs, and my neighbor was stabbed, twice, and the knife narrowly missed crucial organs! I went to his house and prayed for his healing. God answered. Over the years they often invited us to their family gatherings and I often invited the husband to come to my house for some Bible study. Nothing developed. But now, some weeks ago the neighbor came to my house, "I have wonderful news. Sunday, we attended my sister's church, Calvary Chapel in Camarillo and I went forward to accept Christ!" Yes, Jesus urged us not to give up.

GROWTH REQUIRES ENCOURAGEMENT   October 20

"Paul, an apostle of Christ Jesus by the will of God, and Timothy our brother, to the Church of God in Corinth, together with all his holy people throughout Achaia....For the Son of God, Jesus Christ, who was preached among you by us—by me and Silas and Timothy, was not 'Yes' and 'No,' but in him it has always been 'Yes.'" (2 Corinthians 1:1, 19 NIV)

Paul had changed his travel plans, from that promised in his earlier epistle and some critics accused him of being fickle and insincere. But honestly, he was very eager to help them and literally sent 13 associates to Corinth to assist them. This was a beautiful case of convert-care!

When our neighbor, a man in his 40's , told me of his conversion, I offered to meet with him weekly, for one hour, for Bible study and prayer. He eagerly accepted! We have met 32 times. He is determined to live wholeheartedly for Jesus, his Lord. We are learning how to pray, and learning key scripture passages. The 66 books of the Bible are all new to him. On a recent Saturday he came with me to our church's MAN-UP breakfast. Our speaker was the leader of our addiction groups, who testified to his deliverance from drugs and alcohol—the precise help our neighbor appreciated! Each Sunday, since his conversion, our neighbor has taken his family to the local Calvary Chapel for worship. One night was special! Their church had a 5:00 p.m. picnic in the park, and a baptismal service at the community swimming pool. My wife and I attended for support! What a blessed sight. The senior pastor baptized our neighbor couple—jointly—in the presence of the congregation. After the audience clapped, wife and I embraced the dripping-wet couple with joy and affirmation!

PROOF IS SOON NOTICEABLE   October 21

"They had Peter and John brought before them and began to question them: 'By what power or what name did you do this?'....When they saw the courage of Peter and John and realized that they were unschooled, ordinary men, they were astonished and they took note that these men had been with Jesus." (Acts 4:7, 13 NIV)

Peter and John had healed a man and the religious leaders questioned them as to the source of their power. They answered boldly: "In the name of Jesus Christ whom you crucified but whom God raised from the dead..." The miracle could not be denied, as the man was 40 years old. So they threatened them and released them.

As our newly converted neighbor began meeting with me weekly, he reported that at least five persons at his place of employment had asked the supervisors, "What has happened to this man, he is so different—so cheerful!" His answer: "I have Jesus in my life." He is thrilled by this phenomenon. At a recent family-wide birthday party in his backyard, I saw a man, an old-time friend, bring a case of liquor. My neighbor kindly set it on the back patio. He later told me that when that friend left, he attempted to hand the liquor back to him: "I'm a Christian now and don't need this anymore." Why is that so thrilling? Because the neighbor once told me that on his wife's recent birthday, he was drunk already in the morning, he was blacked out all day—and never supported his wife on her special day! He felt so ashamed as he thought about it.

Think of the proof of change in this man: (1) Publically accepting Christ, (2) Weekly going to church worship, (3) Requesting baptism, and (4) Meeting weekly with a mentoring disciple.

VACATIONS HAVE VALIDITY   October 22

"...because so many people were coming and going that they did not even have a chance to eat, he said to them, 'Come with me by yourselves to a quiet place and get some rest.' So they went away by themselves in a boat to a solitary place." (Mark 6:31-32 NIV)

Jesus felt it was necessary at times for his disciples to follow him to a secluded place in order to get some rest. How true that is in our day as well. Times of rest and variation are very therapeutic.

In my first pastorate, in Southern California, when our three sons were in elementary school, we enjoyed camping trips to Yosemite. Our parishioner, named Tony frequently loaned us his trailer with a foldout tent. We camped in Yosemite Valley for the first week, and later moved to a higher campground for the second week. We learned how to make our meals over the campfire. We learned how to scare off bears by clanging our frying pans. As a family we hiked miles and miles of mountain trails. Yosemite is a place of beauty with gorgeous scenery and many delightful things to do.

Recently, our three sons flew in, to celebrate their mother's birthday. We pulled out picture albums, and set up the old projector to view several thousand slides. We enjoyed reliving the days of yesterday. We saw trophies they had earned in their sport events. And we discussed a highlight from their college days—when we flew to Hawaii on their Christmas break. Those family-centered holidays were a very significant element in building Christian togetherness.

Dear friends, don't overlook the grand opportunity to build family oneness during those vacation holidays. They can—forever—be memorable. You will forever reap the benefit of these precious times together.

HELP FOR NEW BELIEVERS   October 23

"Blessed is the man who walks not in the counsel of the ungodly, nor stands in the path of sinners, nor sits in the seat of the scornful. But his delight is in the law of the Lord, and in His law he meditates day and night." (Psalm 1:1-2 NKJV)

When serving as a mentor to a new Christian, we sometimes call this—the art of discipling (Matthew 28:19-20). It is so important that we emphasize the role of Bible reading and scripture memorization. Dwight L. Moody once said, "The Bible will keep you from sin, or sin will keep you from the Bible." Good advice, don't you think?

The first verse of the Psalms gives us three suggestions for happy victorious living. First, don't shape your life by the "counsel of the ungodly." You make many decisions, but don't allow the ungodly crowd to influence them. Find new friends with a Christian worldview.

Second, don't stand "in the path of sinners." Avoid sitting with the ungodly, hour by hour, seeking their advice, leaning on their encouragement. Your church attending Christian friends will give you more wholesome support!

Third, avoid the "seat of the scornful." Why associate with those who ridicule your faith, who mock your God, who enjoy profane language? Don't spend your valuable time in their company. You deserve better.

The bottom line is—how should a new Christian relate to old friends? Does not the Bible require "loving people?" Yes, but when you kindly share with them your new outlook on life—your devotion to Jesus Christ, many friends will quickly and spontaneously drop off. It just isn't their style. But your role is to love them, pray for them and help them. However, your key inspiration needs to come from your new-found Christian friends.

LESSONS FROM GOD'S BIRDS   October 24

"Are not five sparrows sold for two pennies? Yet not one of them is forgotten by God. Indeed, the very hairs of your head are all numbered. Don't be afraid; you are worth more than many sparrows." (Luke 12:6-7 NIV)

According to *Youngs Analytical Concordance* there are some seven verses in the Bible that mention sparrows. The cheapest of birds, the sparrow, is noticed by God. Not that God assigns a guardian angel to each bird, but as God notices details of birds, he knows the number of the hairs on our head. Humans are very valuable to God, so we should oust all fear!

The same concordance lists some 15 verses that mention owls. The strict dietary laws of the Israelites forbade eating eagles, ravens, various owls, ospreys and storks (Lev. 11:13-18). But it was permissible to eat locust, katydid, cricket and grasshopper (11:22). Also sheep, pigeon and cattle were good to eat.

The Great Horned Owl, fascinates me—amazing species of God's creation. According to the National Audubon Society, this owl does not migrate and is found throughout North America. It's diet includes ducks, hawks, skunks, opossums and rabbits. It is the largest American "eared" owl, 18-25 inches. The owl has keen night vision. Feathers direct sound to the ears, so they can hear a mouse rustling in a corn field. They fly silently as they swoop down on prey. My grandson, studying to be a forest ranger, says that the owl's yellow eyes do not turn but the owl can turn its head completely in either direction.

The balance of nature is astounding. As humans live on grains, nuts, fruits and vegetables, as well as fish, chicken, pork and beef, many animals live on other animals smaller than themselves. God's creation is marvelous!

LOST COIN PARABLE   October 25

"Or suppose a woman has ten silver coins and loses one. Doesn't she light a lamp, sweep the house and search carefully until she finds it? And when she finds it, she calls her friends and neighbors together and says, 'Rejoice with me; I have found my lost coin.' In the same way, I tell you, there is rejoicing in the presence of the angels of God over one sinner who repents." (Luke 15:8-10 NIV)

In this chapter of Luke, Jesus gave parables on lost items. This is the second of three. A woman lost one of her ten coins. According to Leon Morris, this coin was the equivalent of one day's wage. For a poor woman this was a precious loss! Eastern homes often had no windows, so even in the daytime, a lamp was needed to sweep and search the house. When she found the coin, excitedly, she told her friends and neighbors.

I myself remember a recent loss. One evening I searched high and low for my billfold, with its money and credit cards. It was nowhere to be found. My wife asked, "Where is the last place you used it?" I said, "Wal-Mart." The next morning I anxiously rushed to Wal-Mart. I asked the clerk at the counter, where I had paid yesterday, did you find a billfold? She replied, "Check with Lost and Found." There it was—money, credit cards and driver's license—all there. And did I ever praise God!

The application is made clearly by our Lord and Savior. There is great rejoicing among the angels of heaven over a single human who repents of his sinfulness. That's the value heaven puts on a soul—specifically, on a converted soul who has forsaken his sinful selfishness, and embraced God's kingdom.

ACCEPTING GODLY WISDOM   October 26

"Yes, if you cry out for discernment, and lift up your voice for under-standing, if you seek her as silver, and search for her as for hidden treasures; then you will understand the fear of the Lord, and find the knowledge of God. For the Lord gives wisdom..." (Proverbs 2:3-6 NKJV)

Life is full of choices and God offers the upright, those who seek to live in God's ways, preservation and protection for the future—"He guards the path of justice, and preserves the ways of His saints" (2:7-8). God promises to lead His saints in good and wise paths.

In one of my ten year pastorates I preached one sermon on the subject of "The Dangers of Tobacco." I spoke of the physical harm caused by this habit, and the fact that we are responsible for our body's health. Did I ever stir up a hornet's nest! At the local coffee shop, numerous men ridiculed the pastor for invading their private lives: "What business does he have in preaching on smoking?" About 20 years later, the man most critical of the pastor's sermon, died in his middle 60's. He is known to have said to a friend, "I wish I had never used tobacco."

The Proverbs state that knowledge, wisdom and under-standing are offered by God to all those living righteous lives. That's a marvelous offer. Every choice we make has an ultimate consequence somewhere down the road. God willingly offers us wisdom to walk on every good path (2:9). How important, it is then, that we face every major choice in a prayerful manner. I admit, I myself have made many choices in life, that were based more on my self-serving motives, than based on a Spirit-led, God-driven conviction. Sincere prayer requires a patient waiting on God!

ACTIVITIES PRODUCE CONSEQUENCES October 27

"When wisdom enters your heart, and knowledge is pleasant to your soul, discretion will preserve you; understanding will keep you, to deliver you from the way of evil, from the man who speaks perverse things....To deliver you from the immoral woman, from the seductress who flatters with her words, who forsakes the companion of her youth, and forgets the covenant of her God, for her house leads down to death; and her paths to the dead." (Proverbs 2:10-12, 16-18 NKJV)

The decisions we make are consequential. When we consider the future, we wonder how our current activities will affect it. These proverbs emphasize that our future will be profoundly shaped by the choices we pursue—whether we live uprightly and righteously or whether we live selfishly and wickedly.

Fifty years ago, when we lived in Southern California, I went to see our District Attorney. I wanted his help. One of our new converts at church had come to me confessing that he had forged four checks. He was willing to go with me and apologize to each lumberyard. The Deacon Board allowed me to pay each debt, providing the convert agreed to reimburse the church. Since the convert had made restitution, I hoped the District Attorney would help keep the man out of prison.

One day I opened the newspaper, with a jolting shock. Our District Attorney was arrested and accused of murder. He had suspected unfaithfulness from his wife; so he hid in his closet, and as his wife and her new lover entered bed together, he stepped out and shot them both! Our proverb above clearly states that adultery can lead to death.

The chapter ends with an admonition: *"So you may walk in the way of goodness, and keep in the paths of righteousness" (2:20).* Deeds have consequences.

THE UNPARDONABLE SIN   October 28

"Therefore I say to you, every sin and blasphemy will be forgiven men, but the blasphemy against the Spirit will not be forgiven men. Anyone who speaks a word against the Son of Man, it will be forgiven him; but whoever speaks against the Holy Spirit, it will not be forgiven him, either in this age or in the age to come." (Matthew 12:31-32 NKJV)

Many people have feared that they may have committed this bad sin which is beyond forgiveness. A young man once came to me for counsel—"Did I commit the unpardonable sin?" He had spoken of the Holy Spirit in a profane way and wondered if there was any hope for him. The truth of the matter is that anyone who worries, showing anxiety, has not committed the "unpardonable." He is still listening to the Holy Spirit's convicting ministry and is eligible for forgiveness.

The Apostle Paul, writing to Timothy said, "I was formerly a blasphemer, a persecutor, and an insolent man; but I obtained mercy because I did it ignorantly in unbelief. And the grace of our Lord was exceedingly abundant, with faith and love which are in Christ Jesus" (1 Timothy 1:13-14).

Those who are in danger have themselves to blame. It is not primarily that God is judging them, rather more accurately, these are persons who have shut God out of their lives. They are like the Pharisees of Christ's day, who accused Jesus of working in demonic power, who blasphemed the Holy Spirit and refused to give God credit for Christ's supernatural deeds. They were basically hostile to God, and had no interest in repenting of their evil ways. They felt proud of their actions that placed Jesus Christ on the cross, and they considered it good riddance!

GETTING GOD'S EVALUATION   October 29

"Then Daniel answered the king, 'You may keep your gifts for yourself and give your rewards to someone else. Nevertheless, I will read the writing for the king and tell him what it means...This is what these words mean: **Mene:** *God has numbered the days of your reign and brought it to an end.* **Tekel:** *You have been weighed on the scales and found wanting.* **Peres:** *Your kingdom is divided and given to the Medes and Persians.' Then at Belshazzar's command, Daniel was clothed in purple, a gold chain was placed around his neck, and he was proclaimed the third highest ruler in the kingdom." (Daniel 5:17, 26-28 NIV)*

The queen told the king that the man Daniel could read the handwriting on the banquet wall. Daniel did! He told the king that his forefather, Nebuchadnezzar, was once dethroned until he acknowledged "the Most High God as sovereign." Amazingly, King Nebuchadnezzar, "was driven away from people and given the mind of an animal; he lived with the wild donkeys and ate grass like cattle; and his body was drenched with the dew of heaven...." (5:21).

Daniel reminded Belshazzar— that he knew all this—and still had not humbled himself, but had taken goblets from God's temple at Jerusalem and drank wine from them with his nobles, wives and concubines. He had praised his pagan gods of silver and gold, and had opposed the God of Heaven—who holds even the king's life in his hands (5:23). That night Belshazzar was slain.

This is such a stark reminder to every king, president or ruler, worldwide, that each is accountable to God Almighty. It also challenges each Christian in America to live godly respectable lives. We must pray that God will provide his choice for the White House, for Congress and for the Supreme Court.

CHURCHES HELD ACCOUNTABLE   October 30

"I know your deeds, your hard work and your perseverance. I know that you cannot tolerate wicked people, that you have tested those who claim to be apostles but are not, and have found them false...Yet I hold this against you: You have forsaken the love you had at first. Consider how far you have fallen! Repent and do the things you did at first...." (Revelation 2:2, 4-5 NIV)

Here the Church of Ephesus is both complimented and criticized by the Risen Christ. Six other churches of Asia are also evaluated and challenged. All Christian churches, worldwide, should ask: "Are we still faithful to Christ?" Today, scores of churches in varied denominations are impacting America greatly and powerfully.

While living in Kansas, I secured Leonhard Sudermann's book, *From Russia to America in Search of Freedom*. Sudermann, at age 20, migrated from West Prussia to Russia and at age 39 became minister of the Berdyansk Mennonite Church. At age 52 (1873) he was one of twelve chosen to spy out North America—since Russia revoked the Mennonite military exemptions. For five months the 12 visited Canada and the USA. Two men even visited President Grant regarding freedom of religion in America. Back in Russia, in his Farewell sermon (07-10-1876) Leonhard urged his flock to follow him to America. Only a few did. Significantly, in 1877, Elder Sudermann settled in Kansas and became the pastor of my home church, Emmaus Mennonite of Whitewater.

I once wrote: "Mennonite folk were planted on these prairies destined by God to share a harvest of food and faith. In America's heartland their Turkey Red wheat created a bread basket for the world and in America's liberties their faith blossomed into worldwide mission and relief, peace and service, mutual aid and disaster care." In a recent year my home church gave $1,000,000 to Missions!

SLIGHTLY SOILED, PRICE REDUCED　October 31

"Catch us the foxes, the little foxes that spoil the vines, for our vines have tender grapes." (Song of Solomon 2:15 NKJV)

Solomon, the writer, refers to the little foxes that bring ruin to the vineyards. However, some scholars think that this may be the "loved one" speaking. She may be referring to some small unresolved irritant, in their relationship, that has not been resolved. She may be speaking metaphorically, not thinking of foxes in a literal sense. In a marriage relationship, love is easily threatened, by some issue and she may be asking her lover to help. The problem might be uncontrolled desire, or jealous mistrust, or pride that refuses to admit fault, or a spirit of unforgiveness. Many little items can rob a marriage of the needed harmony!

I heard a commencement speaker, Dr. Robert McQuilken, speak on the topic—"Slightly Soiled But Greatly Reduced in Price." He had gone to a department store to buy a quality table cloth. He noticed one was drastically reduced in price, but it appeared as good as the others. The clerk explained that there was a slight soil in one corner. So the price was marked down. He went on to say that small deeds of wrong, of evil, or legal violations will drastically harm our reputation. He remembers sitting beside a girl in the second grade. He saw her cheat. Every time he met her in later years, his self-talk was "she is the cheater!" She may have reformed and become an honest noble person, yet he could not forget her misbehavior. She was slightly soiled, but greatly reduced in price. The lesson is obvious. If we want people to hold us in high esteem, we need to be truthful, honest and exemplary.

BEING EFFECTIVELY PRODUCTIVE   November 1

"...make every effort to add to your faith goodness; and to goodness, knowledge; and to knowledge, self-control; and to self-control, perseverance; and to perseverance, godliness; and to godliness, brotherly kindness; and to brotherly kindness, love. For if you possess these qualities in increasing measure, they will keep you from being ineffective and unproductive in your knowledge of our Lord Jesus Christ." (2 Peter 1:5-8 NIV)

The Apostle Peter gives Christians a great recipe for being effective and productive for Jesus Christ (2 Peter 1:1-11). When God gives us this "precious faith" he also gives "precious promises" that enable us to escape the world's corruption. Almighty God provides everything we need for "life and godliness." **THE STARTING POINT: FAITH.** As we declare Jesus the Lord of our lives, we need to progress forward—not stopping or stalling—but improving with great effort! **ADD GOODNESS.** This is sometimes rendered "moral excellence." Every Christian should gradually change and ever more and more resemble Jesus Christ our Lord. **ADD KNOWLEDGE.** Christians must practice thought control. Wisdom requires a good discernment between good and evil. Saints must live with clear consciences. **ADD SELF-CONTROL.** The indwelling Christ is our thermostat for control. One of the gifts of the Spirit is self-control. Sins of anger, greed, and lust must disappear. **ADD PERSEVERANCE.** Satan brings two attacks: worldly opposition from without and fleshly enticements from inside. Handling adversity is a Christian's key task. **ADD GODLINESS.** Godliness is a practical awareness of God in all areas of life. Two areas, stewardship and spiritual gifts, must be discovered and developed. **ADD BROTHERLY KIND-NESS.** Here is Christianity-in-overalls. The spiritual gifts of service, hospitality, ministry, teaching and showing mercy will solve many needs! **ADD LOVE.** Love is not only the motive of our evangelism, it's also the method. Globally, the wholesome way souls are won to Christ is by REDEMPTIVE LOVE.

OUR TEN COMMANDMENTS   November 2

"You shall not make for yourself an image in the form of anything in heaven above or on the earth beneath or in the water below. You shall not bow down to them or worship them; for I the Lord your God, am a jealous God, punishing the children for the sin of the parents to the third and fourth generation of those who hate me, but showing love to a thousand generations of those who love me and keep my commandments." (Exodus 20:4-6 NIV)

The second of the famous Ten Commandments probably does not receive enough attention. Abhorring idols, due to our love for God, carries great and splendid rewards, because of God's love for us!

IDOL: MY HOUSE? In the 50-some years of our marriage, we have lived in eight houses. Three were our own, costing us $23,000, $85,000 and $220,000. Each was modest in the town where we lived, but adequate for the moment. The final house, in California, has some spare bedrooms for children and grandchildren.

IDOL: MY CAR? For 40 years I bought secondhand cars. The last three however were new: 1993 Chrysler Concorde, 2001 Concorde, and 2010 Chevy Malibu. None cost more than $25,000, except for my restored 1947 Chevrolet, which my dad bought new on the farm in Kansas! This "IDOL" of mine, wife approved, but would gladly sell!

IDOL: MY LIFESTYLE? I asked my SS group for ideas: Loving Money, Stock Market, Net-Worth Calculations, worshiping Bank Balances, like the old rich fool still "Building Bigger Barns;" here are real potentials: Television, Cell-phones, Sports, Computers, Face Book, Liquor, Clothing, Beauty Treatments, and Daily Feasting at Swank Restaurants. My dear friend, you and I must each decide—what are our personal idols? What are the items we treasure more than the Bible, the Church and the Kingdom of God?

COMMANDMENT NO. THREE   November 3

"You shall not misuse the name of the Lord your God, for the Lord will not hold anyone guiltless who misuses his name." (Exodus 20:7 NIV)

When people swear in court to tell the truth and then lie, that is misusing God's name. Paul Harvey once joked about folks who raised their hand and said, "I will tell the truth, the whole truth, and anything but the truth, so help me God." My father used to insist that we children always tell the truth, and never deviate with jesting and joking falsely. That was good advice, don't you think?

As a farm kid in the Midwest, I heard many a hired man swear a blue streak. I was fascinated by this, so I tried it out on my mother, "What in the dickens are you doing here?" "Albert, we don't talk that way, that's not nice!" Walking home from school with other boys, when the girls were out of earshot, we used to swear very unashamedly. But in High School, attending a Christian Academy, it dawned on me that if I wanted God to save my soul and ultimately take me to heaven, I had to give up my swearing, whether in word, thought or deed. Yes, it was a no, no!

My mother was strict. To her gosh and golly were derivatives of "God." And dam, darn and dickens were referring to the devil. And even gee whiz referred to Jesus, as did also Christ Almighty. Thank God for a mother who was righteous and upright—who tried to educate us in a Christian manner.

Luke astutely writes, "The good man brings good things out of the good stored up in his heart...For out of the overflow of his heart his mouth speaks" (Luke 6:45).

SOARING LIKE AN EAGLE   November 4

"He (God) gives strength to the weary and increases the power of the weak. Even youths grow tired and weary, and young men stumble and fall; but those who hope in the Lord will renew their strength. They will soar on wings like eagles; they will run and not grow weary, they will walk and not faint." (Isaiah 40:29-31 NIV)

In this chapter of Isaiah, Israel is accused of claiming that God disregards them. Not so—their everlasting God never tires, He knows no weariness in his effort to sustain them! With His strength they can soar like eagles, run like champions, walk like conditioned hikers. Dependence on God, guarantees victory.

Our son Greg ran two 26-mile marathons while at Westmont College in Santa Barbara. The first was at San Luis Obispo. He ran side by side with another runner, until he dropped back. At the 20 mile mark his coach told him that a boy who had been four minutes behind at ten miles, was now only 50 seconds behind. That news energized him—he widened the gap—winning the race in two hours and 39 minutes. He felt royally "pumped up!" In his second race, at El Toro Marine Base, LA, he ran each mile in 5:45 until he hit "the wall," where legs weaken, where carbohydrates in the muscles are exhausted, where the body starts burning fat. His time was two hours and 34 minutes! We were very proud of Greg!

The children of God who make a total commitment have a supernatural energy flowing through their lives. They soar on wings like eagles. They move forward like tireless runners. They work persistently like conditioned hikers on a mountain trail. And who is their coach but the Sovereign Lord Almighty!

EXCITING SUMMER ADVENTURES   November 5

"Take delight in the Lord and he will give you the desires of your heart....The Lord makes firm the steps of the one who delights in him; though he stumble, he will not fall, for the Lord upholds him with his hand." (Psalm 37:4, 23- 24 NIV)

In the summer of 1981, Steve (24) our oldest, and Nathan (19) our youngest did some painting for us. After that they felt they deserved a vacation. Their big desire was to hike the John Muir Trail. So they drove through Fresno, California to Sequoia National Park. They parked their car and hiked 180 miles through wilderness to Yosemite National Park.

They were there with the bears and rattlesnakes. Of course, they were thoroughly trained and well read. They could count on our prayers surrounding them. They knew how to tie food between trees, so no bears could get to it. We hoped they would stay on main paths so they would often meet company. But no, they chose less-traveled routes, and sometimes saw only one person per day. But they saw areas few people had seen! They hiked ten days before seeing their first telephone station called the Devil's Postpile. They said, "We're OK. We're in good shape." They reviewed their daily experiences. In a few more days they reached Yosemite Valley. There they caught a ride back to Sequoia Park to retrieve their car. They had the trail-hike of their lives!

Friends, when we delight ourselves in the Lord, he delights in rewarding us and protecting us. He guards our steps and upholds us in his hand. This mutual delight blesses both of us. God is blessed and honored as we show him love. We are blessed as we feel his presence. Let's both of us delight ourselves in the Lord today.

RENEWED FELLOWSHIP ENJOYED   November 6

"Therefore if you have any encouragement from being united with Christ, if any comfort from his love, if any common sharing in the Spirit, if any tenderness and compassion, then make my joy complete by being like-minded, having the same love, being one in spirit and of one mind." (Philippians 2:1-2 NIV)

Paul and Timothy tell the folks at Philippi, that the encouragement, comfort and fellowship they have enjoyed with the Lord, they should also duplicate in their relationships with one another. Yes, Christian fellowship runs deep. This week we received a surprise phone call from our nephew, Dwight, living in Ohio, whom we had not seen in twenty years. He with family members was vacationing on the West Coast and invited himself to our house for a Thursday brunch, en route to Sequoia National Park. We were overjoyed to entertain this Christian family!

We prepared a great meal: orange juice and coffee, bacon and sausage, scrambled eggs, cantaloupe, french toast and caramel rolls. We had a delightful fellowship around the table with these seven relatives.

Dwight and Ruth live in Northern Ohio, he is a high school music teacher and she works in an office. They are active in their church. Their three sons all graduated from the Air Force Academy in Colorado Springs. Glen, 33, is an Air Force pilot stationed overseas. Paul, 31, also an Air Force Pilot, lives stateside with wife Shelly from Shreveport, Louisiana. Luke, 30, and wife Katie live near Edwards Air Force Base, and both work in Mojave for a company building the world's largest plane (twice the size of the 747). Luke and Katie are very active in their church in Rosamond. Our fellowship around the table was truly God-blessed!

Christian fellowship on earth is a foretaste of the glorious reunions we will experience in heaven!

LOVING OUR NEIGHBORS   November 7

"Do not seek revenge or bear a grudge against anyone among your people, but love your neighbor as yourself. I am the Lord." (Leviticus 19:18 NIV)

The Bible emphatically asks us to love God, but added to that, we are to love our neighbors as ourselves. The book of Leviticus gives strong advice on what this means: Don't defraud him, rob him, nor hold back wages you owe him (19:13)!

One of our neighbors, next door, once joined us in hiring a block-layer to build a six foot fence between us. Otherwise our relationship over the years has been casual, but truly cordial. Recently, the neighbor, a Ford car dealer, said: "Al, my motor home will be gone next week, it might be a good time to trim your elm tree hanging over our fence! My gate will be unlocked."

First, Sally and I trimmed the tree on our side. Sally, my 21 year old granddaughter bravely got on our tile-roof and cut branches. Next we went to the neighbor's side. She held the ladder while I cut all I could reach. To reach higher, we bolted a four foot extension to my 12-foot ladder. Then Sally, the gardener, and I, took turns climbing up and cutting limbs. By noon we had a huge clean-up pile on the ground—a job we postponed until after lunch.

The next day I saw the neighbor's wife. Midmorning, she had stopped by to check on men working in her house. I knew she was oriental, and often went to foreign lands to visit family, but I seldom had a chance to speak with her. I said, "We trimmed our tree yesterday." She looked up at the tree, clenched her fist with a thumbs-up sign. "That looks great," she said smilingly. I was pleased—I had loved my neighbors.

SAFE IN GOD'S ARMS November 8

"For this cause everyone who is godly shall pray to You in a time when You may be found; Surely in a flood of great waters they shall not come near him. You are my hiding place; You shall preserve me from trouble; You shall surround me with songs of deliverance." (Psalm 32:6-7 NKJV)

At a recent annual congregational meeting, our church voted me onto the pastoral staff, with the label of Pastor of Senior-Care. With this honor came added responsibility. This morning I got up at 6:00 a.m. to eat breakfast, and by 7:00 I was en route to the hospital ten miles away. One parishioner, Lynn was scheduled for a double angiogram, to determine whether he needed open heart surgery to replace a heart valve.

Yesterday evening I phoned the house to pray with Lynn, as did Pastor Eric. This morning I made a beeline for the fourth floor, where Lynn's wife was hospitalized for the fifth day, to control blood pressure, to check whether she had suffered a stroke? Her daughter was by her bedside. I read Psalm 32:7, "You are my hiding place; You shall preserve me from trouble; You shall surround me with songs of deliverance." I prayed jointly for Ann and Lynn, these 20-year faithful members of our church.

Next I went down to the Lab Waiting Room, and Ann's daughter, Karen, soon joined me. We had a wonderful conversation, regarding God's daily watch-care over His children! God had recently given Ann a heartwarming assurance of salvation! At about nine o'clock, the nurse took us to Lynn's recovery room. The doctor said that only a single angiogram was performed, and a new valve was not necessary, but a balloon-procedure might help. We rejoice in God's deliverance, a volume of prayers was answered!

WITH ALL YOUR MIGHT   November 9

"Whatever you do, work at it with all your heart, as working for the Lord, not for human masters, since you know that you will receive an inheritance from the Lord as a reward. It is the Lord Christ you are serving." (Colossians 3:23-24 NIV)

In the 2012 London Olympics we saw many contestants compete "with all their might"—in swimming, in diving, in running, in rowing, in cycling, and in other events. Eight USA women won gold in rowing. Michael Phelps won gold in the 100 meter butterfly final. Two runners, trained by Oregon's Salazar won gold and silver in the 10,000 meter race.

While in junior high our granddaughter Cydney heard of the $10,000 Danimal's Yogurt 90-second Internet Video-Contest. Also the winner and family would earn a four day trip to Hollywood to meet Dylan and Cole, from the Disney Channel's Zack and Cody Show. Cydney said, "Dad, lets do it."

First, Cydney, and her dad, Nathan, wrote a song: words and music. Danimal's key products were featured—Crush Cup and Smoothie. Danimal words were used: Natural flavor, Calcium, Vitamin D, Lactobacillis, a Probiotic! In the background were hundreds of Danimal cups and cans. Words reoccurring were: "ONLY THE GOOD STUFF!"

In Nathan's portable home studio he made a 16-track audio recording, and finally a music video. Cydney's sister, Chase, struck the drums and cymbals. Her brother, Cade dramatized the miraculous effect of a Danimal Crush Cup. As a wimpy skimpy boy he drank a cup—and promptly looked healthier! But the heroine was Cydney. What a stellar performance. Smilingly, she sang, danced and entertained with all her might. It was awesome! She advertised the Danimal good stuff. From hundreds of entries, Cydney's was judged best. They flew from Indiana to Hollywood—also visiting the Epp Grandparents in Bakersfield!

THE CHRISTIAN'S MOTIVATION   November 10

"And whatever you do, whether in word or deed, do it all in the name of the Lord Jesus, giving thanks to God the Father through him."
(Colossians 3:17 NIV)

As the athletes of the Olympics strive to honor their own countries, Christians—in their anticipation of the Olympics of Heaven—live and work deliberately to honor their Lord Jesus Christ. All their activities are designed to bring glorious attention to their loving Lord, and to draw their neighbors, friends and relatives to their loving Savior who has fountains of living water.

Another verse speaks to this same issue, whom do we really live for? "So whether you eat or drink or whatever you do, do it all for the glory of God. Do not cause anyone to stumble, whether Jews, Greeks or the church of God" (1 Corinthians 10:31-32). The Pharisees asked Jesus, which is the greatest commandment? His answer, "Love the Lord your God with all your heart and with all your soul and with all your mind..." (Matthew 22:37). Living for the Glory of God must be our highest priority.

This kind of living involves both God and man. We each have a part. When I was a teenager I heard a commencement address at Hesston College. The speaker was the "Walking Preacher of the Ozarks." He told this parable—a preacher and a boy walked across a pasture. A bull started chasing them. The boy yelled "Shall we pray?" The preacher screamed back, "Yes, but while we pray let's run like thunder!" What a beautiful lesson.

God, with all his sovereignty, his power, his protection and his love is part of the picture, while the human element is our part—our praying, our planning, our deciding, and our acting. We must fit into God's will!

THE CALL OF JESUS November 11

"As Jesus was walking beside the Sea of Galilee, he saw two brothers, Simon called Peter and his brother Andrew. They were casting a net into the lake, for they were fishermen. 'Come follow me,' Jesus said, 'and I will send you out to fish for people.' At once they left their nets and followed him." (Matthew 4:18-20 NIV)

The call of God came to Peter and Andrew at their place of employment. It was a working day for them. They were starting to fish. At the bidding of Jesus, they left the fishing to the rest of the crew, and promptly followed Jesus. That day these brothers probably got their first discipleship instruction—the beginning of three years of training!

God's call to service came to me through various sermons I heard. On one occasion I was helping my dad care for his cattle. "Dad, I feel God calling me to Christian service. I plan to go to seminary after college, and then follow the Lord's leading into the pastorate, teaching or missionary work. That means I won't be able to farm with you," I concluded. "If God is calling you, I approve," my Dad said!

Last week I visited a retired Mennonite Brethren pastor, who moved to Bakersfield to be near his two daughters. He quickly told me how he became a pastor. At the end of the Korean War, age 29, he was in the US Air Force, stationed in Japan. He bought a ticket on a charter plane, but was "bumped" for a higher ranking officer. That plane crashed into the ocean, killing everyone. Then he knew, he owed his life to God. Back home he graduated from Tabor College, then seminary at Fresno, and ministered to numerous churches with God's blessing upon his life. My friends, we must all follow Jesus Christ!

HOLY SPIRIT ACTIVITY!   November 12

"Now an angel of the Lord said to Philip, 'Go south to the road—the desert road—that goes down from Jerusalem to Gaza.' So he started out, and on the way, he met an Ethiopian eunuch...The Spirit told Philip 'Go to that chariot and stay near it'...Then Philip ran up to the chariot and heard the man reading Isaiah the prophet..." (Acts 8:26-30 NIV)

In a miraculous way God sent Philip to a desert road to meet the Ethiopian—who embraced Jesus and requested baptism. After baptism, the Holy Spirit snatched Philip away, and the Ethiopian official went on his way rejoicing. What a miracle!

I heard a present day miracle today. My friend Bert, who accepted Christ eight weeks ago, was sent by his employer, Pacific Gas & Electric, to a farm 90 miles north. But the farmer needed no electrical repair. The office gave him a wrong address. He picked a few figs and started back. Instead of going directly to I-5, he took a side road which ends up at Lost Hills. In the middle of nowhere, he saw a lady lying in the shade. He stopped. She was dehydrated. Bert gave her water and figs. Her car got stuck in a hole in a field; So she had walked for help. She got into Bert's truck—they drove seven miles to the car! She told Bert that she was a San Francisco nurse, going to LA to meet her boy friend. She had a Triple AAA card, able to tow 200 miles. Bert phoned a tow truck. In three hours of waiting, Bert shared how he had recently become a Christian, and how Christ had wonderfully forgiven him and changed his life! What a miracle: right road, right time, right woman, right witness. Bert probably saved her life!

GOD'S PROTECTING CARE   November 13

"What then, shall we say in response to these things? If God is for us who can be against us? He who did not spare his own son, but gave him up for us all—how will he not also, along with him, graciously give us all things?" (Romans 8:31-32 NIV)

In yesterday's devotional, my friend, Bert, rescued a lost woman laying by the roadside, miles from any available help. She was from the Philippines, working as a nurse in the San Francisco area. She had not found Highway 58 or Highway 99. But God graciously protected her. When her car left the road and entered a field, her car fell into a shallow hole. Tire marks showed she had repeatedly tried to get out. When she finally got on top, her car was hung up on a ridge. That was fortunate. Had she driven further, she would have driven into a bigger hole filled with water!

When Bert picked her up, he noticed she had slurred speech. As he got to the car he saw the beer cans. He could feel with her—Bert himself had been drunk all day on his wife's recent birthday! He later felt so ashamed because he had invited many friends. He shared with the lady how eight weeks ago he had gone forward at his sister's church to accept Christ, and how God had delivered him from his addiction.

The lady said her boy friend was always kind and gracious. Bert phoned him that the lady and her car would be coming by tow truck. Later we heard that the lady was immediately hospitalized for recuperation. Is it not marvelous how God sent Bert down that lonely road, to rescue this precious soul? God is so good!

UNSELFISH SACRIFICIAL SERVICE   November 14

"We then who are strong ought to bear with the scruples of the weak, and not to please ourselves. Let each of us please his neighbor for his good, leading to edification. For even Christ did not please Himself, but as it is written, 'The reproaches of those who reproached You fell on Me.'" (Romans 15:1-3 NKJV)

The "reproach" quote in verse three comes from Psalm 69:9. Christ's unselfishness is highlighted. William Newell in his book on *Romans* writes: "The constant drawing upon Him by the multitudes, upon His time, His love, His teaching, His healing, was a marvelous proof that they could count on the absolute absence of self-pleasing in Him!"

A striking example comes to us from the sports area. It occurred in the year of 2010. The baseball team was the Texas Rangers. They won their playoff series. On the team was a player named Josh Hamilton. He faced the addicting enemies of drugs and alcohol. So when it came to the postgame celebration, Josh feared the fast-flowing liquor. How could he cope? After all, he was a recovering alcoholic. He was in danger. To his surprise, his teammates showed amazing empathy! As an act of honor to their friend Josh, the players stocked the drinks with ginger ale, so Josh could happily celebrate with them. What a truly unselfish deed—denying their own selves to help a brother.

Each of us as Christians, find in Christ a marvelous example to emulate. He lived to help others, and supremely died to save humanity from their sins. We too need to love God wholeheartedly, and live to please our neighbors. The mark of true maturity—for a Christian—is a willingness to sacrifice any activity, that could be a stumbling block. We must live to build others up.

GOD'S APPROVAL OF JESUS   November 15

"When all the people were being baptized, Jesus was baptized too. And as he was praying, heaven opened and the Holy Spirit descended on him in bodily form like a dove. And a voice came from heaven; 'You are my Son, whom I love; with you I am well pleased.'" (Luke 3:21-22 NIV)

Before Jesus chose his Twelve, taught the crowds or performed his miracles, God the Father, proclaimed his love for Jesus. For thirty years Jesus had worked in Joseph's carpenter shop, and before he began his three-year ministry, at the baptism, the heavens opened—the Holy Spirit descended, and God spoke audibly: "with you I am well pleased." That was before Jesus had accomplished the major tasks for which he came to earth!

Recently, in a worship-telecast from the Crystal Cathedral, Bobby Schuller spoke of his experience at Fuller Seminary. One professor gave incoming students, an amazing assignment: "On a sheet of paper, write what you think God thinks of you." Over half of the students wrote a negative evaluation. Many referred to God's disapproval of their attitudes, actions or their sins. Apparently the professor took notice of each paper that gave a positive response—that God loved and approved them!

Just think for a moment—when you understand Christian theology, the issue clears up. Before you have given any money, attended any Church, or did any deeds of kindness to others, when you accept Jesus Christ as your Savior and Lord, you are forgiven, accepted, and declared righteous in the sight of God—and that through the merits of Jesus Christ, who died for you and arose again! Therefore you have the right to say that God loves you, because you have accepted his redemption, and have submitted to his Lordship over your life.

CHOOSING BEST CHOICES   November 16

"Now fear the Lord and serve him with all faithfulness. Throw away the gods your ancestors worshiped beyond the Euphrates River and in Egypt, and serve the Lord. But if serving the Lord seems undesirable to you, then choose for yourselves this day whom you will serve.... But as for me and my household, we will serve the Lord." (Joshua 24:14-15 NIV)

In the last chapter of Joshua, the fearless leader of Israel, appealed once more to his people, to forsake all the pagan gods and idols, and to serve the God of Abraham, Isaac and Jacob. He warned them that their sins, disobedience, and rebellion would bring further judgment from Almighty God, if they chose the wrong. The people insisted, "No! We will serve the Lord" (24:21).

In our personal lives, we Christians again need to affirm our utter devotion to Jesus Christ. We need to choose whether we put God first, or whether we serve our favorite idols—our houses, our cars, our jobs, our lifestyles. Yes, we need to choose. How we spend our money is solid proof whether we have put the Kingdom of God ahead of our own selfish pursuits!

In the normal cycle, the Republicans and the Democrats have their national conventions. The citizens of America have a choice to make. For Christians this is a crucial time for prayer and participation. We dare not fail our Lord. Our beloved nation is always at a critical crossroad. Our Constitution guarantees life, liberty and happiness. But if we Christians fail to vote for the candidates who stand for high and holy principles, we shirk our biblical obligations. We need to take time to inform ourselves, the best we can, by dialoguing with others. Finally, we must go to the polls to vote.

CHRIST'S SECOND COMING   November 17

"For the Lord himself will come down from heaven, with a loud command, with the voice of the archangel and with the trumpet call of God, and the dead in Christ will rise first. After that, we who are still alive and are left will be caught up with them in the clouds to meet the Lord in the air. And so we will be with the Lord forever. Therefore encourage each other with these words." (1 Thessalonians 4:16-18 NIV)

In theology, the Second Coming of Christ is called "THE BLESSED HOPE." When I was a lad of ten, seventy years ago, our minister, the Reverend J.C. Kauffman, in a morning sermon postulated that he would not experience death, because the coming of Christ surely was so near! Well, he is long gone. Even the Early Church thought that Christ would come in their day.

"THE DEAD IN CHRIST WILL RISE FIRST." One week when I was preparing an Easter Sermon, I came across a sermon written by a pastor, 300 years ago. He said, Suppose you die on a ship, and your body is heaved overboard. Fish will eat that body. Does that disprove the Resurrection Idea? He said—NO! What's the difference: fish eating the body, decay devouring the body in the grave, or the body reduced to ashes in cremation? Who knows? Maybe angels keep track of our molecules, and at the Second Coming all believer's molecules are reassembled. We believe that our Resurrection bodies will resemble Christ's body—not subject to time and space.

What a glorious day when we, who are still alive, "will be caught up with them in the clouds to meet the Lord in the air." This will follow the trumpet call of God. This is OUR BLESSED HOPE!

RELIABLE TRAVEL GUIDANCE November 18

"Trust in the Lord with all your heart, and lean not on your own understanding; In all your ways acknowledge Him and He shall direct your paths." (Proverbs 3:5-6 NKJV)

This verse has been a favorite of mine for many years. Already as a teenager, as I looked for divine guidance in choosing colleges to attend, I leaned heavily on God. I quoted Proverbs 3:5-6 over and over again. In later life, I never moved far from this admonition, to acknowledge God and rely on His leading.

In 2010 we gave our Chrysler Concorde, with 260,000 miles to our son Steven and the car continues to run well. We downsized to a Chevy Malibu—with a six-speed transmission. It has the On-Star navigation system. When we were in Las Vegas for our grandson Zachery's Soccer Tournament, the On-Star led us to the Soccer field on Saturday, and to a certain church on Sunday. The instructions were reliable. Then some months later, coming through Oregon on I-5, we planned to visit some old-time friends in Grants Pass. We followed the On-Star to a spot where the voice said, "You have reached your destination." Really? We had reached a dead end in the road with no houses in sight! We were on the right road but had passed their house five miles back.

A spiritual lesson can be learned. Our lives must point people toward heaven. So many rely on their own piety, their good works, their family reputation, their church denomination. But the Bible states that salvation comes through Jesus Christ alone (Acts 4:12). As we claim Jesus Christ as our Savior from sin, admitting He died for us, and crown Him as Lord of our lives, following Him in obedience, we are on the road to heaven (John 10:27). Praise God.

IMITATE ONLY GOOD   November 19

"Dear friends, do not imitate what is evil but what is good. Anyone who does what is good is from God. Anyone one who does what is evil has not seen God." (3 John 1:11 NIV)

The Apostle John writes this letter to his dear friend, Gaius. This brother in the church had a reputation of standing firmly for the truth, and was leading others to remain in the truth. John called other church members, "my children." These also were walking in the same gospel truth. On top of that Gaius was complemented for showing hospitality to some Christian brethren, complete strangers, who had come into their midst. The Apostle John also names Demetrius, as one standing in the truth—having a good reputation, being well spoken of by everyone. Gaius and Demetrius were therefore two pillars in the church whose influence was very visible. And John was so happy about that.

In that same church was a man named Diotrephes (verses 9-10). He had a bad attitude: (1) He loved to be first, (2) He gossiped maliciously about John, and (3) He expelled from the church those who helped John's men. Diotrephes wanted to control everything in the church for his own self-centered purposes.

What a lesson! It is imperative that we associate most with those enthusiastic about our church. Avoid the grumblers, the complainers, the criticizers, and spend time with those who are positive encouragers. EVERY PERSON THAT GOD BRINGS INTO MY SPHERE OF INFLUENCE—is a person that God wants me to bless! That is a basic presupposition in our witness to the outside world, as well as our technique for building friendships within the church. No one enjoys being around people who drip negative words with every breath. Friends, let's be positive for God!

THE TRIUMPHANT CHURCH   November 20

(Jesus replied) "And I tell you that you are Peter, and on this rock I will build my church, and the gates of Hades will not overcome it." (Matthew 16:18 NIV)

We all want to invest in something that's solid, lasting, and guaranteed! In our world our wealth and worth is not guaranteed. Every earthly thing is fragile. When my forefathers left Russia, and came to America, in the 1800's, the wealthy man who bought up many of their farms, later died of starvation.

The scriptures however promise that the Church of Jesus Christ will prevail to the end of time, to the Second Coming of Jesus Christ our Lord. Hallelujah! Every ounce of effort expended for Jesus Christ and every dollar given to Christ's church will bring rich dividends. The Bible talks about laying up treasures in heaven where neither insects, rust and rot, or thieves can destroy it (Matthew 6:19-21). Investing in heaven is a sure bet. It can't be denied.

Based on this biblical premise, the sooner we and our families open our hearts and lives to our Blessed Lord, the larger will our bank account in glory grow. Whatever is done in the name of Jesus, even giving a cup of cold water, carries a heavenly reward (Matthew 10: 41-42). This biblical assurance is so comforting. The poet states it this way: "Only one life will soon be past. Only what's done for Christ will last."

My friends, never give up. Keep your eyes riveted on heaven. That will be the best investment you ever made. This is promised to us by our Risen Lord. Not only are we promised a resurrection, but also heavenly rewards which no one can strip away from us. It pays to serve Jesus Christ and his church.

324

CONTENT WITH CIRCUMSTANCES   November 21

"Forget the former things; do not dwell on the past. See, I am doing a new thing! Now it springs up; do you not perceive it? I am making a way in the wilderness and streams in the wasteland." (Isaiah 43:18-19 NIV)

Many of us have encountered circumstances which we could not alter. They were not events of our choosing. Truthfully, they were beyond our control. Why God permitted them we do not know, but we were forced to face them and deal with them. A religious American thinker, Reinhold Niebuhr once formulated a petition, later known as the Serenity Prayer: "God, grant me the serenity to accept the things I cannot change, the courage to change the things I can, and wisdom to know the difference."

The prophet Isaiah quotes God as urging us to stop dwelling on the past, the past things we can't change if we tried. No, that is futile and useless. Rather, God's new and better things are symbolized by highways in the desert and rivers in the waste-lands. God arouses our expectations, filling us with new dreams and visions. If we could but perceive, understand and visual-ize the changes God has in store for us, we would be highly blessed. Friends, your future need not be shaped by the limita-tions and failures of your past. God's vision for you is a new life of joy, victory and strength, like you have never known before!

I think of my neighbor Bert, who stopped by this afternoon for his weekly rendezvous with me. You see I am his mentor, and I am helping him with counsel, Bible study and prayer. I'm helping him forget his old life of alcoholism, and now enjoying a new life of freedom. Since the day he opened his life to Jesus Christ at his sister's church, he has made gigantic strides in Christian growth! Praise God.

BARNABAS, THE ENCOURAGER   November 22

"Then Barnabas went to Tarsus to look for Saul, and when he found him, he brought him to Antioch. So for a whole year Barnabas and Saul met with the church and taught great numbers of people. The disciples were called Christians first at Antioch." (Acts 11:25-26 NIV)

Joseph of Cyprus, was renamed by the Apostles as Barnabas, "the son of encouragement" (4:36). That name fit him accurately, according to the book of Acts. When Saul was converted, the church feared him, but Barnabas introduced him to the church as a real believer (9:26-27). When Gentiles turned to Christ by droves in Antioch, the church of Jerusalem sent Barnabas to Antioch to encourage them (11:19-22). He, in turn, invited Saul to come help, so for a whole year the two taught vigorously (11:23-26).

We have a couple in our church named Doug and Myra. Doug retired in his middle 50's, after working for 30 years as a Fireman. They volunteered to go to Portugal, to encourage a missionary couple supported by our church. After two years, they came home for a year. The churches in Portugal testified that this couple was a tremendous encouragement in their work. And our couple was greatly blessed.

This morning we had Doug and Myra at our house for breakfast. What a delightful visit! I asked Doug, "What inspired you to retire early and volunteer for mission work?" He said in affect—as we looked forward to the next 30 years, we didn't want a life of leisure, fishing, boating, golfing etc., we wanted to make an impact for the Kingdom of God! NEXT FRIDAY THEY LEAVE FOR ROME, ITALY! This again is a two year assignment, helping a missionary couple from our church, as they minister to refugees who have fled to Rome. What modern-day encouragers!

PORTRAYING GOD CORRECTLY   November 23

"Thus says the Lord, 'Let not the wise man glory in his wisdom... But let him who glories glory in this, that he understands and knows Me, that I am the Lord, exercising lovingkindness, judgement, and righteousness in the earth. For in these I delight,' says the Lord." (Jeremiah 9:23a, 24 NKJV)

It is often assumed that only the elite scholars should discuss the nature of God. However, Jeremiah the prophet, demonstrates that even the common people should understand theology—what God says about Himself.

In Jeremiah's day, the religious teachers claimed to be speaking for God, but actually they were perverting the truth. Jeremiah, chapter 23, has a lengthy description of how they prophesied lies (v.32), and prophesied false dreams of blessing, which were not from God. Their mental delusions and wickedness stemmed from their worship of Baal (v.13). God's true nature of "lovingkindness, judgment and righteousness" was not being proclaimed.

In our day as well, some folks lay emphasis on God's wrath, teaching that God is waiting to punish every wrong deed, no matter how small. On Mount Sinai God taught Moses that He, the Lord God is "merciful and gracious, long-suffering and abounding in goodness and truth" (Exodus 34:6). This has led others to teach that God is too loving to punish wrongdoing. No! We need to hold a balance between love and justice. God is both a just Father and a loving Father.

The Apostle Peter in the New Testament is emphatic that God does not relish punishing people. He does not want any to perish, but wants all to come to repentance—so He can forgive them (2 Peter 3:9). God's great love has sent Christ to die for us, so we can be forgiven. This is a marvelous truth.

OYSTER-PEARLS VIA AFFLICTION   November 24

"And to Joseph were born two sons before the years of famine came, whom Asenath...bore to him. Joseph called the name of the first-born Manasseh: 'For God has made me forget all my toil and all my father's house.' And the name of the second he called Ephraim: 'For God has caused me to be fruitful in the land of my affliction.'" (Genesis 41:50-52 NKJV)

These verses comprise Joseph's amazing testimony. After his brothers, in hate and envy, had him sold into slavery, and after false accusations had landed him in prison, he was exalted to a position only second to the king of Egypt. He gave God the credit for such amazing reversals—from affliction to this awesome triumph. For seven years his enormous storage of grain fed all of Egypt and all surrounding countries in an era of severe famine! It was all of God's doing, elevating a slave boy to become a famous prince, saving thousands of people from starvation, including his own family from Canaan.

We can take a lesson from oyster-pearls. There are no pearls unless an irritant like a grain of sand, or an undeveloped egg, or a parasite gets lodged between the shell and the mantle. This stimulates secretion that envelopes the irritant. According to the *Americana Encyclopedia*, the Bahrein Island, in the Persian Gulf, is famous for its pearl industry. Boats go out 40 miles, and divers go 30 feet deep to the oyster beds. One week a boat gathered 35,000 pearl oysters, but netted only 21 pearls.

Here is our lesson. We encounter many trials and wonder why. Like Joseph acknowledged God's hand in weaving a beautiful pattern in his life, we too have to look back and admit that God has led us in amazing ways—NO BLESSINGS WITHOUT TRIALS!

HAVING GOD IS ENOUGH   November 25

"Then the Spirit of the Lord came on Jahaziel...'Listen, King Jehoshaphat and all who live in Judah...Do not be afraid or discouraged because of this vast army. For the battle is not yours, but God's... As they began to sing and praise, the Lord set ambushes against the men of Ammon and Moab and Mount Seir who were invading Judah, and they were defeated.'" (2 Chronicles 20:14-15, 22 NIV)

Three nations, Moab, Ammon and Mount Seir had not allowed Israel to enter when they possessed Canaan. Now they amassed a huge army to conquer Judah. King Jehoshaphat cried to God, and God so confused the vast army that they slew each other. It took three days for Jehoshaphat to collect the spoils among the dead bodies. This battle put "the fear of God" in surrounding countries, and God gave Jehoshaphat peace on all sides (2 Chron. 20:1-30).

In the days when this huge army was assembling, Jehoshaphat called his tribal leaders to Judah to fast and pray. They came from every town, keeping their eyes on the Lord (20:12). What a lesson for us! When we face drastic dilemmas, we need to join with our whole family, our whole church, our whole city, our whole state, our whole country—to ask God for his great deliverance. We are helpless and hopeless. We must admit that this battle is God's!

In every family, many of us are self-sufficient. But in the hour of crisis, we are driven to our knees. We remember well, when in desperation, we prayed for a sick family member, or an injured son or daughter. We had no hope, but God; and that was more than enough. We saw real miracles, when God so willed. And how we praised God, knowing no human could have done it.

COMING, JUST AS I AM   November 26

"When he came to his senses, he said, 'How many of my father's hired servants have food to spare, and here I am starving to death! I will set out and go back to my father and say to him: Father, I have sinned against heaven and against you. I am no longer worthy to be called your son; make me like one of you hired servants.'" (Luke 15:17-19 NIV)

Jesus told a parable of "the prodigal son" who rejected his father's authority, grabbed his inherited wealth, and went to a distant country. There he squandered his wealth in wild and wicked living. He ran out of money and found a job feeding hogs. Yes, in a pigpen, he came to himself! There he started his homeward trek.

While still far away, the father saw him. He ran to meet him! The son's clothes were ragged, his robe wreaked with a pigpen odor. Yet his father embraced him and kissed him! The son said, "Father, I have sinned." The father yelled, "Bring the best robe, ring and sandals. Make a feast. We must celebrate!"

One person told me: "I'll come to church when I get my life cleaned up." The Bible says, "Come as you are!" A fisherman, who was also a soul-winner once prayed, "God, I'll catch them, you clean them!" That works—my neighbor recently accepted Christ. God took the anger out of his heart and the alcohol out of his refrigerator. He comes to my house weekly for prayer and counsel!

In one of Billy Graham's LA Crusades, I advised the counselors. Thousands responded to the song: "Just as I am without one plea, but that thy blood was shed for me." Yes, friend, just pray: "God I have sinned, I accept Christ as my Savior!" Come as you are.

FOR SUCH A TIME   November 27

"For if you remain silent at this time, relief and deliverance for the Jews will come from another place, but you and your father's family will perish. And who knows but that you have come to royal position for such a time as this?" (Esther 4:14 NIV)

One of the most inspiring Bible stories is that of Esther becoming queen for King Xerxes in the land of Persia and Media. When Haman was elevated to be the top Noble, Mordecai, a known Jewish noble, refused to kneel before him. This so enraged Haman that he plotted to kill all Jews in the kingdom, not knowing that the queen was Jewish. Mordecai urged Esther to inform the King. Discreetly, she invited King Xerxes and Haman to several banquets. At the second, she disclosed her own nationality and Haman's plot. The king arose in anger, ordering Haman to be executed.

Few words in the book of Esther are as captivating as those spoken by Mordecai to Esther, "Yet who knows whether you have come to the kingdom for such a time as this" (4:14 NKJV)? These words show a dependence on God's providence.

My dear friends, just remember that each of us is here by God's design. God has a plan which we need to seek and joyfully fulfill. Already as a youth, I pondered the danger of coming to the end of my life and realizing that I had missed God's will. That is why two scriptures were my favorites (Ps. 37:4-5; Prov. 3:5-6). I did not want to waste my life. God has promised to lead us and show us His way and His will. Many times I asked God to open and close doors ahead of me. I am confident that God is still leading me today!

CONSCIENCE: FRIEND OR FOE?   November 28

"When the governor motioned for him to speak, Paul replied, 'I know that for a number of years you have been a judge over this nation; so I gladly make my defense...I strive always to keep my conscience clear before God and man.'" (Acts 24:10, 16 NIV)

Is it safe to follow your conscience? That is a valid question. A professor of mine in Bible College in an Ethics class, once tackled that subject. He said it depends on how you define conscience. If to you, conscience is that internal voice that always says—do right, do right, do right—then it is safe to follow. If, on the other hand, your definition includes that mental process of discerning right from wrong, then your conscience is not a safe guide. As a sinful human, your ethical standards can be warped, distorted and shaped by your own self-centered pursuits.

The Apostle Paul told Felix that he sought to keep a clear conscience, before God and man. That was after his conversion. In the early chapters of Acts, Paul named Saul, killed Christians with a clear conscience (7:58 and 8:1), living by the same Jewish theology that the Pharisees and Scribes did—who wanted Christ crucified. His encounter with Jesus, however, brought radical change. He quit killing and started saving people, viewing every man and woman as a potential saint in the church of Jesus Christ. Instead of fighting enemies, he started to evangelize them in the love of Jesus. He became the world's greatest pioneer missionary!

If we could ask Paul today, "How can we live with a clear conscience?" He might say, "Yield unreservedly to Jesus Christ. Obey His teachings in the Gospels. Live by the Epistles written by the Apostles. Interpret the Bible together with Christians in your church."

VICTORIOUSLY FORTIFIED   November 29

"These things happened to them as examples and were written down as warnings for us, on whom the culmination of the ages has come. So, if you think you are standing firm, be careful that you don't fall."
(1 Corinthians 10:11-12 NIV)

The failures of Israel are recorded so we would avoid their pitfalls. They lusted for evil things, even though God had lovingly protected and nurtured them (10:1-5). Some practiced pagan idolatry, some committed sexual immorality, some tested the Lord and grumbled. In each case God's punishment was severe (10:6-10). So Paul warns: "If you think you are standing firm, be careful that you do not fall."

In this context we are given a marvelous verse (10:13), which we can claim anyhow, anytime, anywhere. Here are two solid promises. First, God will not allow a temptation to hit us, stronger than we, as Christians, can bear. And secondly, with every temptation God will provide a route of escape! Our duty is to watch what we desire, what we see, what we hear, what we think, what we do and where we go. The key is—live close to God! He has promised to carry the load of each temptation, and to direct us to the escape routes.

I grew up on a Kansas farm, and the farm is still in my DNA. I can easily illustrate temptations! To catch mice in the granary, we set a mouse trap loaded with cheese. To catch a rat in the barn, we placed a chunk of meat on the trigger of a trap. While trapping for furs, I hung a dead chicken on a fence post, waiting for a skunk to step in my trap.

Friends, Satan allures us with many temptations, but God surrounds us with songs of deliverance (Psalm 32:7).

WATCH YOUR THOUGHTS   November 30

"Finally, brothers and sisters, whatever is true, whatever is noble, whatever is right, whatever is pure, whatever is lovely, whatever is admirable—if anything is excellent or praiseworthy—think about such things." (Philippians 4:8 NIV)

As the Apostle Paul writes to the Church of Philippi, he highlights the importance of thought control. He knows full well, that Satan tempts Christians, with thoughts of evil, of hatred and anger, of lust and sexual immorality, of covetousness and envy, of busyness and daily schedules—things that even crowd out prayer, Bible study, and Christian church activities.

After we moved away from Southern California, I recall that each New Years Day we would watch the Rose Parade from Pasadena on television. One year, at the same time, while my wife was setting together a 1000 piece puzzle, I constructed two artistic posters (22 inches by 40 inches). The first read. **"Life Tends to Follow the Furrow the Mind has Plowed."** The second read: **"the TRUE, the NOBLE, the RIGHT, the PURE, the LOVELY, the ADMIRABLE, the EXCELLENT, the PRAISEWORTHY—Think on These Things. Phil. 4:8."** This Bible witness is still hanging on the wall of my garage!

When you ponder the words of our text, here is a high and holy standard, things that please our Heavenly Father (the true, the right, the pure). Items opposite to this are clearly sinful. The other words that should characterize our mental processes, reflect a lofty wholesomeness (the noble, the lovely, the admirable, the excellent, the praiseworthy). These qualities inspire us to live extraordinary lives—which no one can do in human strength. This requires supernatural strength, namely the filling of the Holy Spirit. Friends, please join me in praying for God's special enablement. We need to live lives that honor God and lives that bless others!

FACING FIERY FURNACES   December 1

"Shadrach, Meshach and Abednego replied to him, 'King Nebuchad-nezzar, we do not need to defend ourselves before you in this matter. If we are thrown into the blazing furnace, the God we serve is able to deliver us from it, and he will deliver us from your Majesty's hand. But even if he does not, we want you to know, Your Majesty, that we will not serve your gods or worship the image of gold you have set up.'" (Daniel 3:16-18 NIV)

These remarkable courageous Hebrew young men, defied the king of Babylon, and refused to fall down and worship the ninety feet high image erected on the plain of Dura (3:1). This made Nebuchadnezzar furious with rage (3:13). He ordered the three men bound and thrown into the fiery furnace (3:23). Then in shock and amazement he leaped to his feet: "Look! I see four men walking around in the fire, unbound and unharmed, and the fourth looks like a son of the gods" (3:25). Promptly the king asked the men to come out. What a miracle! Their bodies were not harmed, their hair not singed, their robes not scorched, and no smell of fire on them (3:27). The king gave high credit to the God of the Hebrews, promoting Shadrach, Meshach and Abednego in the province of Babylon (3:30).

This is one of the most striking miracles recorded in the Old Testament! The three Hebrew men told the king that their God was able to save them from the fire, assuming it was God's will. They were submissive. They did not coerce God! However, for certain, they promised God's deliverance from the king's hand, whatever that meant. For you and me today, we too need to expect great things from God. But prayer must always grow out of a submissive attitude.

THE NARROW ROAD — December 2

"Enter through the narrow gate. For wide is the gate and broad is the road that leads to destruction, and many enter through it. But small is the gate and narrow the road that leads to life, and only a few find it." (Matthew 7:13-14 NIV)

Jesus Christ our Lord contrasted the broad way with the narrow way. He had the perspective of history—thinking of the thousands who had already lived and thinking of the millions yet to come—making a profound observation. He says "many" are on the broad road, and "few" on the narrow road. The obvious conclusion is that hell, will sadly, have a larger population than heaven.

The problem is that few people find the narrow gate that leads to life! Anne Graham Lotz, the daughter of Billy Graham, once appeared on a radio talk show. She was asked this penetrating question: "Are you one of those who believe that Jesus is exclusively the only way to heaven? You know how mad that makes people these days!" Anne gave a brilliant response: "Jesus is not exclusive. He died so that anyone could come to him for salvation."

So today you and I, the church of Jesus Christ, stand on the road of life, at the narrow gate, prayerfully, passionately, persistently inviting people to join us on the narrow road to heaven. Yet it's a narrow gate, a narrow way, and many refuse to kneel humbly to acknowledge that they are indeed needy lost sinners. They can think of many others who are worse sinners than they! The Bible is clear: "All have sinned and come short of the glory of God" (Romans 3:23). Jesus Christ died for all. His invitation is inclusive: "Whosoever will may come!" My friend, are you on Christ's narrow way to heaven?

HANDLE HATRED CAREFULLY   December 3

"Let those who love the Lord hate evil, for he guards the lives of his faithful ones and delivers them from the hand of the wicked. Light shines on the righteous and joy on the upright in heart." (Psalm 97:10-11 NIV)

We as Christians must handle hatred with great care. The 19th Century English writer, Olive Moore, put it this way: "Hatred is a passion requiring one hundred times the energy of love. Keep it for a cause, not an individual. Keep it for intolerance, injustice, stupidity. For hatred is the strength of the sensitive. Its power and its greatness depend on the selflessness of its use."

Our tendency is to squander our hatred on insignificant hurts and differences. Hostile letters written to the editor frequently elevate trivia to the level of significance, simply due to the pathology of our ill-directed hatred. Church splits and divisions happen when hatred is directed at people, rather than at the issues that confront the average church. Such divisions are hazardous to any church because such hatred is rooted in basic personal selfishness—hating persons rather than issues. Yes my friends, the matter of hating evil is legitimate, but must be handled with extreme care.

Too many Christians have not learned the art of forgiveness. That is a colossal mistake. When we differ on issues, we can still love each other. When saints jointly pray, seeking God's will, "light is shed on the righteous" and when finally harmony is achieved, great joy is experienced. With growth and maturity, Christians learn how to hate evil, and still love God and man. It must be admitted that in our day, too many church members compromise with evil and don't hate the things God hates. God have mercy on us and help us!

HANDLING GOD'S WORD December 4

"Keep reminding God's people of these things. Warn them before God against quarreling about words; it is of no value, and only ruins those who listen. Do your best to present yourself to God as one approved, a worker who does not need to be ashamed and who correctly handles the word of truth." (2 Timothy 2:14-15 NIV)

Here is a challenge for all who come to the Bible to learn God's truth. There is such a temptation for each of us to rush to the Bible to bolster our own opinions. But wait—this text has several prerequisites for those who interpret the Scriptures. First, present yourself to God as an honest unashamed student, and secondly, as one who will handle the truth of the Bible correctly.

I remember my high school days in Kansas. I attended Berean Academy. Our Principal was a missionary. One day a complex issue came up, and his wife asked him, "Waldo, what do we believe on that?" We smile. But really, we're all in that same predicament. We are all encouraged to read our Bibles. Yet there are some difficult passages we don't understand. So, what do we do? We go to a pastor, a teacher, or a friend for help. I, myself, when I come to a difficult verse, look at the 2,000 books surrounding my desk and grab five or six to see what these respected scholars say on this subject.

Our scripture warns us about quarreling over words. It has no value. But some critics argue that Bible reading is worthless, since there are hundreds of possible interpretations. I disagree! When we pray for wisdom, and read the Gospels and Epistles with an open mind, the core message is crystal clear: God loves you, Christ died for you, and believing in him gives you eternal life!

A THANKSGIVING THOUGHT   December 5

"Oh, give thanks to the Lord, for He is good! For His mercy endures forever....Oh, that men would give thanks to the Lord for His goodness, and for His wonderful works to the children of men! For He satisfies the longing soul, and fills the hungry soul with goodness." (*Psalm 107:1, 8-9 NKJV*)

I am writing this devotional in the middle of October. This is a beautiful autumn day in Bakersfield. Our front and back lawns have been seeded with winter rye grass. Each day we're gently watering the seed. God has blessed us this year with abundant fruit in our back yard! First came a bumper crop of apricots. Next our new Early Elbertas yielded well. Our tomato plants produced for months. In September our late Elberta tree gave us peaches weighing one pound a piece. Today we're still picking peaches from that tree—smaller fruit, but sweet ripe and delicious! As the early Pilgrims gave thanks to God, so we too, praise God for His blessings. I remember memorizing (Ps. 107:8 KJV): "Oh that men would praise the Lord for His goodness...!"

Beyond our material blessings, God promises spiritual blessings: He "fills the hungry soul with goodness." This is even greater! My wife and I experience good health. When asked "How are you?" I often reply, "I'm still taking nourishment." Seriously, I consider health as a gift from God. I am 80, and this summer my church voted me in as Pastor of Senior Care. I feel greatly honored. As long as the Lord gives strength, I want to serve Him and His church—until that day when others need to serve me. For us as Christians, our spiritual blessings in Christ are countless. My wife and I praise God for His goodness!

THE POWER OF KINDNESS   December 6

"But in all things we commend ourselves as ministers of God: in much patience, in tribulations, in needs, in distresses…by purity, by knowledge, by long-suffering, by kindness, by the Holy Spirit, by sincere love…" (2 Corinthians 6:4, 6 NKJV)

The Apostle Paul commended himself to the saints at Corinth by kindness which was bathed in genuine love, and motivated by the Holy Spirit. In a long list of aspirations, he highlighted the quality of kindness in his dealings with the Corinthian church. What a grand idea to emulate.

I think it was Henry G. Bosch who told a story of the power of kindness. The US President, William McKinley, needed to appoint an ambassador to a certain foreign country. Two men appeared equally qualified. On careful scrutiny, the President finally concluded that one man was very self-centered, while the other was outstandingly kind. That influenced his decision. Here is the true story. Years earlier, while Mr. Mckinley was a congressman, he remembers boarding a street car during the rush hour. He took the last seat. Soon an old washer woman entered, carrying a heavy basket. Not finding a seat, she stood in the aisle. Sitting near her, was one of the two men the President was now considering for the Ambassador job. He moved his newspaper so not to see her. William Mckinley, on the other hand, arose and went to the old lady. He lifted her basket, and ushered her to his vacated seat! What this potential candidate, years later, never realized was that his unkind behavior to that old washer woman, had tipped the scales in the mind of President Mckinley—who gave the honorable Ambassador position to the other man.

My friends, being known as a person of kindness, honors God, and blesses others!

COASTING TO HEAVEN?   December 7

"The righteous will flourish like a palm tree, they will grow like a cedar of Lebanon; planted in the house of the Lord, they will flourish in the courts of our God. They will still bear fruit in old age, they will stay fresh and green, proclaiming, 'The Lord is upright; he is my rock, and there is no wickedness in him.'" (Psalm 92:12-15 NIV)

Where does it say in the Bible that we should retire at age 55 or 65? Nowhere! While many folks get impatient during their regular working years—anxious to retire, and take it easy—their lives may still offer 35 years of productive living. Both of my parents lived to be 94. My father at age 88 rented out most of his Kansas farm land, but still farmed one 80 himself. My mother had one leg amputated at the knee at age 90, and still lived four more happy fruitful years. We praise God that both were blessed with clear minds, almost to the end.

I read of a man named John Kelly who ran 58 Boston Marathons, the last one in 1992 at age 84. He lived to be 96. Keeping active is important. All too many reach middle age and put their mind and body in neutral. Careful eating, proper active exercise, and available medical supervision, keeps most of us energized in body, mind and spirit.

The psalmist suggests that the righteous can flourish like a palm tree and bear fruit in old age (92:14). What a challenge for a Christian! As long as health permits, we can be about: helping, visiting, blessing and serving others. Many who are bedridden are still capable of a phone-ministry and especially a prayer-ministry. It has been wisely said—to stay youthful, stay useful.

BECOMING CHRIST'S MODEL   December 8

"You became imitators of us and of the Lord; for you welcomed the message in the midst of servere suffering with the joy given by the Holy Spirit. And so you became a model to all the believers in Macedonia and Achaia." (1 Thessalonians 1:6-7 NIV)

The Christians at Thessalonica began imitating Paul, and his helpers Silas and Timothy. And not only that—they imitated the Lord Jesus (1:6). Despite heavy suffering, they had received the gospel message with special joy given by the Holy Spirit! In turn they also became models for all the believers in the surrounding region. That is so typical—Christians on fire for Christ always become a pattern for others to follow!

We once visited a church in the Chicago area where Lee Strobel was on the staff. In 1979, his wife Leslie Strobel had become a Christian. She modeled her faith in such a powerful and winsome way that her atheistic husband began a two year research while being a noted journalist at the Chicago Tribune. After his intense study, Lee became convinced in the truth of Christianity, and was converted. He wrote a book entitled *The Case for Christ* wherein he defended the Biblical philosophy modeled by his wife. The change in his life also influenced their five year old daughter, who said, "Mommy, I want God to do for me what he's done for Daddy." So Leslie's faith created a ripple effect that changed the whole family!

In one of my churches, I had a parishioner who effectively used his Gift of Evangelism. However, his favorite advice to converts was: "Don't watch my life, I'm fallible. Keep eyes on Jesus." Yes, a bit of truth. But Paul would say, "Fasten your eyes on Jesus, on Silas, Timothy and me. Our examples are powerful!"

THE SHOCKPROOF CHRISTIAN   December 9

"But He (God) knows the way that I take; when He has tested me, I shall come forth as gold." (Job 23:10 NKJV)

Some 240 years ago America was struggling under the domination of Great Britain. The Revolutionary War seemed to fade after 15 years, and on July 4, 1776, fifty-six noble men signed the Declaration of Independence. The first half of the document explains that they wanted to be free from the King of England, free from oppression. People everywhere crave political freedom. Secondly, humans yearn for spiritual freedom. Worldwide, people sense guilt and do drastic things to appease God, whom they view as angry and vicious. But the Gospel of Jesus offers love, peace, and forgiveness.

A third kind of freedom is unavailable—freedom from future uncertainty. How we long to know the future: sickness or health, death or life, war or storms. To avoid worry, some persons escape into alcohol and drugs, or even sports and business. But Christians need never fear!

When I graduated from high school, I received a wristwatch: 17-jewel, Swiss movement, shockproof, waterproof. One day it failed. Mother took it to the jeweler who said, "Your son must have waved the girls too much!" Her retort: "I thought the watch was shockproof." The patriarch Job was shockproof: "[God] knows the way I take; when He has tested me, I shall come forth as gold" (23:10).

> One ship sails east, another sails west with
> the very same wind that blows
> 'Tis the set of the sails and not the gales
> that tells them the way to go.
> Like the winds of the sea are the waves of
> faith, as we voyage along through life.
> 'Tis the set of the soul that decides it's goal;
> and not the calm or the strife.
> (source unknown)

VERIFIED BY ARCHEOLOGY   December 10

"The Lord is good, a refuge in times of trouble. He cares for those who trust in him, but with an overwhelming flood he will make an end of Nineveh; He will pursue his foes into the realm of darkness." (Nahum 1:7-8 NIV)

The prophet Nahum foretold the destruction of the huge Assyrian city, Nineveh. King Ashurbanipal, died in 626 BC and within 14 years his vast empire fell to the Medes and Chaldeans. Although this Assyrian culture was advanced, the Jewish prophets viewed it as God-defying, ruthless and inhumane. It lacked the love of God and righteousness. And Nahum was gleeful that this brutal regime, judged by the wrath of God, would be toppled never to rise again.

In terms of archeological digs, from 1820 to 1945, the city of Nineveh was the most important location. Scholar R. K. Harrison writes: "The writer has yet to become acquainted with any single archeological find which categorically disproves the testimony of the Old Testament..." It is truly comforting that the findings of archeology have time and again verified our Bible!

Probably the most famous archeological discovery of all times has been the Dead Sea Scrolls found in the Judean wilderness, near Jericho, in the late 1940's. There two tribesmen, herding sheep and goats, found some scrolls in the Qumran Caves. Other nearby caves held more manuscripts of the Qumran Community. By 1948 there were two collections, one contained a complete copy of the book of Isaiah plus a commentary on Habakkuk. The American scholar, W. F. Albright, after examining these scrolls, called it the "greatest archeological discovery ever!" In 1954 the Hebrew University of Jerusalem paid a price of $250,000 for the Dead Sea Scrolls. To put it simply, archeology has played a big role in supporting the truthfulness of the Old Testament.

CROSSING THE CHASM   December 11

"This righteousness is given through faith in Jesus Christ to all who believe. There is no difference between Jew and Gentile, for all have sinned and fall short of the glory of the God, and all are justified freely by his grace through the redemption that came by Christ Jesus." (Romans 3:22-24 NIV)

The chasm between the perfect holiness, the glory of God, and the sinful selfishness of depraved man is enormous. If any human imagines that he or she can bridge that gap by some kind of human effort, they are extremely misguided.

When I was pastor of a parish in Kansas in the decade of the seventies, news flooded radio, television and newspapers that Evel Knievel, on September 8, 1974, would attempt a dangerous daredevil stunt! He was famous for jumping over a long line of cars with his motorcycle, but this time he decided to jump across the Snake River Canyon in Idaho with thousands of spectators watching. The day came. He revved up his motorcycle to an excessive speed and flew over the canyon, only to begin dropping, and his parachute landed him safely in the canyon below. He failed to get across!

Equally, true it is, many a man imagines that he can gain the favor of God by doing some good deeds—that he can cancel all his sins by proper behavior. But our good never cancels out our bad. In our courts, when a law-breaker stands before the judge, he is never asked, "What good deeds have you done in the past?" Rather, he is asked whether he is guilty of this one violation. This chasm between God and man can only be bridged by Jesus Christ. Our scripture states, we are "justified freely by his grace through the redemption that came by Christ Jesus." My friend, are you trusting Jesus Christ?

DEALING WITH DEAFNESS   December 12

"Jesus replied, 'Go back and report to John what you hear and see: The blind receive sight, the lame walk, those who have leprosy are cleansed, the deaf hear, the dead are raised, and the good news is preached to the poor.'" (Matt. 11:4-5 NIV)

Jesus Christ, our Lord, had a special ministry to the blind, the lame, the sick, the deaf, and the dumb. His compassion for the handicapped was beautifully highlighted in the gospels. His pattern of care for the disabled merits emulation.

We attend the Laurelglen Bible Church of Bakersfield, CA and are proud to report that we are one of only a half dozen churches in the USA that has a full-time salaried deaf pastor. Pastor Jeff Jackson, deaf himself, shepherds a flock of 100 deaf folks at our church. In addition, he leads a Bible Study for some 60 deaf inmates at a nearby prison. He was recently honored when Evangelism Explosion of Florida, asked him to create a DVD, for national use, on how to reach the deaf for Christ! He is compassionate, winsome and dynamic in his preaching ministry.

About a decade or two ago, Joni Eareckson Tada, conducted a seminar in the Midwest on how to teach and reach people with disabilities. Jeff Jackson was in attendance. By that time he had mastered lip reading and related techniques. Also in attendance was a lady from our church, DeAnn, Mrs. Michael Sampley, who taught "Signing" at our local college. She invited Jackson to come to Bakersfield to learn "Signing." He came and today is our Pastor for the Deaf. Once a year he Sign Preaches to our larger congregation and a person like DeAnn Sampley interprets his enthusiastic gestures. What a marvelous ministry to the 5,000 deaf people of Kern County—the overlooked segment of our society!

346

ENCOURAGING EACH OTHER December 13

"Now about your love for one another we do not need to write to you, for you yourselves have been taught by God to love each other. And in fact, you do love all of God's family throughout Macedonia. Yet we urge you, brothers and sisters, to do so more and more." (1 Thessalonians 4:9-10 NIV)

As Paul wrote his first letter to his new converts at Thessalonica, he urges them to increase the intensity of their love. Already in chapter three he stated: "May the Lord make your love increase and overflow for each other and for everyone else, just as ours does for you" (3:12). Paul knew that believers who gripe, groan and gossip do not bless others.

This admonition to love more and more is such a warm word of advice. When I think back over my forty years of pastoral work, I can think of various people whose life and service exuded a big doze of love. In one case the church custodian was extremely kind and helpful. He never complained. He worked hard to meet everyone's needs—setting up tables, setting up classroom chairs, and doing all of his cleaning chores with a smile. By contrast in another church the custodian was always grumbling. He was known to flick lights, off and on, to hurry people's exit. A kind person always reaps admiration and appreciation!

In my first church, a 50 year old lady accepted Christ and requested Believer's Baptism. She came from a nearby church which had not taught the joy of the Gospel. Immediately she said, "I must make up for lost time!" She volunteered to sponsor our Junior High group. Her Christian love shone more and more as she sacrificed to serve our youth.

FACING OUR MORTALITY   December 14

"Just as people are destined to die once, and after that to face judgment, so Christ was sacrificed once to take away the sins of many; and he will appear a second time, not to bear sin, but to bring salvation to those who are waiting for him." (Hebrews 9:27-28 NIV)

Each of us as humans has to face his mortality. Many wise people have stated that we are better prepared to live, if we are prepared to die. I remember facing the thought of death when I was eleven, attending my grandfather's funeral on the prairies of Kansas. His pre-selected text for that event was Hebrews 9:27.

My parents both reached the age of 94. They had 8 children. The first to die was my sister Frieda, the sixth child, a retired school teacher at Leavenworth, Kansas. She was a 17-year cancer survivor who died at age 70 of Acute Leukemia with only 60 days to plan her passing—and this she did with meticulous care. Her service was held at the Covenant Church of Lenexa, where she was very active.

My next sister to die, was Martha, age 81, the second child, dying in 2010. Her service was in our home church, Emmaus Mennonite of Whitewater, Kansas. Martha had been a missionary nurse in Ethiopia and the Sudan. She was sent by Wichita doctors to the KU Medical Center to replace two heart valves, but she died of a stroke.

Today my sister Justina, the seventh child, age 72, living in Leavenworth, told me she has Stage four bone cancer and gets radiation daily at KU Medical Center. How do we cope? Honestly, when we live to 80, or even 70, we can be very thankful for those years! As Christians, we're in God's hand. We must be ready to die.

EXPRESS YOUR FEELINGS   December 15

"Yes, my soul, find rest in God; my hope comes from him. Truly he is my rock and my salvation; he is my fortress, I will not be shaken... Trust in him at all times, you people; pour out your hearts to him, for God is our refuge." (Psalm 62:5-8 NIV)

One of my favorite verses in the Psalms is 62:8. When I sign my name in the guest book at a memorial service, I normally add this Bible reference. It urges us always to trust God, and to express to him our deepest inner feelings. This seems so appropriate at times when grief floods our hearts. God is our refuge and he alone can comfort us and give us the peace and tranquility we need.

Pouring out our hearts to God is an interesting concept. We are aware of the advice often given to us that our heavy worries need be shared with a friend, a pastor or a psychologist. This can truly be helpful. However, we seldom hear about this unique spiritual method of how to handle our deepest concerns, namely prayer—pouring out our heart feelings directly to God! This can be very therapeutic. It can give us great peace, security and release.

My friends, have you tried this method of dealing with unsolved burdens? It works! When I was pastor of a church in Southern California, I was on a Mission Committee with pastors from Oregon and Washington. We started a new church in Phoenix, but were extremely frustrated the first year by problem after problem. There was utter disunity. So we each covenanted to besiege God daily for help. God marvelously answered. He led us to hire a couple from Montana who stabilized the work, and stayed ten years to build a solid church!

THE BEE STING LESSON   December 16

"When the perishable has been clothed with the imperishable, and the mortal with immortality, then the saying that is written will come true: 'Death has been swallowed up in victory. Where, O death, is your victory? Where, O death, is your sting?' The sting of death is sin, and the power of sin is the law. But thanks be to God! He gives us the victory through our Lord Jesus Christ." (1 Corinthians 15:54-56 NIV)

My dad maintained several bee hives to provide honey for our meals. He had a spinning machine that extracted the honey out of the honeycomb with centrifugal force. When he harvested the honey, he protected himself by wearing a heavy jacket and gloves. He wore a sting-proof hood to protect his face. He tranquilized the bees with a gadget that puffed smoke. Several times annually he would open the beehives—to feed the bees or to retrieve the honeycombs.

A honeybee stung me on the eyelid. It began to swell. My mother showed me that the stinger was in my skin, torn out of the bee, never to sting again. I recovered after several days.

Here is a powerful spiritual lesson. The sting of death is nullified by Christ's death on the cross. He died for our sins and set us free! Christ's death gave us the victory over sin, hell and the grave. We need never fear. When Christians die, Christ takes them by the hand and leads them into glory. He has removed the sting of death, rising victoriously over it. My friend, do you have the assurance of salvation? Have you invited Jesus Christ to be your Lord and Savior? Have you accepted God's free gift of eternal life? Please do so!

OTHERS DEPEND ON US   December 17

"He took Peter and the two sons of Zebedee along with him, and he began to be sorrowful and troubled. Then he said to them, 'My soul is overwhelmed with sorrow to the point of death. Stay here and keep watch with me'…Then he returned to his disciples and found them sleeping. 'Couldn't you men keep watch with me for one hour?' he asked Peter. 'Watch and pray so you will not fall into temptation. The spirit is willing, but the flesh is weak.'" (Matthew 26:37-38, 40-41 NIV)

At Gethsemane Jesus revealed his extreme stress and asked his disciples to pray with him. Three times he came back to find them asleep. Jesus struggled alone with no assistance from his followers. They utterly failed him!

When it came to parenting, as we raised our three sons, we often discussed the importance of taking an interest in their activities—baseball games, basketball tournaments, cross-country competition, or their track events. We tried to be there, to watch, to pray and to support. The boys would ask. "Did you see my home run? Did you see my ten free throws? Did you see me overtake Jimmy in the mile run?" They expected us to be in the spectator stand! Our encouraging helpfulness was always important to them.

Even more important were those moments of stress? Did we help our child with his math lessons, when his test score came back low? Did we intervene when some bully threatened our sons? Did we keep our promise about fishing or Disneyland? Were we there when it counted? Could we spare one hour, or two?

Bottom line—do we give time to God? Can't we devote 20-30 minutes daily for Family Prayer and Bible Reading? Will we utterly fail our Lord as the disciples did?

MEANING OF CHRISTMAS December 18

"All this took place to fulfill what the Lord had said through the prophet: The virgin will conceive and give birth to a son, and they will call him Immanuel—which means, 'God with us.'" (Matthew 1:22-23 NIV)

Here is a story, told in my hearing, by Robert H. Schuller at a pastor's gathering. One longtime member at his church, Grandma Dorothy, age 72, looking young and beautiful, usually sat directly in front of the pulpit, and seldom missed. Thirty-two years earlier her son went through a bitter divorce, and his wife took their two little girls and moved out of state. So Grandma Dorothy never learned to know her granddaughters. She had heard they were alive, and one worked for Flying Tiger Airlines.

Recently, one Sunday Dorothy came to church early and heard two ladies behind her. One said she had been in Hong Kong and stopped at the Flying Tiger office. Grandma Dorothy whirled around, "I heard that my granddaughter works for Flying Tiger, her name is either Timmy or Marie." "I have a sister Timmy, and I'm Marie." Dorothy jumped up, "I'm your Grandma!" They hugged and kissed. "Marie, what are you doing at my church?" "Oh Grandma, a year ago I was coming apart. A psychiatrist said, you need a religious experience. How could I, I was an atheist? Then, on TV, I heard Schuller invite us to a Christmas Eve service. I came. He urged us to kneel at the altar and accept Jesus Christ as Savior. I went and Christ wonderfully came into my life. Last March I attended membership classes and was baptized!" Today Grandma and Marie sit together at worship. Friends, there is the essence of Christmas—Christ in our lives! Have you opened your heart to Jesus Christ?

HANDEL'S DELIGHTFUL "MESSIAH"   December 19

*"You who bring good news to Zion, go up on a high mountain...
say to the towns of Judah, 'Here is your God'" (Isaiah 40:9 NIV).
"But the angel said to them, 'Do not be afraid. I bring you good
news that will cause great joy for all the people! Today in the town of
David a Savior has been born to you; he is the Messiah the Lord.'"
(Luke 2:10-11 NIV)*

The birth of Christ has inspired earth's most beautiful music!
Handel's "Messiah" weaves together scriptures from Isaiah and
Luke. In 1741 George Frederich Handel was invited by the
Duke of Devonshire to perform in Dublin. For that occasion
he wrote the magnificent oratorio, "The Messiah." At age 56,
he wrote that in the space of two weeks. After the concert, the
Faulkner's Journal (April 17, 1742) wrote, "On Tuesday last,
Mr. Handel's Sacred Grand Oratorio, the Messiah was performed...the best judges allowed it to be the most finished
piece of musick. Words are wanting to express the exquisite
delight it afforded to the admiring crowded audience."

One year later it was performed in London. When the glorious strains of the Hallelujah Chorus burst upon the assembly,
King George II, deeply moved, spontaneously rose to his feet,
and the whole court with him. Ever since, audiences always
rise! Handel is buried at Westminster Abbey. Above his grave is
a statue of the great composer writing "The Messiah," working
on the passage, "I Know That My Redeemer Liveth."

George Frederich Handel, the brilliant musician, has
inspired Christians for two and a half centuries. Any of us who
have sung through "The Messiah" will, over and over again
hum those melodic tunes! They bring praise to our God, and
blessings to ours souls. Of all religions, only Christianity has
produced such beautiful marvelous music!

TIDINGS OF GREAT JOY   December 20

"Suddenly a great company of the heavenly host appeared with the angel, praising God and saying, 'Glory to God in the highest, and on earth peace to those on whom his favor rests.' When the angels had left them and gone into heaven, the shepherds said to one another, 'Let us go to Bethlehem and see this thing that has happened, which the Lord has told us about.'" (Luke 2:13-15 NIV)

If we took to the street with a microphone, asking the question, "Where is the joy and glory of Christmas? What excites you?" Some might say, **"IT'S THE GLITTER."** Sparkling tinsel. Twinkling stars. Flashing lights. Rotating colors. Decorated houses—all aglow with Christmas. Snow glistening on the trees. Jingle-bell music in the stores. Others will say, **"IT'S THE GIFT GIVING."** A generous Christmas spirit. People more considerate. Deeds of unselfishness. Salvation Army bell-ringers reminding us of needy people. Still others will say, **"IT'S GOOD EATING."** Christmas dinners excite us. Grandma's table heaped high with scrumptious food—that's celebrating! What would you say?

Let's be realistic: Does glitter comfort aching hearts? Doesn't gift giving leave many disappointed? Doesn't good eating lead to overindulgence? The shepherds obeyed the angels and found the glory of Christmas, and left telling everyone!

When we lived in Southern California, my brother-in-law, Joe Stahl, a South Dakota teacher and coach, moved his family to live near us. He attended our church, and taught Elementary Schools in Baldwin Park for 25 years. In the 60's religion in schools was a big issue. Yet Joe had a clever way of teaching the true meaning of Christmas. Students wrote essays, "What Christmas means to me?" He took them home and selected the best Christ-centered essays. At school he asked certain pupils to read their essays to the whole class!

NATIVITY EVENTS VERIFIED   December 21

"This is how the birth of Jesus the Messiah came about: His mother Mary was pledged to be married to Joseph, but before they came together, she was found to be pregnant through the Holy Spirit… An angel of the Lord appeared to him [Joseph] in a dream and said, 'Joseph, son of David, do not be afraid to take Mary home as your wife'…When Joseph woke up, he did what the angel of the Lord had commanded him and took Mary home as his wife." (Matthew 1:18, 20, 24 NIV)

All we know about the Nativity, the birth of Jesus, comes from the authentic historical reliable accounts in four chapters of the Gospels, two in Matthew and two in Luke. Matthew and Luke record six things in common. 1) Jesus, born in Bethlehem; 2) Jesus, born of the Virgin Mary; 3) Mary betrothed to Joseph; 4) The conception of Jesus by the Holy Spirit supernaturally announced; 5) the Greek word "Christos" is equivalent to the Hebrew word Messiah; and 6) The child is destined to be the Savior of the world.

Matthew uniquely adds three items. 1) Details of Joseph to whom Mary is betrothed; 2) Story of the Magi and the Guiding Star; and 3) King Herod's attempt to kill the Christ Child.

Luke distinctly fills in four other details. 1) Angel Gabriel's annunciation to Mary; 2) Mary and Joseph forced to go to Bethlehem due to a Roman Census; 3) The inn was full, Christ was laid in a manger; and 4) Angelic hosts appear to the Shepherds.

The precise date of Christ's birth is not known. The earliest reference to December 25 as the date for the Nativity occurs in the Philocalian calendar (A.D.336). Regarding the writing of all New Testament books, Cambridge scholar, J.A.T. Robinson argues that all must be dated before A.D. 70.

JOSEPH: COMPASSIONATE MAN   December 22

"But after he had considered this, an angel of the Lord appeared to him in a dream and said, 'Joseph son of David, do not be afraid to take Mary home as your wife, because what is conceived in her is from the Holy Spirit. She will give birth to a son, and you are to give him the name Jesus, because he will save his people from their sins.'" (Matthew 1:20-21 NIV)

Here is the fascinating story of the young couple named Joseph and Mary. Age wise, some have suggested that Joseph may have been 19, and Mary about 15. As was the custom in Jewish culture, Joseph was betrothed to Mary. This was the preliminary step to marriage. It involved a formal exchange of consent before witnesses, and constituted a legally ratified marriage. From this point the couple was regarded as husband and wife, and the relationship could only be broken by a certificate of divorce. Yet the bride normally continued living in her family home for another year, until the groom takes her to his family home and they start living together as husband and wife.

Apparently, Mary was still living with her family, when Joseph discovered her pregnancy. He was shocked. He knew it was not his child, and suspected Mary of unfaithfulness. Since he was an upright just man, living by Jewish law, he thought of divorcing Mary. But because of his love for Mary, he chose not to embarrass her publicly. At that point God intervened. An angel, in a dream, revealed to Joseph that this was a virgin birth, an act of God—and the child must be named Jesus, "he will save his people from their sins." Israel expected political deliverance, but Jesus was destined to bring spiritual deliverance, for everyone (John 3:16).

MARY: HONORED WOMAN   December 23

"But the angel said to her, 'Do not be afraid, Mary, you have found favor with God. You will conceive and give birth to a son, and you are to call him Jesus. He will be great and will be called the Son of the Most High. The Lord God will give him the throne of his father David, and he will reign over Jacob's descendants forever; his kingdom will never end.'" (Luke 1:30-33 NIV)

After the angel Gabriel had visited Mary in Nazareth of Galilee, and told her of her upcoming pregnancy through the Holy Spirit, Mary hurried to her relative, Elisabeth, in the hill country of Judea. There she spent three months. Elisabeth offered great comfort, since she also was expecting. In Elisabeth's presence, Mary uttered a hymn of praise, a beautiful lyrical poem, known as the "Magnificat" (Luke 1:46-56).

The Roman Emperor Caesar Augustus, who reigned 44 years (30 B.C. to A.D. 14) decreed that a census for taxation be taken. While women were also taxed, only the men were required to go. Joseph chose to take Mary along on the 90 mile journey from Nazareth to Bethlehem, we believe, for several reasons. 1) Her child birth was near. Joseph did not want her to suffer insults from people who knew her marriage to Joseph was less than nine months, and 2) They probably knew that the Messiah was to come from Bethlehem (Micah 5:2).

When Joseph and Mary reached Bethlehem, all inns were full. Baby Jesus was born in a stable, cradled in a manger. He left Heaven's beauty to experience this cruel sin cursed earth, so that all who believe in him, can enjoy the marvel of Christ's heaven! Has Christ saved you from your sins? Friends, accept him today!

CHRISTMAS: FEAR NOT   December 24

"And there were shepherds living out in the fields nearby, keeping watch over their flocks at night. An angel of the Lord appeared to them, and the glory of the Lord shone around them, and they were terrified. But the angel said to them, 'Do not be afraid. I bring you good news that will cause great joy for all the people. Today in the town of David a Savior has been born to you; he is the Messiah the Lord.'" (Luke 2:8-11 NIV)

Few words are more common in our language than fear. Being only one syllable, it extends to every part of life. We have adapted some thoughts from the writings of Psychologist Eric Burn.

Fear at birth – Babies enter life terrified. They gasp for their first breath. They feel helpless. They soon learn pain, hunger, noise and discomfort. Life opens with fear.

Fear at school – For Children, the first day at school is a fearful adventure. They fear nonacceptance from peers, and disapproval from teachers—and fear failure.

Fear as teens – Youth are afraid of ridicule. Their lives are loaded with fears. They are afraid of being called a square, or being different. They're afraid of rejection.

Fear as newlyweds – Couples fear unemployment, high home interest rates and unpaid bills. They fear childlessness, or having an abnormal child. Illness is feared.

Fear of middle age – Couples fear recession, the dissipation of savings. They fear restrictive health factors through arthritis, heart attacks, cancer or strokes.

Fear of Old Age – Retired couples fear rising living costs, leaving jobs and vacating homes. They fear widowhood and loneliness. In final years they fear loss of sight, hearing and memory. They fear being a burden to others!

Christianity removes this fear. Through Jesus, sins are forgiven. Through the love of God, eternal acceptance is found in heaven (John 3:16)!

THE JOY OF CHRISTMAS   December 25

"How beautiful on the mountains are the feet of those who bring good news, who proclaim peace, who bring good tidings, who proclaim salvation, who say to Zion, 'Your God reigns!' Listen! Your watchmen lift up their voices; together they shout for joy." (Isaiah 52:7-8 NIV)

On the very day Christ was born, the angel promised the shepherds great joy (Luke 2:10). On the first day of Christ's ministry he read out of Isaiah 61:1-3 promising good news, favor and comfort (Luke 4:16-19). The salvation of Christ Jesus brings the ultimate joy, now and eternally.

Dr. A. W. Tozer once asserted—in conversion we receive acquittal, acceptance, and sonship. At Christ's Second Coming we're promised perfection, glorification, and eternal joy. In between—in the here and now—Christ's atonement guarantees deliverance, victory over sin, fruitfulness, spiritual growth, and the filling of the Holy Spirit. **BUT, these are ours only if we ask for them, pursue them and sincerely go after them!**

One Christmas, a little girl stood at a gift shop counter. She clutched the hand of a poorly dressed woman. Her eyes were riveted on a beautiful doll. Mother asked, "Can my daughter just hold that doll?" The clerk handed the doll across the counter. The girl gazed with wonder at the doll in her arms. Finally mother said, "Give the doll back." The clerk looked at a man standing nearby. He nodded. She placed the doll in a box and tied a ribbon. "Here little girl, the doll is yours—Merry Christmas!" Mother and daughter left overjoyed. The man paid the bill and walked out. An observer asked, "Who was that man?" The clerk explained, "He comes every Christmas and buys something for somebody!"

Likewise God offers salvation to everyone. Jesus paid the price. This gift of joy is ours for the taking (Romans 6:23).

GOD IN HISTORY   December 26

"After [the Magi] had heard the king, they went on their way, and the star they had seen when it rose went ahead of them…On coming to the house, they saw the child with his mother Mary, and they bowed down and worshiped him. Then they opened their treasures and presented him with gifts of gold, frankincense and myrrh." (Matthew 2:9-11 NIV)

God directed the details of the Incarnation in an amazing fashion. God led the Roman Emperor, Caesar Augustus, to establish peace and order throughout the world. This made future expansion of Christianity possible. At the precise time (Gal. 4:4), he arranged for the birth of the Christ-child. God's angels spoke to both Joseph and Mary. God directed the Emperor to order a census which brought Mary to Bethlehem at the right time (Micah 5:2). God provided a stable for the birthplace.

That night angels, shining in God's glory, appeared to shepherds, breaking the news of the Savior's birth. They hurried to Bethlehem. Finding Christ, they praised God, telling everyone (Luke 2:18). On the eighth day the baby was circumcised and named Jesus. After 33 days of purification, Mary took her firstborn to Jerusalem to present him to the Lord, sacrificing two doves (Lev. 12:8).

Meanwhile, Magi came from Babylon, following a star, seeking the new born king. The star led them to Jesus. They bowed down, worshiping the child, and gifted him with treasures: gold, frankincense and myrrh (Matt. 2:10-11). (The entourage of the Magi was probably large—deserts are dangerous). On leaving, God warned—don't report to Herod! Next, God warned Joseph to flee to Egypt, to escape Herod's execution orders. He fled by night. The Magi gifts were God's provision for living in Egypt. After Herod died, God directed Joseph to return home to Nazareth.

ADVANCING CHRISTIANITY December 27

"Jesus, full of the Holy Spirit, left the Jordan and was led by the Spirit into the wilderness, where for forty days he was tempted by the devil...Jesus returned to Galilee in the power of the spirit, and news about him spread through the whole countryside...and everyone praised him." (Luke 4:1, 14-15 NIV)

Jesus entered his ministry at age thirty, appearing on the scene in a dramatic flash of supernatural power. Repeatedly, he was filled with the Holy Spirit. First, at his baptism, God Almighty spoke. Secondly, at his temptation he overcame the devil by quoting scripture. Bruce Larson condensed Satan's threefold appeal, take care of yourself, be successful, and seek the spotlight. Thirdly, Jesus entered his Galilean ministry with great popularity, "everyone praised him" (4:15).

Now every believer is obligated to advance Christianity. While I was pastor of a large town church in the Midwest, every baptismal candidate was asked to share his or her personal testimony. Here is an example, "When I was about 14 years old, my father and I were irrigating a corn field. While we were waiting for the ditch to fill with water, my dad turned to me: 'Son, have you accepted Jesus Christ as your personal Savior and Lord? If not, would you like to now?' So right there in the cornfield I prayed to ask Jesus Christ to come into my heart." How beautiful when a father leads his own child to Christ!

As we spread the Good News, General William Booth, the founder of the Salvation Army once predicted, "The chief danger of the 20th Century will be religion without the Holy Spirit, Christianity without Christ, forgiveness without repentance, and heaven without hell." My friends, it behooves all of us to be faithful to God's clear biblical revelation!

JUDGEMENT FALLS ONCE   December 28

"When they hurled their insults at him, he did not retaliate; when he suffered, he made no threats. Instead he entrusted himself to him who judges justly. He himself bore our sins in his body on the cross, so that we might die to sins and live for righteousness; by his wounds you have been healed." (1 Peter 2:23-24 NIV)

In 1876 my forefathers, the Harder Family, came to America from West Prussia, seeking religious freedom. This group of families jointly purchased six sections of prairie land, from the Santa Fe Railroad, in the state of Kansas. Using the tall grass, they made haystacks for shelter until they could build houses.

The pioneers heading west—a century earlier—often faced a severe danger when strong winds drove prairie fires across the plains. They had a clever technique of protecting themselves. They burned a backfire around their cabin, or burned a plot of grass and urged their whole party to get on the black scorched soil. The fire would come up to their burned spot and then go around, leaving them safe. The obvious truth is that the grass could not burn twice; they stood where the grass had already burned!

This simple illustration helps us understand the dynamic of our redemption. *"God made him who had no sin, to be sin for us, so that in him we might become the righteousness of God"* (2 Corinthians 5:21). The judgment for our sin fell on Jesus Christ. If we believe in him, taking our stand by the cross, we are safe. The judgment will not fall twice. But if we reject Christ, and spurn his death in our behalf, the judgment will fall on us in the future judgment when God punishes wicked humanity. Salvation is God's gift (Romans 6:23)!

TOUCHING PEOPLE'S NEEDS   December 29

"Then the King will say to those on His right hand, 'Come you blessed of My Father, inherit the kingdom prepared for you from the foundation of the world: for I was hungry and you gave Me food; I was thirsty and you gave Me drink; I was a stranger and you took Me in; I was naked and you clothed Me; I was sick and you visited Me; I was in prison and you came to Me.'" (Matthew 25:34-36 NKJV)

Jesus Christ our Lord, in His ministry, seldom sought out the high society folks, or the wealthy. In His teachings He highlighted the needy, the stranger, the sick and the prisoner! What a great challenge to the Christian world! Jesus once spoke to a Samaritan prostitute, a five time loser. She, in turn, brought many friends to hear Jesus.

I attended a seminar led by Dick Simmons. He told of one prisoner in Washington who sat in jail for three years without receiving one single visitor or letter. So Simmons started the M-2 program, matching a person on the outside with a person in prison. In Washington, 2,000 Christians committed themselves to go regularly on a one-to-one basis to befriend prisoners. The state leaders were so impressed with the M-2 program, that when Seattle had a 20% unemployment rate, the state legislature voted to give six months unemployment payments to prisoners released in Washington State!

In Christ's home synagogue, He identified His mission (Isaiah 61) about preaching to the poor, healing the brokenhearted, and healing the blind and bruised (Luke 4:16f). You can support the homeless at Rescue Missions, or the sick at hospitals, or prisoners through Prison Fellowship, or hurricane victims via Samaritans Purse. My friends, what will you do for Jesus?

LESSONS FROM SHEEP December 30

"My sheep hear My voice, and I know them and, they follow Me. And I give them eternal life, and they shall never perish; neither shall anyone snatch them out of My hand." (John 10:27-28 NKJV)

Some people assert, in a rather careless way, that they can do anything—right or wrong—as a Christian and it won't affect their security. That's not what this verse says. Jesus Christ, the Good Shepherd, says emphatically that the true sheep, will hear His voice and they will follow Him! This offers no solace to straying, sinning, disobedient sheep. Believers are not free to live wicked lives.

An unusual story appeared in the Washington Post. In the country of Turkey, while certain shepherds were eating their breakfast, one of their sheep fell off a 45-foot cliff to its death. Then to their utter amazement, the rest of the flock followed, one by one—all 1500. Only 450 actually died. The reason was that the first sheep that fell, provided a soft cushioned landing for the last 1050!

The Bible frequently refers to humans as sheep (Isaiah 53:6). People tend to follow group influence rather than following God's instructions. It's easy to absent-mindedly follow the crowd. That's a detour Christians must avoid.

So we must ask a crucial question: "Whom am I following?" Sheep blindly follow a leader, but we must choose our leader carefully. The Apostle Paul urged Christians to follow him as he follows Christ. People who are truly godly, who live exemplary lives, become good patterns for us. We must always ask, "Am I really listening to the voice of the Good Shepherd?" The most reliable leader is Jesus, whom we follow via prayer, Bible reading, the Spirit's inner voice and our church fellowship groups.

READING MY WITNESS   December 31

"You yourselves are our letter, written on our hearts, known and read by everyone. You show that you are a letter from Christ...written not with ink but with the Spirit of the living God...on the tablets of human hearts." (2 Corinthians 3:2-3 NIV)

What a powerful concept—my life is a letter which is read and written in the hearts of people! The Holy Spirit imprints it on the consciousness of others. They detect whether I'm kind or critical, loving or demanding, giving or grabbing. Each thought and action is quickly judged by what was my mother's favorite verse as she was raising us: "Abstain from all appearance of evil" (1 Thessalonians 5:22).

Simon Peter once denied his Lord and soon wept over it. Years later he urges us to submit to Christ's lordship, being prepared always to explain the reason of our Christian hope—when persons ask (1 Peter 3:15). Their inquiry is a grand open door for a witness. Then Peter adds: "Do this with gentleness and respect."

You and I need to learn how to move from a casual conversation to a "witness" topic. David Branon, in a devotional for *Our Daily Bread* gives a clever example. His friend was speaking to a guy with little regard for Christianity. After general talk, he suddenly said, "Hey, do you know where sinners go?" The man replied, "That's easy, you're going to tell me they go to hell." "No," replied the friend, "They go to church!" The man was speechless. The friend continued that all people are hopeless sinners. Churches are really hospitals for sinners, not holy clubs for saints! He explained God's grace, the unmerited favor which God extends to all of us (Ephesians 2:8-9).

PRAYER: "Dear God, help me be a fearless courageous witness for Jesus Christ."

THE INDEX TO FIND QUOTATIONS AND ILLUSTRATIONS